This Book Belongs To:

Miss J Shults
31A Lyford Road
London
SW18 3LU

More
Variety Days

More
Variety Days

*Fairs, Fit-ups, Music Hall, Variety
Theatre,
Clubs, Cruises and Cabaret*

Edited by
Frank Bruce & Archie Foley

Tod Press

First published 2000 by Tod Press, 21 Joppa Road, Edinburgh, EH15 2HA

Copyright the authors and Tod Press

ISBN   0 9537789 0 8

Contents

Preface

More Variety Days, like its predecessor *Those Variety Days,* is primarily a collection of personal reminiscences written by performers and theatre-goers. *Those Variety Days* focussed on the Scottish variety scene. The scope here is wider. We start with showman Billy Purvis in early nineteenth century fairs and fit-ups and end with television and cabaret in the 1980s. On the way we take in revue, cine-variety, working mens' clubs across the UK and travel as far afield as Budapest and Alaska. We meet magicians, dancers, scriptwriters, producers, theatre proprietors, singers and comedians. Nevertheless, there is a common thread running through the book. As all the contributions illustrate, from the beginning of our story to the present, showpeople have had to follow the opportunities and adapt to constant change and innovation. Much of the excitement of the whole experience was the uncertainty. As one showman put it 'everything was fresh again, fresh again'.

Thanks to our contributors, special thanks to Margaret Paterson and Angela Oswald for typing and transcription, to Vicki McDonnell for generous access to her father's papers and grateful acknowledgement to Jim Pratt for the Walford Bodie poster and additional information.

Frank Bruce & Archie Foley, Edinburgh, 2000

Magic entertainment – three extraordinary showmen

Jim Cuthbert

This chapter looks at the careers of three Scots-born performers who were exponents of stage magic and illusion. All three also had their own touring companies with supporting acts and as we trace their careers we also track the movement of popular live entertainment from the fairgrounds and race courses to the variety and music halls of the towns and cities.

The first is Billy Purvis. He was born in Auchendinny near Edinburgh in 1784 but when he was young his parents moved to Newcastle where he was based all his performing life. Writing about him in the *Newcastle Journal* in 1987 Keith Gregson characterised him as Les Dawson, Roy Castle, Paul Daniels and Laurence Olivier all rolled into one.

Billy started working life as an apprentice joiner with John Chapman at Biggs Market, Newcastle but any spare time he had was given to anything related to the stage and entertainment. He practised tightrope walking in the joiners' shop by using a rope slung between two workbenches. He took a job as a call-boy at the local Theatre Royal, which was under the management of Stephen Kemble, and was soon given small walk-on parts. He trained in the local Militia as a drummer and he also became a very accomplished Northumberland Pipes player as well as a good fiddler. It was an interest in dancing, however, that led to the start of Billy's stage career. Having become a very accomplished dancer he set up his own dancing school in rented premises. Visiting entertainers sometimes found it difficult to get rooms for rehearsals and so when his dancing classes were not using them, Billy would offer them to the touring entertainers. When business was poor and money tight he did not charge for their use but often these entertainers taught Billy some of their skills as a token of their appreciation for his help.

This act of kindness brought him into contact with many entertainers, including Monsieur Peru from France, Shanshias from Germany and Mr Hunt from England, all of whom were magicians. His discussions with them interested him so much that he studied the skill of legerdemain and became a very accomplished magician. He soon created his own magic act and included this with his other skills to create his stage shows.

In the early days Billy took his one-man show to the nearest village where he would make contact with the local hostelry or village hall and hire a room from them. After putting out the advertising himself, he put on a show that night for an entrance fee of one penny. If he had a large turnout he would stay and perform till the numbers started to reduce and then move on to the next village to go through the same process. By 1818 he had his own show and booth and his travelling theatre company could be seen at all the fairs and race meetings all over the north of England and Scotland. In Scotland he was a regular visitor to Kelso, Edinburgh, Glasgow, Paisley, Kilmarnock, Ayr, Greenock and Dundee. His company included Tom Matthews, Ned Corvan, Billy Thompson, Harry Wadforth, Emma Atkinson and their repertoire included plays such as *Hamlet, Othello, The House that Jack Built, Turnpike Gate, The Miller and his Men.*

A regular sight would be Billy standing outside his pavilion doing his spiel to attract the customers. He would sometimes dress in a very distinctive clown costume but, no matter the costume, his Geordie accent and patter attracted the crowds. Soon his booth was filled and the show would begin. The entrance fee was a penny or tuppence. Larger and more elaborate booths and well-known entertainers of the day set up in opposition to him but the rapport between Billy and his supporters would soon have a packed house for his show.

If Billy had one weakness it was his generosity. Meeting a fellow entertainer fallen on hard times he would give him the full income of that night's show to help him on the way to recovery and he was well known locally for his donations to Newcastle Infirmary. When he did not raise much money from his show he would always see that his staff were paid first. He had very high religious morals and did not like to see others treated unfairly. If he arrived at a fair to find a group who could not get a site, he would offer to share his site with them or offer to include them in his show and pay them.

One of Billy Purvis's best-known routines was called 'The Bundle' and as described in Mr Stephenson's *Recollections of Billy Purvis* went as follows.

The scene was set in the country with a cottage on the right hand of the stage. A ploughboy played by Tom Matthews comes from the opposite side, peeps through the window and expresses in pantomimic action that he sees his sweetheart inside. Placing the bundle he carries by the door, he claps his hands together three times as a signal for his ladylove to come out. She does so; then after some pantomimic lovemaking they enter the cottage. Enter Billy, the clown, dancing round the stage until his toes kick the bundle left by the ploughboy. He looks at it, then glances slyly around to make sure he is not observed, picks it up, says ' By gox! It's a bundle!' and begins to undo the knots with his teeth. The ploughboy opens the cottage door; they look at each other; Billy drops the bundle, whistles and with a shuffling step dances off. The ploughboy watches him, then indicates his doubt as to the clown's honesty and determines to watch him. Billy returns cautiously and in a loud whisper exclaims,' By gox ! It's there yet; as mun ha' it!' He wags his finger and whistles to the bundle as to a dog he wants to entice. Just as he reaches the door it is opened suddenly, and the ploughboy deals him a blow on the mouth, at which Billy stammers out 'Da - da - da- am the man! Wha - wha- wha - t did you de that for?' then sneaks off, holding his hand to his mouth. When the stage is clear, he returns, says 'By gox the beggar is there yet; as mun ha' it this time'. He dances cautiously round in the opposite direction to his former movements, succeeds in kicking the bundle away, then calls out, 'Stop thief!' The ploughboy runs on and misses the bundle. Billy points off, shouting 'Stop thief!' 'Stop thief!' The ploughboy runs off one side and Billy picks up the bundle and runs off the other, saying, 'By gox, some gentleman lost his bundle and another gentleman has fund it!'

There is a painting by Ned Corvan titled 'Star Turn' showing Billy outside the inn used as the back drop for his famous bundle routine. A local art historian suggested that it was painted around 1840 and it was last seen at a sale by Anderson and Garland the auctioneers in Newcastle on 10 December 1996.

When Billy died in 1853 at Hartlepool, the Sanger Brothers put on a special show and presented the money raised to erect a memorial at his grave. The inscription on the stone reads: 'This stone was erected by J G Sanger, circus proprietor, to mark the last resting place of him who was always a friend of the fatherless, the widow and the distressed.' In Hartlepool on the day of the funeral all the boats in the harbour flew flags at half-mast and all the house shutters were closed.

If we move on just another few years we can see how the theatre and its performers adapted to meet the needs of the audiences. Our next star is John Henry Anderson who was born plain John Anderson in Kincardine O'Neil in Aberdeenshire on 16th July 1814. Anderson used various titles including 'The Caledonian Magician', but he was probably best known as the 'Wizard of the North'.

He started his performing career in a Penny Rattler owned by

Big Scotty Longhurst in the Old Bool Road, Aberdeen around 1829. Scotty sometimes went under the names of 'Emperor of all Magicians' or 'Baron Munchausen'. The Penny Rattler was a small wood-built theatre with a stage outside the auditorium. This outside stage was used to provide a sample of some of the wonders that the patrons would see inside after they had paid their penny entrance fee. A few years later John married Hannah Longhurst, Big Scotty's daughter and assisted his new father-in-law with his magic act also playing small roles in plays. Longhurst was one of the earliest magicians to perform the famous bullet catching trick which was recorded in Phillip Astley's book *Natural Magic* published in 1785. In his early years as a performer John Henry Anderson was an actor and only later became a magician. He toured with theatre groups organised by Benjamin Candler, Mullinder, Halloway and Parish, and Manley.

He decided to add magic to his skills after seeing Signor Blitz, a well-known magician and ventriloquist of the time, performing in a theatre in Hull. Anderson soon had a magical act put together and was performing it regularly around the country. He returned to Aberdeen to give his first magical performance in the city in the Morrison Hall and it was during this time that he became friendly with a young Frenchman in the confectionery trade in Aberdeen who had gone to see him perform. Anderson, in fact, helped him start his career in magic and when the young man returned to France he became one of their best magicians. His name was Jacques Noe Talon better known as Philippe.

Now on the way to becoming a great magician, Anderson by 1831 was to be seen with his horse and cart and all his magic props on the highways and byways touring his own show all over Britain. By 1838 he was performing in venues such as the Victoria Rooms in Hull, Exchange Rooms Manchester, Tyne Theatre Newcastle, Waterloo Rooms and the Adelphi Theatre, Edinburgh. He had a stay in Glasgow where he rented a two-thousand seat theatre and named it the Temple of Magic. This extract from an advertisement, which he probably wrote himself, in the *Scotsman* on 29 December 1838, gives an insight into how he promoted himself and his show:

The Great Wizard of the North

MR J.H. ANDERSON has added to his before UNIQUE EXHIBITION, wonders unparalleled...The sensation caused in the towns and cities of England, by the incredible feats and wonders of the only Scottish magician, has gained for him the cognomen of THE GREAT WIZARD OF THE NORTH.

He will, for a short time only, in the ADELPHI THEATRE, EDINBURGH, perform his Wonders! Mystery! Magic! Legerdemain! Necromancy! And the Wonder of the Age, THE FAR FAMED GUN TRICK!... Mr J.H.A. will allow any gentleman to charge a fowling-piece with bullets in the presence of the whole audience, previously marking them so as to ascertain them again. He will be desired to fire at Mr A. who will receive the Ball in his hands, his face, or any other part of his body the audience may direct; being upwards of the 1000th time of his attempting the experiment. Ladies not wishing to witness the Gun Trick, are respectfully informed that it will not be performed till all other deceptions are finished.

In 1840 at the age of twenty-six Anderson took the ultimate challenge when he decided to go to London. During his season, which opened first in the New Strand Theatre and later moved to the St James Theatre, he was invited to Windsor Castle to perform in front of Queen Victoria and Prince Albert and it is recorded that Prince Albert actually assisted him with one of his effects. The Anderson show ran for six months, which was the pattern in London theatres since most theatregoers usually left the city for the summer season. It was so successful that he returned to London for a similar season for the next four years. Immediately after the London season Anderson toured the rest of Britain and Ireland.

When he was in Glasgow in 1844 Anderson decided to build his own theatre at Glasgow Green. Named the City Theatre, it was the largest theatre in Scotland at that time with a seating capacity of around five thousand. On the opening night in May 1845 the Laurie family, who were acrobats, the Ethiopian Minstrels and a campanological orchestra supported Anderson. The cost of entry was: boxes - two shillings, pits - one shilling and the gallery - sixpence.

This venture was short-lived as the theatre was destroyed by fire in November 1845 and it was suggested at the time that the fire was started by a disgruntled member of staff. This was the first but, as we shall see, not the last time that Anderson lost all the money he had because of an accident outwith his control. The theatre had cost over £5,000 to build and furnish.

This loss could have been the end of many a man but not Anderson. As well as planning his European tour to begin in 1846 he took time to write the ninth issue of his book *Handbook of Parlour Magic* which described two hundred and fifty tricks as well as several gambling exposures. The three card trick or 'chase the ace' was a popular gambling trick used around the fairgrounds and racetracks and Anderson revealed how cheats would always win.

He was soon on the road again calling at Hull, Hamburg, Sweden, Norway, Denmark, St Petersburg, Vienna, Berlin, England and returning to Scotland and Balmoral Castle. It was during his Scottish tour in 1848 that he performed for Queen Victoria and Prince Albert and as part of his act he made a bottle of whisky appear. It was a new whisky on the market by Begg and Byers called Lochnagar and after the company heard of this it regularly delivered cases of the whisky to Anderson for his act.

Late in 1848 Anderson was back in London but this time he had strong magical opposition which included Philippe, Hermann, Herr Dobler and Robert Houdin. The quality of his magic and talent for attracting publicity soon had Anderson as the top man in town again.

By 1851 he was on his travels again, only this time to America. The first engagement was in New York, where he ran for one hundred nights. It was reported that only Jenny Lind had attracted a larger audience into the theatre. It was on this visit that he started to look at the fraudulent spiritualists performing in the area. He issued a challenge to any spiritualist that he would duplicate any-

John Henry Anderson - 'Wizard of the North'

thing that they would do as part of their seances. The challenge was never accepted.

When he returned to London in 1856 he first appeared in the Lyceum Theatre before moving to the Covent Garden Theatre. *The Times* wrote, 'Anderson was, if we are not deceived, the first among the present generation who practised legerdemain in the grand and brilliant manner.' Again he had bad luck when the Covent Garden Theatre caught fire. Once more he had lost a lot of money but this time the situation was worsened by his bank, the Royal British, going into bankruptcy a short time after. He was left penniless but as on previous occasions he was soon on the road again, New York, Australia and Honolulu and back to San Francisco all in one year and down the Pacific coast to Mexico.

Another tour of the USA in 1861 had to be reorganised and curtailed due to the start of the American Civil War. In Richmond, Virginia, which was the capital of the Confederacy, the townspeople were so enraged with his title, 'Wizard of The North' that they ripped down his posters and forced him to retreat over the Mason-Dixon line. Having all his plans made and publicity printed only to have to cancel, cost him $5000. He made alternative plans to perform in Boston, Baltimore, Cincinnati, Louisville, Chicago, St Louis and back to New York but because of the Civil War Anderson decided to return to Britain. It was calculated that by 1863 he had travelled over 235,000 miles during which he had donated over £4,030 to various charities. When this amount is added to the cost of his Glasgow theatre loss, prop loss from the Covent Garden Theatre fire, the bank bankruptcy, and the American disaster Anderson had lost in the region of £26,526.

Although Anderson is well known for his magic few current magicians know of his acting skills but Scottish theatre-goers of his day knew him as a leading actor in plays such as *Rob Roy, Black Eyed Susan, Pizarro, Wandering Steenie* and *The Rose of Ettrick Vale*. It was taken for granted that he could fill any theatre where he performed. Although popular, one critic stated that Anderson took bad acting to its highest peak but while many of us have heard of Anderson, the 'Wizard of the North', nobody can remember the name of the

15

critic.

The next few years were not kind to Anderson. A number of friends to whom he had entrusted and forwarded money for safe keeping during his Australian tour, had either committed suicide after spending all his money, or moved from the area without leaving forwarding addresses. His health was poor and he was burdened with debt. He continued to tour but on 3 February 1874 he died in the company of his friends Margaret and Charles Foot. It was his wish that he be buried in St Nicholas Churchyard in Aberdeen next to his mother and on the day of his funeral thousands lined the route to the churchyard gate.

The great escapologist Harry Houdini declared that Anderson was one of the greatest advertisers of magic there had ever been. Anderson pioneered the use of billboard advertisements, he also sent out promotional material such as butter pats to leading dairymen which had a shape of himself and an invitation to come along and see his show. He had processions of vehicles and men with sandwich boards parading the streets to display information about his show and where it could be seen. Anderson used top-class lithographers for his publicity such as Miller and Buchanan in Glasgow and Keith and Gibb in Aberdeen (examples of these can be seen in the book *The Great Wizard of the North* by Constance Pole Byer). To attract the public into the theatre Anderson used his fertile imagination and copy writing talent to devise exotic names and enticing descriptions for his magical effects. Audiences flocked in to find out about the *Telescopic Tell Tale*, the *Rings of Poo*, what was in the *Cabinet of Confucius* or see the 'magician command a card to fly at the rate of one thousand miles in a minute'. Anderson was also a prolific writer of books on magic of which the most popular was *The Fashionable Science of Parlour Magic* which went into over 150 editions as well as booklets and pamphlets which could be bought for a few pence at the theatre after his show.

If John Henry Anderson is quite rightly regarded as being responsible for bringing magic and illusion out of the cold and into the theatre then the person who took it to the top of the bill and made himself a huge box office attraction was Dr Walford Bodie.

Bodie was born Samuel Murphy Bodie in Aberdeen on 11th June 1869. Despite pressure from his parents to train as a minister, or study medicine, he decided that his future lay in the growing field of telecommunication and got employment with the Scottish National Telephone Company. Here he increased his knowledge of electricity that was to serve him well in his future as an entertainer. Bodie was so interested in the new medium of telephony that he installed phones in the houses of four of his friends who stayed near him in Aberdeen. He wrote a book about the telephone and at one time was working on an invention that would cause the phone to automatically ring if a fire started in a house.

Away from work he was interested, and proficient, in magic and ventriloquism and his first professional venture on to the stage was at Stonehaven Town Hall. Here he performed magic and ventriloquism one weekend and gave a talk on South Africa on the second weekend. It should be said that at that time he had not been out of Scotland and knew little about the country but this did not deter our self-confident entertainer.

By 1897 his performing career had taken off. He had taken up the job of theatre manager at the Connaught Theatre of Variety in Norwich but soon discovered that front-of-house work was not as interesting as being in front of a live audience on the stage. He had changed his name to Walford Bodie, Walford being the name of his brother-in-law for whom he had a great respect and also added the letters MD CS (USA) after his name. These letters were to raise problems at a later date.

A Walford Bodie performance would show off his skills in ventriloquism, hypnotism, telepathy, clairvoyance, cartoon sketches and magic. The following effects were all part of Bodie's stage show:

He would invite a female member of the audience onto the stage, move forward, touch her hand and her hair would stand straight up.

Other members of the audience would be invited to inspect all the apparatus on the stage, which Bodie was about to use. He would then allow thousands of volts of electricity to flow through his body without causing any harm to himself. He would then encourage the volunteers to try the same but despite their efforts they could not accomplish the feat.

A man and woman would be asked to kiss on stage but as their lips drew closer sparks would flow between them and prevent them kissing causing great hilarity in the audience.

The chair that he used in his electric act was presented to him by Harry Houdini and was used for the first electrocution of a murderer in America. This part of the show was billed as 'the man they could not electrocute'.

An essential part of the Bodie act was his demonstrations of 'healing' using 'Bodic Force' (hypnotism) and 'Bloodless Surgery' (manipulation) and by passing an electric current through his body into that of the volunteer patient from the audience. It has to be said that some of these 'volunteers' were plants but as Bodie's reputation as a healer grew he expanded his interest into electric medicines which included Electric Life Pills and Electric Liniment and Bodie's Health Spa.

Bodie was always a controversial character and soon found himself being taken to court over some of the cures he claimed. The medical profession in particular took umbrage and the fact that he had MD after his name did not improve their opinion of him. He did go to court over this issue and was discharged after his explanation that the MD meant Merry Devil but this was not to be the end of his problems with the medical profession. Bodie broke new ground in a court case brought against him by performing a demonstration of his extraordinary resistance to electricity. His apparatus, called the Death Cage Experiment, was set up in the London court for the purpose of the demonstration. The lawsuit successfully over, Bodie was left to count the cost of the action, in the region of £10,000. This was not to be the last time that Bodie would find himself in Court.

After the court case in London, Bodie came to the Glasgow Coliseum in November 1909 with his show. Demonstrations by medical students against him started early on the Monday with innuendoes and insinuations flying around Glasgow and eggs and pease meal in the theatre. Tuesday was similar to Monday and Bodie was warned that further demonstrations were being planned. Thursday came, as did the riot. Having been warned the police were in the theatre in large numbers standing by waiting for the troubles to start.

It was known that the medical students had had a planning meeting in the University earlier that day. Preparations were made as to where and when the groups would meet and march together to the theatre and the entire circle of the theatre was pre-booked as well as any other seats that were available. It was estimated that one thousand undergraduates were in position when the curtain was raised.

All went well until it was time for Bodie to come on stage. This was the signal for the throwing of fruit, eggs and all kind of vegetables. The orchestra left the pit in case of injury. All this time more students were waiting outside.

While this was going on, one of the student leaders, the police, Mrs Bodie and Walford Bodie were all trying to negotiate a way out of the problem. The students demanded an apology from Bodie. He did attempt to give some kind of one but was shouted down. After the police moved in and cleared the theatre, some of the students then decided to take their wrath out on a medicine vendor in the West End of the City.

Mrs Bodie states that the demonstration was more under the direction of the university medical staff rather than students. The Glasgow demonstration was co-ordinated to include medical students from other than Glasgow University. It is doubtful if there were 1000 medical students in Glasgow University at the time, therefore medical students from further afield must have been brought in. Bodie tried to put out to the public that the letters after his name stood for Merry Devil and that they were not in any way meant to infer a medical degree but to no avail. Some of the students involved in the riot or disturbance were charged and taken to court. They were found guilty and fined but when they went to pay their fines these had already been paid. It was suspected that the university medical lecturers had paid their fines but no proof was put forward. This whole affair affected Bodie greatly. He cancelled

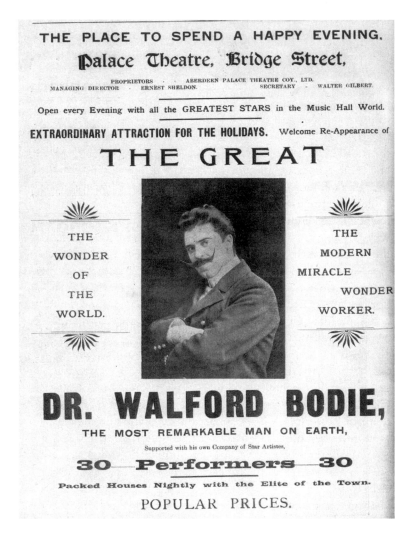

Typical Walford Bodie poster in Aberdeen, 1903

some of his bookings excusing himself on the grounds of stress and neurasthenia, bordering on collapse.

Although all of the above played an important part in Bodie's life it was not all of his life. He toured Ireland where performers had to perform in any hall available to them. Sometimes it was a village hall others it was the courtroom or even the local chapel. In Cork he was made a Life Governor of the town. He also visited India with shows in Bombay and Calcutta. It was on one of these journeys that he missed serious injury when the train he was on stopped suddenly because a length of rail had been removed from the line. He then visited Ceylon where he contracted malaria. During these visits he tried to identify the origin of the Indian Rope trick but came to the conclusion that it had first been reported by a drunken soldier.

During these travels he always made a point of meeting local magicians to discuss magic and exchange ideas all of which were written down by him in notebooks. On his return journey in 1916 the ship in which he was travelling was torpedoed. All of his company were rescued but unfortunately all Bodie's notebooks with the records he had made and all his materials were now at the bottom of the sea. He was soon on board again on his way home and again the ship was torpedoed. This time he was landed on Malta and eventually got home safely.

Bodie was a master showman and with his dark, piercing eyes, waxed up-turned moustache and monocle, he cut an imposing figure. He was also a flamboyant self-publicist who wrote most of his bill material and could use his artistic talent to produce colourful, dramatic posters. On stage 'The Most Remarkable Man on Earth', as he described himself, played to packed houses all over the country with his mixture of healing, scientific novelty and sensational illusions such as the 'Cage of Death'. Although he was the major attraction, Bodie's touring company always contained a full company of variety artistes and he employed many performers who were later to gain worldwide recognition. Harry Lauder was part of Bodie's show for the enormous fee of four pounds and ten shillings. It was Bodie who cajoled the theatre agent Foster to see

Lauder perform, which was the start of a three year run that was also the start of Lauder becoming one of the highest paid entertainers of his time.

Be that as it may, for a number of years before his death Bodie did not appear in the number one halls but was content to work wherever he could, be it a third rate theatre, public hall in a small town or even the fairground.

Like John Henry Anderson he wrote a number of books. Various editions of *The Bodie Book* appeared and his book of *Valuable Prescriptions* was very popular. Bodie also wrote a detective type story, which was compared favourably with the Sherlock Holmes books. In *Harley the Hypnotist* the hero used hypnosis to help him solve the murders and both Bodie and his wife believed that hypnotism as they practised it could be a help in detecting and preventing crime. They also suggested that personal magnetism should be studied by the police to help in identifying criminals.

Bodie was a complex character but was he just a fantastic self-publicist and charlatan? Certainly, many of his demonstrations of the effects of electricity and mesmerism were performed on 'stooges' well rehearsed, for example, to jump from the 'electric chair' when the doctor stretched out his arms and pointed at them. However, although he made outrageous and ridiculously false claims about his academic qualifications, he always kept himself well informed on scientific advances so as to include some of them in his act. Did he cure people? The answer probably is 'Yes' and 'No'. He believed wholeheartedly in his methods and spent a lot of time and money trying to prove his critics, especially doctors, wrong. The judge in the 1909 court case said that there was evidence of cases 'which had been cured as a result of Dr. Bodie's treatment.' He was an entertainer ahead of his time but was overtaken by it. As knowledge and use of electricity became more and more widespread its novelty value got less and less. In the late 1920s and into the 1930s 'movies' became 'talkies' drawing audiences away from live theatre and he was a tired sick man when he died in a theatre in Blackpool in 1939.

In almost 150 years we have tracked the movement of magic

and illusion on stage from the fit-up theatres and booths of Billy Purvis to the grand variety halls occupied by Walford Bodie. All three of these performers not only were supremely talented show-men but also had a dogged determination to keep on going when the odds were stacked against them. In addition, they were skilled practitioners of the arts of self-promotion and publicity, making sure that their names were in the forefront of the public mind.

I remember, I remember
Kit Peters

I t was finding my old make-up box that brought back the memo
ries with a rush. The smell of greasepaint, dressing-rooms, back-
stage, the wings, cheap scent and cheaper digs.

Suddenly I was back in childhood, when it all began. I was eight
years old when a magical moment shaped my destiny. Twelve dancers in a flurry of silver and white captivated me as they dipped,
high-kicked, twisted and twirled and all too quickly vanished, leaving me in a state of delight whispering to myself 'That's what I'm
going to be... a dancer.' My father was roaring with laughter at
George Robey who came on stage looking so silly in those large
boots, wobbly hat and enormous eyebrows. I dreamed away in a
world of my own, until all too soon the heavy crimson and gilt
curtains closed and the matinee of *The Bingboys on Broadway* was
over. It was farewell to the Alhambra Theatre as we stepped out into
the chilly November air and made our way to Victoria Station.

*Just a few years later, the sixteen year old Kit (by this time adopted by
a wealthy cousin 'Poppy' when her mother became ill) had realised her
ambition. Having trained at Madame Judith Espinosa's Academy of dance,
along with her friend Jacqui she successfully auditioned to become a 'Jackson
Girl' for 30/- per week rehearsals and £3 per week performance in the
1927 Julian Wylie 'Humpty-Dumpty' in Liverpool. This was the first of*

several professional engagements recounted in the following previously un-published extracts from her autobiography 'I remember, I remember'.

It was five minutes to ten when Jacqui and I walked back into the theatre and reached Bill's cubbyhole. We paused to thank him but he waved us on with a peremptory 'Go on, only five minutes to go, first right, up the stone stairs, first floor, fourth on right ... move' he winked, and we made for the stairs taking them in twos.

We hardly had time to cherish the moment of seeing our label 'The Jackson Sisters' on the door, because a vulgar voice from within was shouting. 'Oh Piss 'orf Miss Hoity-Toity, who d'you think you are?' It was certainly none of the Jackson girls. We opened the door to see a half-naked girl, arms flaying, feet stamping and eyes flaring. On the other side of the room were nine dancers, wide-eyed and open-mouthed, watching Gloria, who, in a commanding voice was saying 'If you don't mind ladies, this is our dressing room and I am trying to arrange my girls into their positions for making-up.' Jacqui and I squeezed into the two places to which Gloria pointed and set out our make-up boxes and towels (no tissues in those days) on the shelf in front of the enormous wall mirror. Reflected in the glass we were able to watch the showgirls who giggled at their own filthy jokes and sleazy ditties, whilst chain-smoking and drinking themselves into idiocy.

When the call 'All down for rehearsal' echoed through the corridors they staggered to their feet to be first out of the door. With a faint whisper of 'Good riddance' from all twelve, we joined the others from adjoining dressing room and went downstairs.

The theatre seemed to come alive to the sound of high-pitched chattering, banging of doors, clicking of heels on the stone stairs, and tuning of instruments drifting upwards from the orchestra.

Jacqui and I were excited at the thought of meeting the pro ducer Julian Wylie, because Madame Judith had told us that he was a man with great sensitivity and kindness beneath a brusque exterior, very talented and versed in the theatrical mechanics which go to make good productions. He was not called 'The King of Panto-mime' for nothing she told us. He had worked his way up the ladder from being an 'illusionist', inventing a unique act called 'Talking heads'.

'Mind you girls, his capacity for work is boundless, never forget that, but you should consider it an honour to work for this Lancastrian, who at a guess I should think is nearing fifty. You'll like him. He always boasts that he has never really grown up, which gives him a deep empathy with children and the secret knowledge of how to make then laugh. When you come back to me you will have learned a lot from that master of his profession.'

Comparing notes later, Jacqui and I came to the conclusion that it was too much to expect to meet the great man on the first day of rehearsals. We did think however that the portly man with greying hair and puffing on a large cigar, sitting in the auditorium might be our Boss.

He was in deep conversation with his choreographer Eddie Dolly and seemingly unaware of the confusion an stage, which was a madhouse of jabbering stage-hands, scene-shifters, electricians (known as sparks), stage manager and cast. It was not long before Eddie rose, clapped his hands and in a strident voice shouted 'Everybody on stage, please.'

There was an immediate silence. It was a strange feeling standing in my new world of magical back-stage with its smells of paint, wire, ropes, greasepaint, brilliantine, scent and humanity which hung on the air. The masses of scenery being painted, moved, and placed, the electricians positioning the effects, the stage manager busily moving from man to man and the orchestra tuning their instruments. It was an entertainment in itself and 'all for free'. Suddenly a grinning Gloria touched my elbow to say 'Could you come out of your trance Kit, we would like to go through our routine.' 'Sorry' I muttered and followed her.

Sometime around mid-morning there was a lull. Jacqui and I were munching biscuits when I suddenly spied a short figure in a blue reefer coat, wearing a tweedy cap and carrying a load of newspapers under his arm. Naturally I suspected he was a paper-boy come to sell a few papers to the cast and pulled Jacqui's sleeve. 'Look Jacqui, a paper-boy, I'll go and get one' but before I had gone a step she pulled me back. 'Not unless you want the sack, you won't' and then I heard someone say 'Oh good, Georgie's here, now we can get on' I nearly died. I had mistaken that great star 'Wee Georgie Wood' for a paper-boy and, what was more, he was walking in my direction. I slid into a drop split to hide my reddening face.

Later after a short lunch-break we had a session with our wardrobe mistress. It was horrifying to discover that our costumes were hand-me-downs from previous years. It set my mind racing, thinking of all the awful germs which might be lurking in those clothes, had they been cleaned or washed? The shoes, oh the shoes they scared me to death, hadn't anyone in this profession heard of athlete's foot and why had all the dancers before me had such small feet? I had a lot to learn.

Yes, I had a lot to learn; how to keep awake until the early hours, rehearsing, rehearsing and rehearsing until we were all dropping an our feet. With whom to speak and who to leave alone, to know your place in the presence of the un-approachable stars, to yield to the kindness of many others like Billy Leonard the Pantomime Dame, Hal Bryan the Panto King and the Conquest family with their darling Chimpanzee 'Daphne.' These were the real Showbusiness folk and a joy to know and work amongst. They had time to stop and talk, chuck you under the chin, tease and leg pull and protect you if need be from those in the profession who believed young girls were easy prey and theirs for the taking. It was the feeling of comradeship that prevailed in our dressing room that helped me through my initiation days and helped tremendously when the dress rehearsal day arrived.

I sat before the large mirror in an attempt to apply my first professional make-up, but with a host of first performance emotions mocking me I could not control my trembling hands. I was sensing ecstasy, fear, nervousness, doubt, and curiosity as to what and who, would be beyond those twinkling footlights?

I managed, however, to cream my face and apply grease-paints numbers five and nine just as Elsie had demonstrated before I left home; add a touch of carmine number three to my now seemingly suntanned cheeks, make a cupid's bow of my lips, cover my eyelids with a mixture of green and brown to improve my rather small hazel eyes, and even paint little red arrows at the corners. But, oh dear, it was the water black eyelash make-up that defeated me. After stabbing my eyes with the blackened brush a dozen times and making them smart like mad, I ended up looking like someone with an acute attack of conjunctivitis. Gloria came to my rescue steadying my hand and when she thought I looked alright she patted me an the shoulder saying 'Forget the hot black for tonight honey.' I was so relieved because I hated that horrible performance of lighting a candle, digging a match into a fat tube of black grease-paint to extract a blob of the messy concoction, heat it in the candlelight and then 'Hey Presto' lay back your head and drop the blob on to an eyelash. If you were lucky it landed in the right place, if not, it was in your eye and you were screaming.

I was well aware that I was suffering from 'dress rehearsal' nerves but was surprised when I looked through the mirror to discover I was not the only one. Even the old hands were showing signs of being ill at ease by either chattering overmuch or dissolving into an unnatural silence. But of course the unaffected were the four show-girls who by now we had nicknamed 'The bitchy quads.' Well, they were drinking themselves into a stupor on 'port and lemon' and among a series of sentences which all began with 'Have you heard this one', and lewd songs came a giggly slurred version of:

Once I was young and beautiful,
Nobody called me a cow
My face was as fair as a rosebud,
But look at the bloody thing now.

'Don't you dare laugh at them' Gloria had ordered 'or you'll make them worse'. I stifled my giggles as I pulled my frilly dress over my red briefs, squeezed my feet into the one-size-too-small red shoes and pinned a floral garland to my short hair. Then I smeared 'wet white' all over my legs looked in the mirror and wondered who I was? At that very moment what I like to call 'the voice of the theatre' the young Liverpudlian call-boy calling 'Overture and be-ginners', all along the corridors sent my pulses racing and heart thumping. I will never forget that first thrill of hearing the theatre coming alive, doors banging, raised voices and heels clicking on the stone stairs. Never having seen anything like this before Jacqui and I pressed our backs against the wall letting the brilliantly coloured fairy-tale pageant of the cast of *Humpty-Dumpty* pass before our eyes.

There were show girls, their half naked bodies barely covered in shimmering blues, golds, silvers, red, and daring flame all balancing feathered headdresses of great height. They were all shivering and swearing at the icy blast whizzing up the staircase. Following them came 'All the King's men' smart in scarlet jackets, blue trousers and black busbies leading the way for His Majesty dressed in royal purple velvet knickerbockers and jacket under a cloak of the same shade and trimmed with ermine. On top of his white curled and powdered wig he wore his jewelled crown which wobbled dangerously with every step he took. Twenty excited kids, acrobats and clowns followed in his wake along with the great 'Dame'. This jolly actor, who monopolised the width of the stairs with his billowing green cotton skirt, huge boots, large unsteady hat partially hiding his brilliant red wig, came laughing and joking as he swirled his mop and bucket. I couldn't help thinking 'How the kids will love you.'

Somewhere tucked in this medley of colour and turmoil was the Principal Boy and Girl. I just managed to pick out Molly Seton the ballet dancer in her white tu-tu and Sheila Dexter the high-kicking queen in a flouncy white dress trimmed with little black bobbles (She was the girl I wished I could understudy, but it was only a wish.) We joined the colourful cavalcade wearing very short (mini to the twentieth century) sleeveless cherry red and orange dresses with skirts of flower petal- shaped frills. Our shoes and floral head garlands were of matching colours. Listening to the orchestra beyond the small curtain in the wings where the stage manager stood 'on guard' daring you to peep, I could not help thinking of some of the famous pantomime stars who had trodden these boards many times.

Names that come to my mind are Grimaldi, Dan Leno, Marie

Lloyd, Florrie Forde, George Robey, Little Tich, Billy Bennett, Maisie Gay and many more. I whispered my thought to Jacqui who stood nervously twisting her fingers and looking so pretty with the red flowers on her wavy blond hair, her blue eyes shining. Suddenly the music changed. Twelve whispers of 'good luck' filtered along our line of dancers as twenty-four feet and legs went into action. I was so ecstatic that I had forgotten this was only a rehearsal and that beyond those twinkling footlights stood a stern-faced producer and his hawk-eyed team who missed nothing.

Julian Wylie is a perfectionist, Madam Judith had said, and by three a.m. when at long last he called a halt and ordered hot cocoa for all of us, I truly believed her. Jacqui and I dragged our aching limbs homewards. Within minutes were in bed and fast asleep.

★

'Ta-ra-ra-boom-de-ay, we've got-a matinee, Ta-ra-ra-boom-de-ay, we've got a matinee' I sang as I leapt from my bed on Boxing day morning.

Jacqui thought I was mad. She was right, I was mad with excitement. Bare-footed and still in my pyjamas, I danced across the bedroom floor singing my song swirling a stocking around over the top of my head only stopping to say 'Gee, it's good to be alive'.

My very first concern when I got to the theatre was mastering those infernal 'black eyelash blobs' before the afternoon performance. Luck was on my side, our rehearsal was short, this meant I was able to escape to the dressing-room unnoticed. I sat in front of my mirror for hours, digging a match-stick into that fat tube of black stuff, warming it in candlelight and then 'hey presto' to be or not to be I let it drop, After a series of 'Ouch. I missed that one,' I seemed to get the hang of things and as I was starving I blew the candle out and went in search of Gloria.

Jacqui and I had been sent food hampers from home and we had invited Gloria to Boxing Day lunch. Maree had cooked the turkey to perfection serving it with little bacon rolls, roast potatoes, sprouts, bread sauce and cranberry jelly followed by Christmas pudding, mince pies and a lovely big cup of tea. We all felt a bit full up after that, so we ran the short distance to the stage-door, changed into practice garb and did a thirty minute stint of limbering up.

Even that did not suppress my exuberance. I was over the moon with the picture I was fantasising of a real live audience.

I finished my make-up (blobs and all) much too early, dressed and jigged around annoying everyone until Gloria shouted 'For God's sake Kit keep still' I sat down trying in vain to be demure, crossed and uncrossed my ankles and hands a dozen times, added carmine number three to my already red lips and did battle with the hundreds of butterflies having a 'ball' inside my tummy. Would that call of 'Overture and beginners' never come?

When it did, the banging of doors and raised voices was twenty times louder than two days before Jacqui and I scuttled 'clickety-click' down the stone steps to the wings. Right in front of us on the walls were huge notices. One which was above a mass of electrical gadgets and switches read, 'Danger do not touch' the others were 'Silence' and 'No smoking'. When everyone had assembled in this small fusty space where once again I smelt all those smells that only live in a theatre, the waiting was becoming intolerable.

I stood first on one foot and then on the other, tried in vain to settle those uproarious butterflies in my solar plexus, smiled as I heard the 'Jackson girls' whisper of 'Good luck' pass from one to the other until it reached me and thought if something didn't happen soon I would die of frustration.

At last the orchestra completed its medley of introductory pan-tomime melodies and the applause from the audience and cheer-ing of children sounded encouraging. The curtain rose and a great roar of singing broke loose from all on stage. Then came Humpty-Dumpty thrilling the children, who loved the story of the 'Egg' who got broken, and adored all 'The king's horses and all the king's men....' and Wee Georgie Wood was perfect for the part.

After a wait that I thought would never end, we suddenly heard the change of music and that was our cue. By this time we had formed a line with our arms linked behind each others backs and were dancing our way on stage

The thrill of facing the twinkling footlights of blues, ambers, greens, and reds made me forget all my nervousness. I smiled as I kicked, turned on the 'It' (old fashioned word for sex appeal) and revelled in the sight of the sea of faces beyond the musicians.

Half-way through our routine I spied a sad looking old gentleman in the front row of the stalls. It was uncanny because he was so like my grandad, except that there was no smile. I kept looking at him because for some reason he aroused my pity. I was overcome with a desire to cheer him up. Being the last in our line I was able to throw him a special smile, blow a kiss and perform a saucy little back kick as I tripped behind the curtain.

Hearing the wolf whistles and applause was so elevating I simply raced up the stairs to get ready for our next number the 'Under the Sea' ballet. I loved it; there was a certain element of wickedness in this scene, which appealed to my nature. The scintillating green costumes sexy and body-tight, the green satin ballet shoes and the cute green skullcaps all very daring. That was not all. When we had been rehearsing this number the 'devil' got into us. Unbeknown to the musical director or the producer we had written our own words to this tantalising music and every one was a swear word. Lots I had not known before, but I was learning fast.

There was no devil in the scene that opened the second half of *Humpty-Dumpty*. There was the beauty only found in the glorious land of sweet smelling heather and bagpipes - Scotland. The audience were gazing at a lovely scene of hills and dales over which, to the playing of the 'pipes', came a large party of people.

Little did they know of the death trap those people were having to ascend and descend walking over a rickety rostrum which moaned and groaned under their weight. The descent was the most treacherous, especially for us dancers, because on reaching stage level we had to position ourselves in readiness to perform the 'Sword dance.' (Land an the wrong foot and you were in real trouble, not only getting yourself back in step, but the wigging that would be waiting for you back stage). Despite the perilous journey, this was the most exhilarating scene of all it was full of fun, lively music and movement and our costumes were a joy.

Swirling tartan-kilts worn with black velvet jackets, flouncy white jabots, saucy tam-o-shanters, long gartered white socks and soft black dancing pumps always got us a cheer, whether executing the intricate steps of the sword dance, or happily leading others of the cast in 'reels' and 'flings' The dancing ceased, Wee Georgie Wood went down on one knee to sing his song to Baby Love, while those of us who had been dancing, silently dissolved into his very large supporting cast.

Seventy years of living is a longish span to cover when trying to remember, which is the reason why, try as I will, the intervening scenes in the pantomime between the 'Scottish' and the 'finale' unfortunately escape me.

The 'finale' that brings forth the most vivid of memories is that which brought me a surprise after the matinee which I have been describing.

The stage was filled with the entire cast all singing and swinging to that rousing old favourite *Side by Side* with audience participation. I had joined hands with the Dame, played by Billy Leonard, who was dressed in a bulky, gaudy red dress, and white apron, still wearing his ginger wig which by now had an acquired an additional circlet of tatty flowers upon it. On centre stage was our darling chimpanzee 'Daphne' dancing in her best monkey-like fashion holding the hands of her owners Arthur and Betty Conquest. Looking towards the stalls I noticed my sad old whiskered gentleman has disappeared, I know it was stupid but I felt hurt. But not for long, because after we had taken several curtain calls, Julian Wylie had come on to take his bow and say a few words. Everyone had left the stage and I collided with Tommy our call-boy.

'I think you've got yerself a date luv' he grinned and produced a large box of chocolates, decorated with a red bow and gift card attached. 'Don't be so daft' I said 'You must be mistaken it must be for someone else'. 'Don't think so luv, it was you who blew a kiss and did a back kick weren't it?' We laughed and I pretended to kick him. 'Cheeky devil' I said, grabbed the chocolates, looked round to see if the 'Bitchy quads' were anywhere to be seen. They were not so I ran upstairs as if the devil was after me, hearing a very faint 'Don't forget to give us one luv.'

I made a bee-line for the toilets, hid my lovely gift beneath a stack of towels in a cupboard while I read my card. 'You smiled at me, blew me a kiss, you made an old man happy, God bless you child, don't ever grow up'. I stuffed the note up my knickers and made for the dressing room. ' 'Where the hell have you been?' asked Jacqui. I covered my lips with my fingers 'Ssch, I'll tell you later' I whispered, and when I did her eyes nearly popped out of her head.

Jacqui and I collided with an excited Gloria at the stage door next morning. 'Got any newspapers yet?' 'No'. 'Get some fast will you. I'll pay you later, the old man wants to see me' and with that she was gone.

We ran to the paper shop, bought every local paper on sale, and hastened back to a scene not unlike Lewis Carroll's *Madhatters tea-party*. Papers were being tossed in the air, cries of 'Hey, look at this', 'Listen, this is good', 'Girls they loved the Sword dance.' Wee Georgie and Baby Love were being hugged, kissed, congratulated, Vera Pearce (Principal Boy) was chortling with delight because a reporter had praised her for her vivacity, sex appeal and legs as lovely as those of Clarice Mayne (Clarice Mayne renowned for her Principal Boy parts and known as the girl with the gorgeous legs, captured London by storm when she sang '*I was a good little girl till I met you*'). Stella Marris cooed with delight finding her voice compared to 'The song of the lark'. All the time Jacqui and I stood staring in wonderment and 'Daphne' bored with the whole affair squatted at the feet of her master and mistress with a look saying 'Hasn't anybody remembered the monkey?' Hal Bryan (King) and Billy Leonard (Dame) well-seasoned pros had seen it all before so when Hal said 'Come on mate let's go and get a drink' they vanished.

Everyone else was going down into the stalls to offer Julian Wylie and Eddie Dolly their congratulations. I didn't see why I should be left out of that piece of fun. I pulled a reluctant Jacqui with me and stood shyly waiting until the Maestro had finished talking. Then with commendable decorum I offered my congratulations. He beamed and patted my cheek 'Thank you child, but remember it is as much your glory as mine'. When he asked my name I blushed and answered. When he asked me my age, I lied. 'Eighteen' I said. Through the cloud of bluish smoke curling upward from his cigar I saw his eyes twinkle. 'Pull the other one' he teased. I longed to kiss him but I didn't dare.

He was a wonderful man that 'King of Panto'. It has been said and I feel it must be true, that his success laid in the fact that at heart he was still a child and was known to adore children. He made a point of using them in every one of his pantomimes. He engaged twenty for our *Humpty-Dumpty*. By law they were only allowed to appear in the first half of the performance.

Unlike the men who had gone to the pub to celebrate, Jacqui and I went to a nearby café and ate sticky doughnuts and drank hot creamy chocolate before going to the 'flicks'. Those were the days when I was still young enough to swoon at the sight of Rudolph Valentino or Ramon Novarro. I didn't go to the pictures (for six-pence) just to see the film, I went to live in it. I watched Rudolph as 'The Sheik of Araby' and imagined it was I he cradled in his arms, bestowing passionate kisses upon my willing lips, and carrying me across the desert on his magnificent white stallion which I called 'Pegasus.'

As the notes of the Wurlitzer organ died away Jacqui and I walked out of the cinema in a dream and back to our digs in silence. Neither of us wanting to break that magic spell which held us so tightly in its grasp.

It was after our third cup of tea that wearing a soulful look Jacqui said 'Umm, I could die for that gorgeous Italian, couldn't you?' and with that we both roared with laughter.

The next great excitement was 'The Pantomime Ball' to be held at the Adelphi hotel immediately after Saturday night's show. We may have been the two youngest members of the cast to be invited, but by the time we had spent hours in Woolworths (the nothing over sixpence store) selecting long dangly earrings, strings of beads, slave bangles, hair-clasps and a bottle of that cheap and nasty perfume 'Phulnana', ransacked the alley-ways for 'nothing over two guineas' dress shops, painted our shoes with cheap silver paint and written home to borrow evening cloaks we eventually showed ourselves to Maree. 'You both look stunning' she said hugging and kissing us as we got into Gloria's taxi and sped away.

I will never forget the sense of freedom that flooded through me as, unchaperoned, I acknowledged the Commissionaire who opened the Adelphi Hotel door for us and walked as confidently as any other teenager of the 'twinkling twenties' into the brightly lighted foyer.

When Jacqui had handed her mother's lovely green moire cloak to the attendant and I, Elsie's cloak of coral velvet trimmed with silver fox fur, we stood gazing at the pleasing picture of two young girls reflected in the long mirror. Jacqui the blond looking sensational in her short emerald taffeta dress and dazzling jewellery and I, the brunette wearing a striking silk dress of coral colour. It was in Charleston style having a deep fringe that swung cheekily as I moved. The necklace Elsie had brought me from Italy of chunky coral completed the picture. Hoping to live up to the image I wanted to convey of being very grown up, I carried a pretty beaded evening handbag. Jacqui and I moved to join Gloria looking lovely in a seductive black dress with a full swirly skirt. With such attractiveness I caught myself wondering how an earth she had managed to stay single? 'Come on' she teased 'We all look gorgeous and I'm starving?'

We walked into a room where high pitched artificial blabberings of 'Darling how marvellous you look' and 'Reggie darling, my hand bag please sweetie' floated across the layer of cigarette smoke coming from the newly fashionable long cigarette holders, commonly referred to as 'the ladies weapons' because many a male had gone home with a burn on his cheek having got just that little bit too near the deadly weapon.

Through the babbling crowd came the welcome sight of a waiter carrying a tray of drinks one of which I accepted.

I appreciated the elegance of the dining room, the light from the crystal chandeliers casting shadows across the festive tables as I took my place between two men.

On my left was 'Frank', a chatty fellow who looked good dressed in his dinner jacket and smelt of a good cologne. On my right was a feeble kind of chap whose hair smelt of cheap violet scented brilliantine (used in the days before Brylcream was known). He spoke with an effeminate lisp, wore lipstick and had his finger-nails varnished. I turned my attention to Frank for amiable conversation, enjoyed a delicious meal, drank a little wine and learned more about him. At a guess I would say he was about forty years old. In a mellow well-educated voice he spoke of his years on the stage management side of the profession and his eyes met mine with a trusting smile. After the dessert had been served, the port passed and speeches completed, he and I danced.

As we danced we talked and found we had several interests in common. One especially was that of the recordings of Jack Smith the 'Whispering baritone'. Frank was a good dancer, a fun person. I enjoyed his compliments, he admired what he called the passionate colour and swinging fringe stuff of my dress which he said with a squeeze of my elbow made me look seductive. I felt myself blush as the music ceased and we walked back to our table to join Jacqui and her partner.

The next dance was a *Paul Jones* which Frank and I decided to give a miss. As we sipped our drinks he told me was staying in the Hotel and in his room he had a portable gramophone and his collection of Jack Smith's records . 'How would you like to sit out a few dances and come and hear some?'. Had I been older I might have heard those alarm bells ringing, and seen the amber lights turn to red. But being obsessed with the 'Whispering baritone' and very naive, walked upstairs with him joking and laughing. My laughter stopped abruptly as we entered his room and I saw him turn the key in the door.

I was very frightened so I asked him where he kept his gramophone. He smiled and took my hand 'You didn't really think I kept it here did you?' and with that he gripped me round the waist and marched me towards the side of the bed. As he lowered his body to mine. I begged, pleaded, hit, scratched, and kicked him to no avail. His eyes had lost their attraction; they had become hungry and vile. I attempted to scream but he covered my mouth with his, I felt stifled and terribly scared.

Suddenly I remembered Elsie's warning and advice, which she had said she hoped that I would never have to use. It was a miracle that I was able to recall everything she had told me, because I didn't always listen to good advice. Nor was I certain I should have the courage to relax in an attitude of submission, draw the beast's lips to mine and bite him. But I did and as he jumped upwards I lifted my knee with all the force I could muster making him spin backwards across the room holding himself.

'You bitch' he spat. I didn't care what he called me as long as I got free of him. With my heart pounding I grabbed my shoe which had fallen to the ground and managed to reach and unlock the door ahead of a pathetic panting Frank. I ran to the nearest cloak-room as fast as my wobbly legs would carry me, silently thanking and blessing Elsie every step of the way.

After the pantomime Kit returned home to stay with Poppy full of excitement about her adventure, but learns of her father's death. Her next engagement was a cine-variety tour with producer George Leyton.

George Leyton's Cinema tour took us to places like East and West Ham, Whitechapel, Finsbury Park, Leytonstone and many more. In the East End, part of the thrill for the audiences was to stand in their seats, throw rotten eggs, squashy tomatoes, boo and yell their heads off. We got used to dodging the missiles and living in the smells of the eggs and the audiences' eternal feasting on fish and chips and oranges.

But one thing we could not get used to was sharing our dressing room with 'All creatures great and small'. That was too much. Stamping on cockroaches, beetles, and covering the floor and shelves with Keating's flea powder was comparatively simple, but how to deal with the rats and mice was a matter for complaint to which the managements lent but a deaf ear.

We bought ourselves a brush and dustpan which disposed of unwanted 'droppings' but their unsocial behaviour of nightly visits to our primitive dressing rooms was not appreciated. It took but one night to discover how greatly our nocturnal visitors enjoyed the flavour of greasepaint, teeth marks showed the signs of their feasting as authentically as the 'finger prints' of a human thief might lead to the offender. Despite brave pretences we really were scared of these verminous creatures and always crashed into the dressing room 'en bloc' shouting, stamping and clapping. We would switch on the light and watch these horrible monstrosities scuttle down their holes quicker than lightning.

I recall one particular night that was different. We stood staring in disbelief at one fat, pregnant rat, moving more slowly than her thinner friends, doing her best to balance a candle between her paws. We must have terrified the poor pregnant mum with our shouting and stamping (yet determined not to drop the lovely long greasy object she had purloined) she pushed and shoved until only her long brown tail was visible, and this Phyllis helped an its way with a mighty swipe with the end of her umbrella.

Many of the cinemas included on our tour were infested with vermin. The newer ones like Ilford, Richmond, Kingston, Croydon and Finsbury Park had made preparation for the new innovation of 'live-shows'. These were a delight in which to work, they smelt deliciously of fresh paint and carbolic soap, had airy dressing rooms, new mirrors above the make-up shelves, clean floors and windows through which we could actually see. A pleasant change from the lacy pattern of cobwebs we had found elsewhere.

It always amused me when I heard one of the Cockney stage hands say things like 'Thanks Guv, you're a real gent.' I knew exactly what they meant because George Leyton was just such a man. Nice to work for, and with, nice to talk to, a person to be respected and with whom one felt safe. For example after the show he always escorted us until we were well on our way and out of danger from the stage door Johnnies. These Johnnies were the young men waiting like birds of prey to pounce on any of us girls who they fancied to complete their night of revelry. It was terrific fun to see their eagerness change to anger as George walked in the middle of his team of 'young ladies' raising his hat and proffering a wave to those who had waited in vain. He made us feel we were special and that he cared about us.

George was not only a powerful singer but a man of striking stature and good middle-aged looks. I once heard him referred to as 'a symphony in grey', so apt a description because as he walked on stage the spotlight lifted the silver-grey of his hair, spotlighted the grey hat he carried and the finely cut Edwardian suit of the same shade. Only his silver topped stick and black patent shoes broke the symphony. His selection of songs included many reminiscent of the war like *Tipperary, Keep the home fires burning, Pack up your troubles in your old kit bag* and many others.

As his supporting cast, we were kitted out accordingly. In one scene we were smart marching soldiers in the scarlet jackets and uniform of the King. In another, 'Jolly Jack Tars' dancing the 'hornpipe' in baggy trousers and jaunty pork pie hats. One night just as our lively performance of the 'hornpipe' came to an end an inebriated old 'Sea-dog' rose from his seat and shouted 'Ow abart splicing the main-brace lads?' George immediately rose to the occasion 'Good idea Skipper' he replied 'See you later.' How the audience loved that. We had to wait a long time for George that night we thought we would have to face the 'Johnnies' on our own. But not a bit of it, back came George smelling of whisky and still laughing at the jokes the old Skipper had shared with him.

'Come on, share the jokes' we teased as we strutted towards the tube-station. But he was not playing. With a wicked twinkle in his sharp blue eyes he insisted 'You're all too young.'

We are so used to seeing and hearing of the wonderful achievements of the Royal Air Force, Red Devils and Fleet Air Arm these days, that it seems hard to believe that when we kids were performing with George, the Flying Corps was the baby of the services. Imagine our delight in facing the footlights in cheeky air force blue forage caps, natty, snugly fitting uniform to do a high-speed number of tap-dancing, Charleston, cart-wheels and somersaults as 'the flyers'.

In sharp contrast to all this merriment George took a great risk in the finale, but it proved highly successful. He chose to switch the mood to 'pathos' in a scene where wounded soldiers lay on camp-beds, in a field hospital. The lights were dimmed to a night-time blueness, just subtle enough to reveal the whiteness of the long aprons of the 'Florence Nightingale' nurses swinging their lanterns as they moved silently from bed to bed. As if from a long way away, George could be heard ringing *Keep the home fires burning*. Slowly his voice came nearer yet even softer until it was almost a whisper and he was singing a lullaby. Unexpectedly a brilliant spotlight cast its rays on to the pale angelic face of a young nurse standing in the wings cradling a new-born baby in her arm.

The emotion, which swept across the footlights in the direction of those of us on stage, as the last notes of the lullaby died away and the spotlight faded from the face of 'the angel of mercy' was unbelievable. Quietly handkerchiefs fluttering in the audience and gentle sobs were heard before the explosion of applause for George's rendering of bringing the boys back to 'Blighty'.

It was just before Christmas when George Leyton's Show cane to an end at Finsbury Park, a night of mixed emotions for me. I had so enjoyed being with George and the girls, all so different doing the round of cinemas after the hugeness of the Empire in Liverpool. I was glad George took my mind off my doubts and fears for the future by taking us all to the West End for a meal at the Trocadero in Shaftesbury Avenue. We drank wine, danced and chatted until it was tine to say good-bye. George hugged us all in turn and to our surprise even his cheeks were damp.

As I called a taxi I felt as if I had just closed 'my book of life' on one more chapter. I wondered what surprises life had in store as I moved towards my eighteenth birthday? I cannot help thinking how free and easy were those far off days in comparison to today. There were but few dangers for young girls travelling alone by train, tube, or bus; no bombs, rapists, muggers, or raving lunatics or druggies lurking in dark corners ready to knife you. Even stopping at the roadside 'Coffee-stalls' as late as midnight held no fears. My favourite was the one at Hyde Park Corner. I have stopped there many a time, sometimes as late as midnight, drank my coffee, had a chat with the 'cheerful chappie owner' and his customers and walked on my way totally unconcerned and unworried. If I had to pass a pub at turning out time, especially on pay nights I would walk on the other side of the road. But in any case there was that feeling of safety in the knowledge that your friend 'the bobby on the beat' was never very far away.

Kit went on to attend dancing academy run by brother and nephew of Madame Espinosa. Eddie Kelland, the nephew 'took me right back to basics. He had me standing for hours tapping first my left and then my right foot over the top of a match laid horizontally on the floor. He worked out new routines for me, showed me how to improve my Charleston, Black Bottom and Varsity Drag dances. I was having fun, but not working nearly as hard as I did with Eddie's Aunt, Madame Judith'. She stayed at home and took a break from dancing to enjoy life in London. Then on a trip to Berwick Market she decided for old time's sake to drop into Jones' in Leicester Square, a regular meeting place for theatricals. A couple of chums who brought her up to date with the news and a slightly tipsy acquaintance from 'Humpty-Dumpty' told her 'Hey sweetie, hear you've left the rat race for better things, bully for you honey'. Kit bought a copy of 'the Stage' on the way home, saw an audition for an Albert de Courville revue, worked out a snappy routine and was accepted as one of the six dancers for the 'Whirlwind Revue' to tour the provinces.

When I entered the rehearsal room, I knew the *Whirlwind Revue* was going to be a happy show. The atmosphere was alive, Alva and Johnnie, a couple of Cockney acrobats, were fooling about midstage, Gene and Vera were nigh strangling an invisible animal rehearsing their 'Cowboy-girl' act. Midge Bradfield the short dumpy soubrette was practicing a series of tricky movements called 'cobblers'. Being short she seemed to have no difficulty in shooting her little legs out in a squatting position like the Russian dancers. This scared me, because I was her understudy and I always found my legs too long when I tried these antics and try as I would I could never get up any speed without landing on my sit-me-down.

Fun and leg-pulling in the form of Johnny the acrobat looked up as he turned out of a 'butterfly turn' to what is commonly called 'Check the chicks'. His big blue eyes long floppy brown hair, rubber-ball-body and cheeky little-boy expression as he came forward to say 'Hello' contained a sense of danger as I was later to learn. His partner Alva, a cockney with a small body, big heart, and a grip of iron as he shook hands turned out to be a great little guy, and a friend. Midge, a neat little performer with a 'not too bad' voice had a bubbly personality but was not much of a mixer after that first meeting.

There was a sudden hush as Albert de Courville entered the auditorium with an extremely chic young lady, introduced as Yvonne, whose carriage, poise proud tilt of the head and general demeanour suggested she was a dancer from France, even perhaps from the Folies Bergère where de Courville collected many ideas and costumes which he brought over to the UK.

The couple could have walked straight off a fashion plate; Albert impeccably dressed in a beautifully cut grey suit, lavender-coloured silk shirt with a tie of a deeper shade from which a diamond tie pin scintillated. His companion showed off her well-shaped legs by wearing a short flapper style tight skirt with a magyar scarlet jacket and jaunty black beret.

Yvonne lost no time in throwing off her jacket and asking the dancers to 'Follow me, merci.' It was the other kind of 'mercy' we needed when she had us walking in ever decreasing circles like the legendary cat 'Felix'. Only he, lucky devil, did not have to balance books on his head, we did. 'You know why you have to do this eh?' she asked in her broken English, 'No?... because you will be wearing the most beautiful Folies Bergère de Courville headdresses which will make you, up, up, up to eight feet tall, n'est ce pas?'

What a morning. We took our aching backs and feet to Lyons corner house where never had a large coffee and ham sandwich tasted so sweet.

The whole wretched merry-go-round began again after lunch when suddenly Yvonne yelled 'You call yourselves bloody dancers, ach, you wilt like ze wet cucumbers. Now try again, and this time, no bloody wilting eh?' This produced a fit of the giggles. Yvonne was not amused; 'You no take your job seriously, you no want your job with the great Mr de Courville ... you do... then bloody walk straight, and remember you have a gorgeous 'eadress on your 'ead. Now' she clapped her hands and looking at the pianist she commanded 'After trois'. With the aid of a pianist who cast a wink in our direction the tinny old piano produced a rendering of *Tell me pretty maiden are there any more at home like you?* Time and time and yet time again we walked wearing the invisible headdresses, until we were ready to drop.

At five o' clock Pedro's café in Wardour Street was our salvation. We slumped into our seats and ordered rare beef rolls with plenty of french mustard, and large cups of strong coffee.

The next morning Yvonne arrived 'daisy fresh.' She had a smooth ivory skin which she enhanced with a delicate addition of rouge to her cheeks, big brown eyes which looked wickedly seductive under mascara-ed lashes (not real mascara that was unknown, it was wet-black) and a crimson red 'cupid bow', wickedly kissable. Yvonne thawed during the next two days and every time we mastered a new routine she would throw her arms or cardigan into the air, laugh and shout 'Oh la la, my wilting cucumbers they got it'.

On the third day we rehearsed with the complete cast, eleven of us and it soon became apparent that the *Whirlwind Revue* was to be a fast, slick show of colour, beautiful dresses, many from France, with interludes of comedy such as 'the Cowboy' scene, and whirlwind acrobatics by the two Cockney lads.

We enjoyed the de Courville touches of politeness like 'Thank you all, you may go now' which of course was all part of his skillful way of endearing us to him, to encourage our loyalty and make us proud to work for him. On the last day before our departure to Wales, Yvonne had us all sitting around her cross-legged on the floor. 'Now you must remember' she said, her eyes twinkling mischievously 'You must always be a leetle bit naughty on stage. You turn on, what you call 'It', you be like ze teasing little devils to ze gentlemen in the audience, but you never, never show too much, you just keep them guessing, you understand? And' she added wagging her tiny finger 'That means off stage as well, then you catch see big fishes, with ze big bank accounts'.

She told us she would not be coming with us as she had another bunch of 'wilting cucumbers to what you say in English, lick into shape.' She kissed us all affectionately on both cheeks and with a wave and 'Bon voyage' she was gone. I was almost sorry when the rehearsals came to an end. I liked our 'Bossman' who, with his suggestive smile, dancing eyes, and gentle manners, could make my

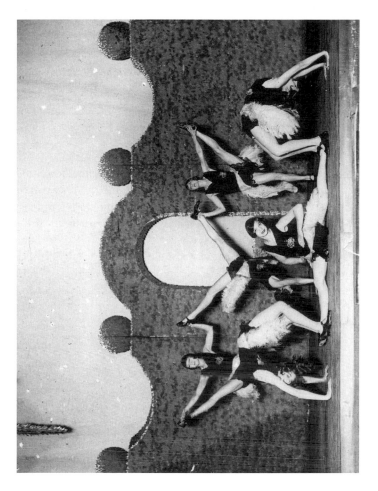

Scene from Whirlwind Revue, London

heart turn over.

Penarth was our Welsh destination. We were engaged to be there for the opening of the new Pier Theatre after a fire had destroyed the original building. Ruby was my new room-mate. She and I and were delighted with the warm welcome from our Welsh landlady and the delicious meal she had prepared for us.

The first morning on our way to a rehearsal we watched mighty waves lashing the pier. The relentless wind that blew across the Bristol Channel made us hold tightly to our hats and turn up our collars against the stinging spray. Struggling against the elements meant a wearisome operation of 'one step forward and two back' until at last we reached and opened the stage door assisted by a mighty gust of wind.

What bliss to walk into the new building away from the wind and to find it so warm, fresh smelling and light. A soft Welsh voice greeted us and directed us to our dressing room. As we passed along the corridor we could see the angry grey sea through the windows. 'I hope it subsides soon Ruby, it scares me'. Don't be daft'. We found the door marked 'the dancers' and on opening found a large lofty room. There were the usual mirrored walls, a long shelf to act as our make-up table, mobile costume rails, two wash basins and an adjoining toilet. This was dressing room luxury.

One of the most exciting moments in a new production is being fitted for your wardrobe. For de Courville's revue our Folies Bergère dresses, and headdresses were as fantastic as Yvonne had described. The headwear was made of a silver material in the shape of a peaked 'tam-o-shanter'. One half was in a slanting position, the other sufficiently erect to take the weight of long, coloured feathers, to raise our height to eight feet. The colours were blue, green, orange, lime, red and pink. Smaller feathers of the same colours were attached to the silver lace capes we would be wearing for the opening scene of *Tell me pretty maiden are there any more at home like you?* These capes were to be attached to our wrists by ribboned loops and held open showing us in the briefest of body tight costumes made of silver lamé with spangled fringe skirts.

Everything about this revue was a little bit daring with a French flavour of extravaganza. For one dance we were issued with natty little black velvet v-necked numbers, brief like bathing suits, with striking pink feathers that would be swathed around our hips ending suggestively in front with a teasing upliftment. An added touch of naughtiness was the effect of an edging of narrow black lace peeping from beneath each leg.

Our third outfits, in which we were to appear twice, were of silver lamé, very short, snappy and evocative with pastel-shaded frills hardly as long as decency permitted in England in the twenties. Despite the brevity and skimpy though they were, these exciting little suits gave me a sense of 'joie de vivre'. I always wished we could have been told the history of our costumes, did they come from Paris, London, or New York?

As usual, finding shoes to fit my long foot was a nightmare. I managed to stretch the silver pair issued to me, but had to coax the 'powers that be' to send for a larger size of the black ones worn for tap-dancing with the black outfits.

The back-cloth, which was used throughout the entire performance, was a patterned green hedge. It was attractively arched, which gave the impression that a garden lay beyond. The top was carved like an inverted scallop, with a ball made of hedge resting on each point.

Many of us began to hope that everything would be 'alright on the night.' The dress rehearsal had been frightful. The lighting failed twice, the orchestra either played like the Salvation Army outside a pub on a Saturday night, or a runaway hurdy-gurdy. Time and time again we missed our cues, Gene and Vera fuddled their words, Johnnie and Alva trying to catch up with the music which was being played too fast, missed a somersault and landed on top of each other.

Talk about first night nerves! The only good thing about the beginning of the evening was the weather. The wind had dropped, the sea had calmed, and the people came out in droves.

Never had I known a dressing room so quiet. We cast anxious glances at each other as we faced the mirror to apply our make-up. We saw ourselves reflected in our 'silver ensemble' making nervous, last-minute gestures of adjustment, when suddenly that cry I loved so much came along the corridors. 'Overtures and beginners'. Waiting in the wings there was the usual nail biting. Between whispers of 'Good luck' Johnnie tip-toed over to kiss us all, Alva blew a kiss and Gene playfully smacked everyone's bottom. Then suddenly as the orchestra finished their introductory music and the applause died away it was our turn.

The curtain rose on a picture of six shimmering silver statues. This brought forth deafening applause. With our capes held open we smiled, moved upright and graceful to the music of *Tell me pretty maiden are there any more at home like you?* The music, soft at first, changed tempo as we removed our capes. We came to the front of the stage to dance the liveliest of high-kicking routines. The music rose to a great crescendo giving our performance a grand finish. It gave us a feeling of intense joy to hear the hand-clapping and feel the warmth coming from the audience across the footlights in waves.

To our surprise when we returned to our dressing room we found a tray of drinks with the manager's compliments waiting for us. 'Well' gasped Maureen 'There's a turn up for the book?'

Quickly following on our act came our two chirpy acrobats Johnny and Alva. Laughing, making funny faces, tossing each other about as if they were rubber balls and looking so smart in dinner jacket suits, worn with soft collared white shirts, and black bows.

'Whirlwind by name and whirlwind by nature'; the show was snappy, slick and speedy. No sooner had Johnnie and Alva disappeared than Midge ran on stage vivacious and bubbly in a stiff taffeta scarlet and primrose-coloured mini-dress. She beamed at the audience sang and danced to the tune of *Marvellous*, finishing with a series of 'cobblers' at tremendous speed. I was watching her from the wings saying 'heaven help me.' As I have already mentioned I was her understudy for this number and for the life of me I could not see my five foot six inches getting into her dress, she was under five feet tall. To make matters worse, I could not imagine myself so near the floor in that semi-sitting position shooting my long legs out one after the other at anything like the speed which Midge attained.

It is not easy to reflect over so many years but I am of the impression that we six girls closed the first half of the revue. We came on in a great swish of sensation wearing those wickedly sexy black dresses with the enormous pink feathers which I have already described. Penarth was to see how de Courville's girls danced the Charleston, Black bottom and Varsity Drag dances, which had only recently been released from the USA.

In the second half of the evening Gene and Vera kept up the pace as a witty, 'Cowboy and Cowgirl'. Vera having a slim figure and a positive stance made a dashing young cowgirl in long boots, short tight fringed leather skirt, broad leather belt, white shirt, leather waistcoat and saucily turned up felt hat -they loved the way she thrust tormenting dialogue at her partner hardly stopping for breath. He in typical 'cowboy' attire with fringed trousers, red spotted kerchief and revolver in hand, stared under his slouch hat to retaliate when he could get a word in. The girls out-front cheered when Vera scared off Gene making the act a great success.

Outside, the rows of coloured lights twinkled from one end of the pier to the other. The *Whirlwind Revue* moved from scene to scene, glasses were raised in the interval to celebrate the re-opening of the Pier Theatre. All too swiftly the evening drew to a close and the yellow moon rose over Penarth.

One morning after a rehearsal when we were playing a childish game of 'tag' with Johnnie and Alva on the pier I slipped, Johnnie picked me up and to my surprise kissed me warmly on the lips. 'Thanks' I said 'but what brought that on?' His big blue eyes looking at me beneath those curling black lashes made my heart turn over. Quickly as if nothing had happened I ran to 'tag' Ruby, but I could not forget that kiss and the twinkle in those eyes. I was happy but petrified. Ruby and I had not yet grown as close to each other as Jacqui and I had been when in pantomime, I could not confide my fears to her. It was the memory of Frank's behaviour that haunted me and made me fearful. I liked my young Cockney admirer, he was fun, he was kind and showed concern over my frigidity. One afternoon in a quaint cafe over tea and buttered Welsh tea-cakes I told him my 'Pantomime Ball story'. He looked at me over the rim of his teacup and said 'trust me'. That was the beginning of a happy light-hearted romance that carried me more or less all over England throughout the tour.

During the course of the Revue we were all invited to perform a charity show at the Red Lantern Club in Cardiff in aid of the local hospital. We had been told in Penarth of the forthcoming election and seen bunting festooned across the main streets of Penarth. There were shops filled with flags and people wearing rosettes of their parties' colours. We had no conception of the pitch of 'election fever' that we would encounter on reaching the city.

We were provided with a coach and enjoyed a three mile singsong drive until we reached the city. Here election fever was in full sway. Our coach crawled, swerved to miss the hordes of people with their enormous rosettes who were yelling, screaming and waving flags. Suddenly we saw a bunch of hysterical drunks come lurching towards the coach and three policeman waving truncheons. In a short time the gallant 'men in blue' had led them away and returned to escort us to the Red Lantern. On arrival the proprietor came running out to meet us, he ushered us through the mob and indoors to a small room. He told a saucily dressed waitress to bring us refreshment. He was so apologetic, insisting that before we performed we must have a meal, it would be ready in five minutes. What a meal that was!

By the time we had changed into our costumes, applied make-up and were shown into the club-room we were in high spirits (in more ways than one), as were the club members. Our show went so well that the enthusiastic audience simply would not let us go. They called us back time and time again until the kindly owner took pity on us. He spoke his words of thanks which was followed by more applause and then escorted us to our changing rooms, where more drinks and sandwiches were offered and accepted.

Nobody could resist the temptation to gaze out of the window at the revelry below. Wild crowds were throwing their hats in the air, cheering, letting off fireworks, releasing balloons, flinging streamers, singing and dancing. We saw a policeman come to the club and, minutes after George, the proprietor came to tell us it was too dangerous for us to leave. He fussed round us like a hen with her brood, turned on a gramophone so that we could dance with each other or members of his staff. Drinks were constantly replenished until the clock struck three and we were all beginning to yawn. George looked out at the crowds still celebrating and turned to whisper something to his manager. As if by magic we were supplied with mattresses, pillows, blankets and rugs, shown where we could wash and within a very short time we had each selected our corner and were fast asleep.

We awoke to the sound of a team of whistling road sweepers, and a soft knock on the door. As we chorused 'Come in' a porter with a tray of morning tea arrived 'Wakey-wakey' he trilled as he poured from the biggest brown teapot I had ever seen. 'Plenty more in the pot, help yourselves' he said as he took his lively self out of the door. Shortly after George's wife appeared and showed us where we could have a bath, and some place where the men could shave. She and her husband insisted we had breakfast before we left. Trestle tables had been laid and plates of sausages, eggs, bacon, tomatoes and fried bread, with piping hot coffee, toast and marmalade were the 'joy' which began our Sunday morning.

The next seven days flew by. On the last Saturday morning Johnnie and I were staring out to sea; 'Why do all the good things have to come to end?' I knew exactly what he meant and went on gazing and gazing at the calm blue waters and wondering if I would ever see them again?

Little did I know in those far off days of nearly seventy years ago, that in my retirement, I would often sit looking across the Bristol Channel from the Somerset shore at Porlock Weir, to the Welsh coastline and re-live those happy youthful days once more.

To say I could remember the chronological order of our 'Stoll Tour' would not be truthful. However, the memories which spring to my mind come from, Nottingham, Manchester, Birmingham, Yarmouth, and the thrill of appearing in London's Alhambra, Coliseum, and Holborn Empire.

Nottingham was really special. Not, as would be expected, for its wonderful cathedral, cigarette factories, lace-making or even its colourful legendary tales of Robin Hood, but for the happy hours spent on and by the river Trent the excellent 'digs' and new experiences.

Our taxi pulled up outside a delightful Georgian house in an avenue of lime trees. It was so grand we thought the taxi-driver must have made a mistake. Not so. Immediately the door was opened and the smell of home-cooking wafted in our direction we felt at home. Ruby, Ethel and I were allocated a three-bedded room with windows looking down upon those glorious green limes. Maureen and Sylvia were next to us, and Pat and Midge were up one more flight of stairs. There was a large bathroom 'With constant hot water my dears' our landlady assured us and a separate toilet. We shared a sitting room with nothing that resembled previous lodgings except the aspidistra. The chintz covers on the chairs and settee, the highly polished oak dining table, filled bookshelves, and big copper bowl of flowers standing in the fireplace suggested to us that our landlady had fallen on hard times. Surely nothing else would make her let these well-furnished rooms.

We hoped she had not seen the surprise on our faces when we found our table laid for tea on a white linen tablecloth. The china was of good quality, the cakes and raspberry jam home-made, bread and butter in plenty and I will swear the milk had come straight from the cow. Cool, creamy and delicious. I stared at the large brown teapot just like my gran's and to cover my rising tear said 'Who is going to be mum?' All in all everything seemed heaven sent and unbelievable!

When we arrived at the theatre the next morning we were amazed at the majestic beauty of the building. It had Georgian windows, impressive entrances, balconies, and handsome columns, six of which were placed at intervals to create a dignified scene. To call it beautiful is an understatement. It was a living monument demanding admiration. I was very impressed by the atmosphere inside the building. I know it sounds ridiculous but I felt as if I were walking with the ghosts of great artists like Vesta Tilley, Lily Morris, George Robey, Little Tich, Marie Lloyd, Florrie Forde as well as many more. Had I dared to let my imagination run rampant I could have visualised Nellie Wallace wearing her saucy feathered hat, and hear her singing 'You don't know Nellie as I know 'er, it's the naughty little bird on Nellie's at'. It's fun to indulge in a bit of sentimentality and to know that when you stand statue like in your silver dress, holding out your cape in your opening number, your feet are where once the famous stood.

Touring the remainder of the provincial towns leaves me with a sense of happiness, but a few poignant memories. Birmingham: I recall we had by law to wear 'tights', and we did a charity performance with 'Billy Cotton' dressed as 'Spooks'. Yarmouth: smelt of bloaters. Manchester: Students' Rag Day when the University students got up to all manner of tricks to collect money for the hospital. It was one of the craziest days of my life. From early morning some of those enthusiastic young men in fancy dress were laughing, joking and waving collecting tins under the noses of the passers by. Others equally madly dressed were racing through the city in open lorries, trucks, cars or buses singing, waving banners and flags, throwing streamers and letting off balloons. It was pandemonium but we, and hundreds more young people got caught up in the excitement of the day. We followed and cheered the students for miles. In the evening the 'ragging' came into the theatre. Young men in 'drag' burlesqued our opening scene by appearing in paper dresses and capes, replicas of ours. They dashed in and out of us, lifted us off our feet to kiss us, pulled our huge headdresses from our heads to plant them on theirs, making the audience howl with delight before standing shoulder to shoulder to bar our exit roaring 'Stand and deliver ladies'. The great roar from beyond the footlights must surely have split every hovering decibel in the house. They had terrific fun with Midge. The audience couldn't hear her singing her song, *Marvellous*, for the din the lads were making. When they squatted, fell over, and rolled on the ground pulling her with them in their stupid endeavours to emulate her little legs shooting out from underneath her like speeding arrows to do the 'cobblers' they landed in a glorious heap in the middle of the stage. Meantime, other young men who were weaving their way through the audiences on all floors cheered and shook their collecting boxes with gusto. It was a 'rave up'. The revelry went on all through the performance, Gene and Vera came in for mimicry and gun-sling-ing, the Alva Brothers were propelled from one to the other and as for our 'Charleston' scene. Well! They tagged themselves on to each end of our line dressed in black shorts, with huge pink paper bows across their hips made to look like our feathers and wearing great heavy black boots. When Ethel and I came forward-stage to do our 'solo' which included the *Varsity Drag* they clod-hopped around us yelling the 'drag' chorus as did the audience who by this time had got caught up in the spirit of the 'Rag'. The blighters invaded our dressing room bringing flowers, chocolates and 'booze'. Did I say that was the craziest day of my life, well, that was an under-state-ment.

Sheffield was the city that made me weep for a family I saw living in poverty even worse than that which I had seen in Liver-pool. The mother of six let out rooms to theatricals. I had booked with her and had no complaints whatsoever. My rooms were clean, the food was plain, but nicely cooked and they even had a bath-room, primitive but adequate which was reached through a corri-dor. One night when I returned later than usual and wanted to go to the bathroom, I lighted my way with a candle and as I was pass-ing along the dark corridor I heard something move. Scared it might be a rat or a mouse I stopped and listened. It was then that I heard soft breathing near my own ear. I held the candle higher hoping to trace the sound of breathing, what I saw brought tears to my eyes. There were children sleeping on wooden shelves on either side of the corridor with only a thin blanket for covering. A flaxen-haired girl was curled into the back of her brother, her blond curls tum-bling across her face. The twins whom I had seen playing bare-footed in the street in the morning were locked in each other's arms on a shelf on the other side of the corridor. I presumed the two older children were on the shelves I could see above me. I lay awake for hours that night trying to think how I could help those poor little mites and their mother who must be worn out with work and worry. Poppy came into my mind, I got out of bed re-lighted the candle and wrote a letter to her at once, then and only then would my conscience let me sleep. I tried to get my landlady to talk about her miserable state of living, but she was a proud northerner. However, she did tell me that the children's' father had been killed in the 1914-1918 war.

Weeks later when I was home again Poppy passed me an almost unreadable letter in shaky writing. It was from my poor 'Sheffield mum' saying 'thank you' for the parcel of blankets, which I had no idea Poppy had sent. I was overjoyed.

'Thank you for doing what I couldn't do darling' I said hugging her. 'Living here in luxury we don't know how the other half lives' she nodded, turning from me to wipe away a tear.

How I wish I had kept a diary of my Showbusiness days because I know we 'played' in other towns and cities but no names will come to my mind except the biggest thrill of all - the Alhambra theatre in London. I had a great affection for this theatre, not only because of my visit there with my father in 1919 when I was dazzled by the glitter of Showbusiness and dreamed my dream of going on the stage, but because of the many visits with Poppy and of it's history. What fascinated me was the 'Moorish-Oriental' atmosphere created by the huge elephant heads protruding from the side walls, the ornate circular dome, the 'fairy-lights' linking the boxes to the balcony, and the deep crimson plush seats and rich velvet, fringed stage curtains. I loved this old theatre as much as any Londoner and when it came to my appearing there in the *Whirlwind Revue* I could hardly contain my excitement.

We met Clarice Mayne when rehearsing on the Monday morning. I thought her blond pianist looked a bit effeminate, Ruby thought him 'dishy' and Johnnie and Alva were dying to cast their eyes on the renowned legs belonging to one of Pantomime's best loved Principal boys. Clarice Mayne was such a nice person. She chatted for a few moments and as she left the stage for our rehearsal to begin, she waved, saying 'See you tonight.'

Having been away from London for quite a while and being in no mood to rush home after the rehearsal, I wandered around theatre-land. Finding myself outside the London Pavilion in Piccadilly Circus, where lights shone over the marquee illuminating the words 'the centre of the world', I lingered to look at the photographs of the stars in C B Cochran's production *This Year of Grace*. I could not look away from the elfin face of the young girl with enormous eyes and a cute little page-boy fringe. She was of course London's new star Jessie Matthews about whom the critics raved and the newspapers wrote reams. Time and time again I had read about the Soho child, who lived over a butchers shop and was dragged by her sister to dancing classes. How she turned cartwheels and danced on her toes in the back streets, and had the courage and guts to cheek the great C B Cochran without batting an eyelid. Lost in my thoughts of admiration for the young star who had jumped from the chorus-line to stardom in such a short time, my mind filled with a thousand 'ifs'. Dare I even hope that one day I too could attain such heights? In the meantime as just one dancer in a troupe of six, it was time to stop dreaming and have a bath, a meal and return to the Alhambra for the evening performance.

When I reached the dressing room I was astounded to find tension, excitement, high-pitched unnatural chatter followed by long stretches of silence, and something I failed to understand, no gramophone was playing. Until that moment I had been quite calm but suddenly I also got an attack of first night jitters. I gave extra care to my make-up, smoothed the wet white on my legs making sure I had not left any smears and poured myself into my slinky dress. Without the feathered cape and headdress, which would complete this ensemble, I slung a gown around my shoulders and with Ruby and Ethel went down to the wings. We were just in tine to watch the very talented coloured duo Layton and Johnson whose act always brought the house down. Next came Clarice Mayne. It was a great feeling to be appearing alongside these stars and as I heard her sing her three most popular songs *I was a good little girl till I met you*, *Put on your ta-ta-little girl* and a soulful rendering of *Every little while*. For the second time that day I was being confronted by 'star quality'. After taking several curtain calls and doing an encore she walked past us. 'Good luck girls' she chirped and then came the long, long interval wait.

At least we had something to do, to keep us occupied and help pass the time away. We went upstairs to our dressing room to put on our capes and headdresses. Too fidgety to hang around upstairs we went back to the stuffy, smelly wings and back-stage. Midge came down to make sure we got our positioning right for the opening. I stood still like the statue I was meant to be, thinking with envy of those lucky people up there in the bar, laughing, joking, smoking and drinking. Suddenly I heard the bell calling them back to their seats. Within seconds, which seemed like hours, *Tell me pretty maiden* was being played softly by the orchestra. The curtain rose to reveal de Courville's six silver statues looking just the same as the audiences had seen them in Penarth, Nottingham and all the other places we had visited but London, being special, was playing havoc with our nerves.

After those few moments of standing still and posed with arms outstretched were over, we walked sedately with our heads high in the opening parade. On reaching the wings we handed our capes off-stage and formed ourselves into a line, linking our arms with each other behind our backs. In the blues, greens, reds and ambers of the footlights, with the nervousness gone, we beamed at the sea of faces in the auditorium, looked up to the lively crowd in the gods and danced our hearts out. Somewhere out there mingling with beautifully gowned women and men in evening dress sat a very important man. It was our producer Albert de Courville and we were anxious for him to feel proud of his touring revue.

I too had a, secret desire, to do my best for out of the corner of my eye I had seen a party of young revellers occupying a box. Two waved, one whistled and I felt myself go hot. How on earth had Ronald, my cousin, escaped from Rugby for the night? When the show had finished I found him waiting just inside the stage door. I ran into his arms. We hugged and as he said 'You were great Kiddo.' I nearly died with love for him. He nudged me through the stage door and introduced me to his friends, who, with him, dined and wined me at my favourite club, the Kit-Kat, where we danced away the night until it was time for them to leave. I went to the station with them and as Ron embraced me once more he looked at me very directly 'Don't you dare tell Mum... promise' 'Cross my heart' I promised and stood waving until the train disappeared into the darkness of the night.

Poppy had refused to tell me which night she would come to the theatre. When Saturday came I was feeling disgruntled and let down. It was hopeless to expect her to come on a Saturday; that was her special night for making up a party and going to the Victoria Palace.

I loved watching Clarice Mayne, so I wandered down to the wings. Catching sight of me as she came off stage 'Hello there' she said and chucked me under the chin, 'Lovely audience tonight'. 'Yeah, yeah' I thought and went to take my place back stage.

When we were doing our opening parade my eyes were focused on a bunch of happy youngsters in the stalls. I was so fed up, I wished I were down there fooling the evening away with then. But just as we turned the corner of the stage I looked up to the stage box and quickly changed my mind. My Godmother looking 'regal' was smiling down at me. She had George, Brownie and Brownie's son with her and Brownie gave a saucy wave as I discarded my cape ready to dance.

I was always a little embarrassed about my home life of luxury, because I knew some of the dancers were quite poor. There was nothing I would have liked to have done more that turn half a dozen cartwheels and yell 'See that lovely lady up there, she's my God-mum' but I held my tongue. Was I glad, when after our last curtain call flowers were presented to our two leading ladies and huge boxes of chocolates to each of the dancers. They could have come from any of those lovely people applauding so vigorously, but I knew by the mischievous wink which came from the stage box that in a few seconds I was going to have to find an excuse to hide myself in the toilet for awhile or I would give myself away.

When I had calmed down I removed my greasepaint listening to the 'Whoever could have sent them', 'Couldn't be the bass could it?' 'Not Pygmalion likely', 'You're very quiet Kit what do you think?' 'A fairy Godmother I should think'. I grinned, pushing my arms into my coat. 'You're in a hell of a hurry, got a date?' 'Yes, with an angel' I retorted and made for the door. I raced down the stairs and along the passage to the stage door and who should be there but

George.

'This 'ere bloke says ee's your Godfather' said the doorman. 'That's right' I retorted 'Well, I'm the bleedin' Prince of Wales then'. George pushed me through the door and into the waiting taxi which took us home. 'Go on scram, get yourself into your glad rags, Poppy's waiting at the 'Kit-Kat'. 'Why didn't you tell me?' 'Oh go on -and not too much lipstick.'

'Oh golly' I thought remembering Monday night with Ron and his friends 'Oh golly Moses'. What am I going to do, supposing someone mentions that they saw us? I've never changed so fast in my life. When we arrived at the club I walked in serenely with George, but hung back, as he went to take off his coat, to see if I could spat Pierre, our favourite waiter. Fortune favoured me; Pierre was coming in my direction carrying a tray of drinks. I beckoned him cautiously and when he reached me I said 'Pierre I want you to do me a favour, please?' He gave me a very funny look 'Don't you dare say you saw me here on Monday night or I'll kill you.' With one of his most seductive smiles he placed his hand on his heart 'My lips are sealed, my naughty little one'. What a perfect ending to a 'dream week'.

After all those weeks of touring it seemed strange to have a free Sunday at home. I felt quite lost without finding myself standing on some strange railway platform watching the scenery, props and huge wicker baskets packed with our costumes being lifted into the luggage vans.

After the Alhambra, 'Whirlwind Revue' spent a week at the Coliseum and then the Holborn Empire.

When Monday evening came I was as excited as those who had been queuing for hours to see Maisie Gay and I was about to see her 'for free' from the wings. Maisie Gay was the funniest woman entertainer I had ever seen, she was vivacious, bright, and terribly funny. Her act was performed when taking a bath that was partially hidden behind a screen. She sang, shouted, and carried on in an hilarious fashion. Suddenly up would come a bare arm waving a bath brush, followed by some bits of lingerie. Then, with the audience splitting their sides with laughter, out would come a soggy wet wig, which got put back on her head when she poked her head round the corner of the screen bare footed and wrapped in a bath towel. Holding on to the towel and her soggy wet wig she crept and crawled about the stage searching and shrieking for her 'damned slippers,' and not for a second did she let up on her jokes and singing.

Later when I stood on stage that first night as a statue and was supposed to look serious, I could feel ripples of laughter gurgling in my 'tummy' every time I thought of her. She was the best female comic I have ever seen. No-one to my mind as ever reached her capacity for keeping her audience rocking in their seats from start to finish as she could. She was the greatest. Layton and Johnson were in the programme and The Houston Sisters whose voices so adorably Scottish made them very popular. Billie, the fair-haired sister with an Eton crop was the boy; the curly haired red-head played the coy little cutie. She wore a childish dress and toyed with the hem as she twisted, turned and played up to 'big brother'. It was a smart, slick, well-presented act and so delightful as to be in strict contrast to another popular sister act, The Dolly Sisters, who were glamourous and sophisticated.

Very often at the Coliseum and other variety theatres in the twenties, well-known dancing troupes like the Tiller girls, Sherman Fisher dancers, Hoffman girls and Rodney Hudson girls would regularly make appearances. So, with the weight of Mr de Courville's reputation on our shoulders, we took up our statue positions with trepidation.

For our last week in London we left the grandeur of the Coliseum and Alhambra behind for the cosy, warm, happy-go-lucky atmosphere of the Holborn Empire. Long after this story of mine ends in 1961 this 'Darling of the peoples' theatre was demolished. Sadly, it was the end of an era; the Holborn Empire was the last of the London theatres to stage variety shows.

I think that of all the seven nights when we appeared at the Holborn Empire, the last was the best for me, because with Rob

Wilton on the bill, my Godmother could not resist coming.

Rob Wilton, England's funnyman who coined the phrase 'The day war broke out my missus said to me' topped the bill with his 'Fireman's Act'. The back-cloth was of a semi-detached house with smoke streaming from an upstairs window. In comes Rob in fireman's garb, in an endeavour to get his stumbling, tripping self plus ladder, bucket, hatchet and long, long hose to the burning house to the tune '*Keep the home fires burning…* mate'. His legs get caught in the ladder as he leans it against the house, he squirts more water over himself and the musicians in the orchestra pit than down the chimney as he struggles, sings, loses his steel helmet and wellies and eventually lands in a great crash on the stage. The London audiences know his act so well they all shout 'Fire, fire, fire'. He scrambles up helmet awry, and one wellie back to front, 'Wait: wait: don't panic I'm coming' he yells lurching and falling to off stage noises of clatterings and screamings. From where I stood in the wings I could just see Poppy in one of the boxes she was absolutely hysterical, Brownie was mopping her eyes and I guessed was keeping her legs tightly crossed and George was getting up in that 'I need a drink' attitude that I knew so well.

Shouts of 'Encore, encore' came from the auditorium, screams for 'My Missus said to me' from the 'Gods' for their favourite monologue until Rob stepped from between the drawn curtains took off his soaking wet helmet, dropped his hatchet and with a wry smile began 'The day war broke out the missus said to me…'. It was the most riotous of acts to follow, but the seductive Australian Albert Whelan swaggered on whistling *Sleepy time gel* with his pretty female assistant following. His routine accompanied by soft music and his whistling was always the same. He would remove his white gloves and pass them to his female assistant, then his top hat, cane, white silk scarf, and cape. When he finished his act in such a manner that female pulses had quickened their pace, and 'desire' was not too far away he would accept his cape, scarf, top hat and gloves from his assistant and whistled himself away into the wings.

It was horrible to think this was the last time we would be performing in the *Whirlwind Revue*. It had been such a happy tour.

After we had taken our last curtain call and I had waved to my family, I walked slowly and sadly to the dressing room, removed my greasepaint, changed into my own clothes, put my salary of £5 in my pocket and went to say good-bye to Johnnie. We kissed and thanked each other for lovely memories. I had said my farewells to everyone else, swapped addresses and telephone numbers and that was how I found myself standing outside the stage door with nothing else to do but call a cab.

After another break from the stage, Kit was inspired by seeing a 'Solo' acrobatic dancer to have a go at developing her own dancing act. She enrolled with dance teacher and champion ballroom dancer Tommy Askew in Cheniston Gardens, South Kensington, who worked on using Kit in one of the fashionable 'Sister' acts. When Kit's partner dropped out, however, she joined Archie Pitt's 'Lido Follies' at Clacton-on-Sea.

Whether it was intuition, conceit, positive thinking, or fate, I do not know but I was convinced I would be one of the lucky ones, chosen to join Archie Pitt's cast for the *Lido Follies* to be presented at Clacton-on-Sea for the summer season. Happily I was right.

Iris, another of the dancers and I had booked single room in a small guest house on the sea front within easy walking distance of the Westcliffe Gardens Theatre where we were to appear. During rehearsals in London I had chummed up with Iris. I liked this long-legged, big-busted girl with rapid mood changes and large green eyes. At the time when I met her, her hair was blond. 'It could be any colour next week' she would boast and by the sight of her hair roots I believed her. Some shunned her, some seemed in awe of her, I befriended her, sensing that beneath that secure sophistication there was a restless unhappy girl, who had suffered many disappointments and had to fight to survive.

On my first morning after settling into the guest-house I awoke early and lay listening to the sea lapping lazily on the shingle and the lovely crunching sound as it rolled back again. I fell to thinking what I had left behind. My thoughts were not however of home or Poppy, Ronald or Brownie but of Tommy, the man who had become big brother, friend and someone very special of late. As I lay drinking my early morning tea brought to me by a young waitress I could not help thinking of Tommy. He had kissed me good-bye and wished me luck.

I knew I had to pull myself together and forget him, but it hurt.

I wondered if my 'stable-companion' had been awakened by the screech of the gulls and the sounds of the sea. Was she also thinking the early hours of the day away? Would she be remembering those glamorous nights in Paris dancing in the Folies Bergère?. Were there secrets of love, or despair, hidden behind those luminous green eyes (which, in the light of day after being expertly mascara-ed, looked at the world beneath long curling lashes)?

When I was dressed and ready to go downstairs I knocked on her door and we went down to the dining room together. A smartly dressed young maid wearing a black dress and well-starched white cap and apron showed us to a table. It was occupied by a man who rose politely and introduced himself as 'Mac'. Had it not been for Mac, an easy going man of the world with a terrific sense of humour, the derogatory sniffs, the whispered 'tut-tuts' and 'They're in the Show that's coming to the Westcliffe, you know the one Gracie Fields' husband has produced, never can remember his name' might have annoyed or even worried us, but not with Mac there. He laughed everything off. It did not take long for the residents to realise that we did not eat our peas off our knife, or wipe our mouths on the back of our hands, that our table manners equalled or in some cases surpassed their own. So perhaps the 'stage folk' were not as 'bad as they were painted after all'. I think it came as a bit of a shock to them to discover we were not novelties, but normal human beings with families, feelings and morals.

On that first sunny morning in Clacton, Iris and I strolled leisurely along the sea front and following the directions given to us by Gordon Courtenay the writer of our sketches, lyrics and music, we found the theatre easily.

It was the dearest little theatre, jointly owned by Bert Grahame and Will Bentley who also owned the famous Bentley's Oyster Bar in Swallow Street, London. Even more interesting to us was the fact that he had three grown up sons.

I hate the expression 'We're like one big happy family'. It usually means that everyone fights like cat and dog. Strangely enough, in our set-up we really were a happy family. There seemed little distinction between the six stars and the rest of us.

Rehearsals of four different programmes each to cover a period of a week meant a lot of hard work. Yet, under the direction of Archie Pitt's two brothers Bert and Pat Aza, and Gordon Courtney, and the promise of enough time to go for a swim later, everything became fun. I especially liked the idea of the four dancers playing small parts and being given slots for our solos. I enjoyed the involvement and found it very rewarding.

The title, the *Lido Follies,* said everything about the Show. It was written and designed for fun by the sea. It opened with a colourful beach scene of three pretty girls in bathing suits, sitting at umbrella tables casually helping themselves to fruit drinks from glass jugs and another girl was sun bathing. They were singing the opening chorus *On the Lido* in a casual manner when interrupted by the comedian Eddie Garr in his act *Rough Stuff.*

Connie Rhodes and Len Clifford followed him in a song and dance duet *Bathe away your blues* with a supporting cast of The Lido Bathing Girls. Various sketches always followed interspersed with solos or duets sung by Madge Luya, soprano, and Booth Hitchen whose tenor voice was strong and very dramatic. A well-loved performer and friend to all of us.

The next time the dancers appeared 'en bloc' was in front of the drop curtain in a number *Sunny Days.* I loved this. We wore brilliant ginger wigs, short silk jade green Jazzy dresses, with flared skirts lined with orange. It was a typical high-kicking troupe number designed as an eye-catcher and sexy to per-form.

I enjoyed all our numbers because the choreographer had kept the movements, costumes, and songs quite distinctive from each other. For instance, the closing number of the first half involving the entire company was *Sunny Hawaii.* The attractive setting was of a South Sea island swaying palm trees, miles of golden sands, and a rolling ocean seen as if at low-tide.

Kit Peters in her specialty costume in 'Lido Follies'

We four dancers were the dusky maidens revealing a great deal of our honey-coloured bodies beneath grass skirts and richly coloured bra's. On our arms we wore native bracelets, on our legs anklets, and round our necks rows and rows of beads and floral garlands. We were fortunate that a new kind of sun-tan-coloured lotion had appeared on the market, which aided by the predominant amber foot lighting gave a sunny hue to our bodies. Everyone sang *Underneath the moon in Honolulu* while the rolling hip swaying of the bare-footed dancers, the sound of their jingling beads and armlets and muffled drum beat from Barney made the 'Land of the Coconuts' seem very real. It was a perfect ending to the first half of the *Follies*.

During the interval the Lido Baltimore Band consisting of four musicians played one of Gordon Courtenay's lively compositions *The Show's the thing* thus leading the show into the second half *Carnival time at Chez-nous*.

The carnival was being held at night in the 'Hotel Excelsior'. It was the usual kind of dimly lit cabaret scene with drinks, glasses, ashtrays and things on tables. A few chairs here and there, couples drinking, chatting and dancing created a very happy picture of an evening's enjoyment when on holiday. It was all so natural, and as you watched the ladies in their pretty or striking, long evening dresses, it was easy to imagine these ladies taking a lot of trouble to make themselves look attractive for the evening out.

I have very good cause to remember my long shot silk blue-green dress with a plunging neckline, tight waist and voluminous long skirt. Every night my partner guided me past the candle-lit tables in the direction of the wings to make a surreptitious exit for a quick change for my dancing solo. Maud our dresser and I had worked out an infallible routine of six easy movements to be performed at great speed, in the smallest and darkest of changing rooms by the wings. Movement number one, Maud would undo the hooks at the back of the dress (I am of course speaking of the days before we had zip fasteners or velcro), number two, I would let the dress drop to the floor. Number three; Maud was to slip a thin multi-coloured muslin dress over my head.

66

One night our infallibility went sadly wrong. I had, inadvertently, forgotten to remove the thick clumsy bra I had worn for the Hawaiian scene. I was so horrified, I wrenched it off with such gusto that it and its lightweight counterpart worn beneath, suddenly became as airborne as pair of turtle doves. The two bras floated up into the 'flies' until coming to rest clinging amorously to one of the ropes. 'Charlie, Charlie' I yelled to the stage-hand who was a habitual 'peeper' and 'eavesdropper' from above. No answer. The seconds were ticking away, I panicked and Barney who was the caller of my cue 'Hey, hey Charleston' was already shouting. I nearly died. But Maud, great old trooper that she was, grabbed me. 'Come on gel' she said 'Stick this 'ere dress over yer 'ead, stick yer nose up in't air and go on stage as if nuffin 'ad 'appened'. With Barney yelling 'Hey, hey, Charleston' for the third time, she shoved the muslin dress made of layers of frills over my head, pulling the neck frill down as low as it would go. 'Never got a bloody safety pin when yer wants it' she muttered giving me a mighty push. I faced the audience, heard the great roar and the wolf-whistles as the power of the spot lights fell across my chest lighting up the two dainty little rosebuds beneath my lemon yellow muslin bodice, revelling in their new found freedom. As brazen as a couple of early Victorian tarts they bobbed up and down in perfect time with my tapping feet, until at last my embarrassment over, I dropped into the splits to an ecstatic round of applause. I had never been a greater success with the lads. I guess I was all kinds of an indecent hussey with the élite.

Tears of shame were very near when I walked into the dressing room. Maud put her arms round me; 'Never mind ducks...'. Her sentence remained unfinished as the door was flung open and a very red faced angry manager yelled 'What the hell do you think you're playing at?' 'It weren't 'er fault, Sir' interrupted Maud. 'Shut up you'. By this time I was sitting down, Maud was standing by my elbow and the Manager was still ranting and raving. Infuriated by the way he had shouted at Maud, and thinking 'well I'm going to get the sack anyway, so what' I rose to my full five foot six inches to say, 'Excuse me Sir, but with such excellent applause tonight I am surprised at your anger. Perhaps you should recall the words of that famous poet Rupert Brooks who wrote 'He wondered whether to praise or blame her''.

The other girls had returned to their dressing tables by now and I knew they were stifling their giggles, but the manager glared. 'Don't you get smart with me you brazen bitch' he shouted and turning to go bumped into a cheerful, grinning, Charlie who was dangling my two bra's before his eyes, and singing 'Here's a thing, a very pretty thing, who is the owner of this very pretty thing?'

I tossed and turned all that night wishing I had not tried to be clever and asking myself a thousand times what had got into me? I thought of the disgrace of being sacked, what would Poppy say? What would Tommy think of me? Oh hell, what had I done? I could not face breakfast, I walked over to the sea and gazed and gazed until I felt a hand on my shoulder and heard a soft Scottish voice saying 'Come on old girl, it's not the end of the world'. It was Mac. He had brought me a lovely bacon sandwich and a cup of coffee. 'Iris told you'. 'Yes, don't be angry with her' and with that Iris arrived and I munched away realising the truth in that grand old saying 'What are friends for'.

There was a note on my dressing table when I got to the theatre. 'Come to my office' it said. Meekly I did and was ready to apologise, but before I could open my mouth, the manager who was seated at his desk threw a black and yellow dress at me. 'Here, take this' he grinned 'It might keep you decent'. 'You mean you are not going to sack me.'

'Well, what would your deceased friend Rupert Brooke say if I did?' With my usual impetuosity I ran to his desk and hugged him. 'Hey steady on old thing' he chuckled and kissed my cheek.

Normally I was a very happy person, but Bognor depressed me. On the last night, I had a curious kind of premonition that I would never appear on stage again. The tears rolled down my cheeks and the girls teased me, 'Don't be so daft, don't be so theatrical, who do you think you are, Greta Garbo?' This wretched depression refused to go, even in the atmosphere of my own home. I decided to go up to Cheniston Gardens, to see if Tommy had come back from America and pick up on the news. As usual, I went down the basement steps and to my surprise the door was locked, I could see a faint light coming from the room beyond the office so I rang the bell. Olive, Tommy's secretary came to the door, her eyes were red. I could see she had been crying. 'What an earth is the matter?' 'You'd better come in.' Through more weeping she told me things I had never suspected. To those of us, who shared in the happiness of Tommy's Academy, spoke of him proudly as the champion ballroom dancer, choreographer of the famous Gaston and André acrobatic dancing act and teacher of every kind of dance, he was on a pedestal from which he could never tumble.

Poor Tommy had tumbled. I listened as Olive raved about his qualities, his generosity, how women had robbed him, and brought him to bankruptcy.

All the time she was speaking, I was remembering his touch, his tuition, his bedroom, his farewell kiss, and my spirits were sinking further and further. 'Where is he Olive?' 'Nobody knows dear, he has gone into hiding and the receivers have taken possession of everything. I am here just to answer callers, hand over the books and close the door for the last time this coming Friday.'

I cried with Olive, I said 'good-bye' walked up the basement steps and stood for several minutes gazing at the place I had learned to love as much as its master. 'What now?' Poppy seemed to understand why I felt so unsettled as we talked over my future. 'I want you at home more darling' she said 'You are at a very vulnerable age'. I thought that remark was a bit outdated, I had been vulnerable for several years. However, I made no reply and scanned the pages of the *Stage* newspaper for the announcements of forthcoming auditions.

Throwing the paper into the air, and yelling 'Whoopee' I showed Poppy what I had found. 'Look, look, dancers wanted for Julian Wylie's London production of *Mr Cinders*. As was my habit I clasped my hands together, looked heavenwards and mouthed 'please, please.'

When I reached the theatre, where the audition was being held, I nearly ran home. There were well over a hundred dancers all nervously dropping off their day clothes to slip into audition garb, put on their dancing shoes, add a extra touch of lipstick or eyeblack, and wait and wait and wait for their name to be called.

I was thinking how much I would like to work for dear old Julian Wylie again when I spotted Eddie Dolly in the auditorium. Eddie had choreographed *Humpty-Dumpty*. I was dying to go down to him and say 'Hey, remember that dumb kid of the Jackson girls in Liverpool, a few years back, that was me'. My courage failed me.

After what seemed a life-time later I heard him call 'next please' and as I was that person. I handed my music to the pianist, sang a chorus of *Annabelle Lee* and high kicked, back-bended, cartwheeled and tapped danced myself into a final split, raising one arm and throwing Eddie a most daring smile, all of which got me on to his short list.

Those of us selected were to line up for Eddie to come and talk to. When he reached me he smiled 'I know you' he said pushing back his hair as he thought 'I know, *Humpty-Dumpty*, Liverpool'. I felt myself blush. 'What a memory' I said. 'Nice to have you around again, good luck'. He passed on. I raced hone to tell Poppy and hoped she would not stand in my way just because I would have to go to Manchester for six weeks for the opening.

I got a letter of confirmation and informed of contract signing day and the first rehearsal. It was wonderful to walk into a theatre and hear again the familiar sounds of hammering and whistling workmen. There were my new companions, who like me, were rubbing their hands and jumping up and down to get the circulation going.

A London show, a Julian Wylie production, back again with Eddie Dolly and to work close to such a star as Bobby Howes, how could I be so lucky? Every step I took homewards had a special spring to it; I turned into Collinghan Place feeling on top of the world. When I was almost there I saw a familiar figure whom I recognised, he was wearing a long dark grey coat, carrying a doctor's bag and putting on a black trilby hat as he came down our front steps. I ran towards him. His grave face told me something awful had happened'. 'Who is it Doctor?' He took my hand in his as he told me gently that Poppy had been taken very ill and was on the danger list. I thought I should faint and leaned against the railings of one of the houses 'Would you like me to come back with you?' 'No, 'I'll be alright Doctor, thanks' I said.

As I ran I fumbled for my key, let myself in and found George pacing the music-room. He came towards me 'It's alright' I said 'I know, I met the Doctor' and with that I left him and went to Poppy's bedside. Anybody looking more like a corpse I had never seen. Her skin was translucent, her breathing hardly audible, her eyelids closed. She was under heavy sedation, all I could do was sit on a chair beside her bed and hold her hand. I sat there for hours. Sometime in the early part of the night, after I had undressed and moved to the big pouffe in her bedroom, I heard her breathing change a little. I went to her and she opened her eyes and gave me a weak smile.

The next day when Dr Lund and the Surgeon came I was told that a few days ago she had fallen awkwardly and twisted her intestine. The damage could be fatal, particularly as she was too ill to move for an X-ray. She was only to be given sips of water or orange juice, nothing else. How different it would be nowadays?

It was seventeen days of constant nursing care before she found her voice and was allowed to suck barley sugar sticks, drink, rather than sip orange juice and sit out for a short while in a chair. I knew I could never tell her how, with my heart breaking, I had been to see Eddie Dolly. How I cried all over his shoulder, how he released from the contract I had signed which would have given me the chance of my young life. As I looked at her, so frail, and heard her words of appreciation because I had never left her, I felt as if I was being split in half. I adored the stage, and wanted more than anything in this world to be a 'star' one day. On the other hand I loved my Godmother more than words could express and she loved me. As she progressed and was out of danger she became more and more dependent on me. Life was cheating me and making me feel bitter. One afternoon when Poppy was asleep, I felt as if I could not stand this trapped feeling another minute. I went upstairs to my bedroom, but instead of staying inside I went out on to the balcony. How long I stood watching the clouds scudding across the sky above the rooftops, I have no idea. My vision was blurred with images of all the people, scenes, loves and excitements that had made up the last eight years of freedom and happy living.

Now, I would have to play another role, that of being a dutiful daughter. I sighed. As I did, a magnificent silver lining split the clouds and a gentle hand touched my shoulder. Lost in the beauty, I had not heard Brownie's step. We stood hugging each other for several minutes; she was so understanding and seemed to know exactly what I was feeling. She rested her tiny head against me; she was much shorter than I and pointed to the sky. 'You see that silver lining darling'. I nodded. 'No matter how long you have to wait child, or how many miles you have to travel. One day you will find your silver lining and when you do, it will be as bright and beautiful as that lovely light smiling down upon us.

After many turbulent years I found Brownie's silver lining, which has stayed with me for the rest of my life. Poppy died in 1953, I married in 1957 and owing to my husband having a serious accident and injuring his spine, I became our bread-winner in 1959. It was then I found my niche in a caring for the elderly job. By the time my husband Jack died in 1969 I had been in charge of an establishment for the elderly for eight years. I continued working in this capacity for the East Sussex County Council until I retired in 1976. My retirement has surpassed all my expectations. I give thanks for a wonderful life.

Memories are made of this

Randle S Cutts

On 22 June 1926 Walter Henry Butler from Birmingham married Margaret Kane from Byres Road, Glasgow in St. Peter's Church in that city. The groom was better known as Wal Butler, a revue and variety comedian, and the bride as Ida Lyndon, a soubrette and dancer. Neither had come from theatrical families. Wal had been a member of the 48th Divisional Concert Party during the First World War and after demob gave up his job in an engineering factory to become a full time performer. Ida Lyndon had been on the boards since joining Harry Loman's dancing troupe at the age of fourteen after graduating from 'back-court concerts'. After his marriage to Ida, Wal was booked to appear as Buttons in *Cinderella* at the Glasgow Queen's opposite the great Scottish comedienne, Doris Droy. It was during this run that Ida gave birth to their son who was named after his father but designated Wally to prevent confusion. Soon after his birth, in true theatrical tradition,

Wal, as Buttons, brought his son on stage and held him up to the audience amidst thunderous applause.

Looking at the date-books of the various members of the Butler family is a revelation. We learn, for instance, that Ida spent some time in the resident circus in Glasgow. In one Wild West scene she played an Indian maid who dived from a waterfall into a tank below. As principal comic, producer and manager of the company Wal had copious date-books which included such essential information as the names, addresses and telephone numbers of landladies and theatres in each town he visited.

Wal and his family made their base at Ida's family home at 73 Byres Road, which was also theatrical digs for artistes performing at the Empire, Theatre Royal and other Glasgow theatres. They would have had only a light tea before going to the theatre and Wally Butler well remembers being made to rest in the afternoon before evening performances. After the show, as was common, they brought their own food back to cook for supper. As most of the numerous theatres in the suburbs and around Glasgow were a mere tram ride from the city centre, performers on the circuit could stay at Byres Road for weeks on end and commute easily to and from work.

Wal Butler had only played Edinburgh and Glasgow but Ida had toured all over Scotland including summer seasons as a featured performer in the Harry Gordon company at the Beach Pavilion in Aberdeen where, as well as singing and dancing, she acted as a feed for Harry Gordon. Young Wally went to school in Glasgow but during the long summer holidays toured with the family company to north of England resorts such as Blackpool, Lytham and Scarborough. In winter he often appeared uncredited in pantomimes, coming on in the schoolroom and ghost scenes. He learnt his trade well during these summer seasons and in pantomime. So much so, that after first joining up in a Scottish regiment at the start of the Second World War he found himself drafted to the *Stars in Battledress* company and spent the rest of his service travelling with morale boosting shows to soldiers in all sorts of locations.

After demob Wally went back on the Scottish variety circuit

Wal Butler as Buttons

but finding that he was having too many weeks with no work decided to widen his scope, reckoning that he would be more bookable if he had more to offer. Using his gratuity he enrolled at the Royal Scottish Academy of Music and Dramatic Art in Glasgow for a course in music and left as an accomplished pianist and composer. Adding these talents to his ability as a comic feed and all round utility man Wally was able to get pretty steady work with road shows headed by a number of top Scots comedians. He worked at the Aberdeen Tivoli as a pianist for Andy Stewart in his early days but this promising partnership ended when Andy was given the role of Widow Twanky in *Aladdin* in Glasgow. Andy could only offer Wally a job as his dresser so he was forced to look for pastures new. After a lean period his college music qualification stood him in good stead when he got a job in a revue starring Grace Clark and Colin Murray. He was to be their pianist, utility artiste and also to help in the general production, but there was a problem. The show was opening in the Tivoli theatre in Aberdeen and Wally was in Glasgow without the money for the rail fare north. Fortunately, the Scottish Variety Artists' Benevolent Fund came to his rescue by giving him a railway warrant so he was able to take the job. Clark and Murray paid his digs and he paid them back out of his first week's wages.

It was this, and other similar experiences, that prompted Wally later in his career to try to do something for fellow artistes down on their luck. He learned that *Laudervale*, the former home of Harry Lauder on the Dunoon seafront, had come up for sale. It had been run as an hotel for a number of years and standing in two and a half acres of grounds had unsurpassed and uninterrupted views of the Firth of Clyde. Wally thought it would be ideal as a rest home for variety performers temporarily having a hard time; not a retirement home, but somewhere they could go for a bit of looking after until circumstances took a turn for the better. He was working at Scottish Television at the time and set about trying to interest individuals and organisations in his proposal but met with very little success. He was particularly disappointed with the lack of interest shown by the Scottish Variety Artists' Benevolent Fund and the top of the bill performers. The ordinary rank and file turns couldn't afford to sponsor it so the pipe dream died. Eventually the building was pulled down, after a fire I think, and all that remains of its former connection is the name, Lauder Close, given to a group of maisonettes that now occupy the site. Wally's father, Wal Butler, had known and worked with Lauder and some years later when Wally was at Granada Television in Manchester he directed a programme on the great entertainer starring Jimmy Logan.

Going back to the early days in variety, Wally's break came when he met and formed a double act with a young comedian called Johnny Beattie. They called themselves Beattie and Butler and Wally played the piano and feed while Johnny did most of the comedy. Wally testifies that it is no easy task being a comic's foil and that timing is all-important. You have to know just when and how to feed the right line to him. A successful partnership is like a good marriage where each partner almost instinctively knows the others thoughts. Wally at the piano was often the butt of Johnny's jokes but every so often would come back with a riposte to which Johnny would react with a double take. It seemed very impromptu but was honed down to the last detail. Their material was mostly domestic in content, designed to appeal to Scottish audiences.

One other comic who often appeared with them in sketches was Hector Nicol who also subscribed to the view that Scots had a great sense of humour and could laugh at themselves. Many of the jokes in the sketches were at the expense of their own countrymen but still got gales of laughter because they were delivered by fellow Scots. The same material in an English accent would been booed off the stage.

Butler and Beattie played the Glasgow Empire but the Glasgow theatre where they played most often was the Empress. They still had to take some very indifferent dates at number three theatres, what Wally calls 'tat' weekends and church halls. Some of these week end bookings were set up by the blind agent, Christopher Morrison known simply as 'Stopher', one of whose top of the bill acts was The Zangler Brothers. This was a mind reading duo whose bill matter read, 'Like nothing else on earth!' and Wally says that this

Wally Butler at Scottish Television

was indeed true. Wally and Johnny also worked on occasion for the Maitless Brothers who once booked them into the Roxy theatre in Falkirk. When they arrived at the theatre they found that the show was called *Hollywood Doubles* and they had no idea whom they were to 'double'. Nothing daunted, Beattie and Butler borrowed a couple of bowler hats, improvised and appeared as Laurel and Hardy. Also for the Maitless Brothers they found themselves sharing Friday night bills with pie eating contests. According to Wally they were often paid in pies if too few contestants turned up to eat what had been ordered. Perhaps their strangest booking was as part of a company put together to tour and provide entertainment for the patients in what were then called Lunatic Asylums. Despite having what Wally calls 'captive audiences' it was an unnerving experience. There were tours round the hinterland of Scotland and Wally has happy memories of the bonhomie and camaraderie of these. Dancing and other forms of entertainment were usually included with everyone joining in the fun.

After the double act broke up Wally Butler found employment for some time in the 'straight' side of the business. He was invited to direct a production of the Emlyn Williams thriller *Night Must Fall* at the Kilmarnock Palace and made such a success of this that he remained there for fifteen months. He also produced for quite a while at the Rutherglen Repertory Company. Then he moved to Scottish Television where he wrote scripts and produced for their popular show, *The One O'clock Gang* for four years. Here, remembering the time when he found work hard to get, he made a point of bringing in many of the performers of his variety days to let them play before the large lunchtime audience that the programme pulled in. An example of this was singer Monte Rey who after he retired from the stage became Pier Master on the Isle of Arran.

Several seasons ago Wally with his wife, Joyce was on holiday at the Cowal Highland Games and took the opportunity to renew acquaintance with his old partner, Johnny Beattie who was appearing in the New Pavilion, Dunoon. After the show they talked long into the night about the 'good old days' and the many theatres in which Beattie and Butler appeared. All are recorded in Wally's date-books but not many of them remain - perhaps only the Ayr Gaiety and the Glasgow Pavilion. Wally has mixed memories of the old days, some fond and some, like the soul destroying trek around the agents in Sauchiehall Street, not so fond.

While directing *Coronation Street* for Granada Wally renewed family links with one of the great music hall stars, Randolph Sutton, who had been a friend of his father. The Butler date-books and papers contain many references to Sutton and G. H. Elliot and to this day Wally has some silverware given as a present to Wal Butler by Randolph Sutton. In two episodes in the one week there was a segment in which Ena Sharples, Minnie Caldwell and Martha Longhurst went to the nearby Viaduct Club to see Randolph Sutton perform in person. In each of the two episodes he sang one of his popular numbers. By having these scenes in the soap opera Wally was keeping faith with the music hall tradition while acknowledging the dominance of the social clubs which had supplanted it.

When they were still performing Wal Butler and Ida would return to Byres Road two or three times a year for short breaks between tours in England. As well as performing Wal was responsible for all aspects of his touring revue company from stage production to organizing bookings and travel arrangements. Ida not only performed but trained the dancing troupe in all forms of stage dancing from ballet to tap. Being Scottish to the core, her girls could also perform a handbell routine to traditional airs like *The Bluebells of Scotland*. She was also an accomplished seamstress and as wardrobe mistress designed and made exceptional costumes for herself, the troupe and even Wal. The demise of variety began first in England during the 1950s and Wal found himself working more and more in the clubs of Yorkshire and Lancashire. Because of this Ida retired from the stage and opened theatrical digs in Wakefield although the long established digs in Glasgow were kept on. Wal's main base was Wakefield but he also used Byre's Road until after Ida's death when the flat was sold. Wal Butler died in 1974, ten years after his wife.

What of Wally Butler? After his spell as a television producer of light entertainment and drama first at Scottish Television and then

Wally with the "One O' clock Gang"

at Granada, he went back to College. This time it was as a member of staff and he finally retired as Chief Lecturer at the Manchester Polytechnic School of Theatre. In recent years he has made a point of renewing old friendships when the Scottish Variety Artistes' Benevolent Fund brought parties for a week's break at Blackpool. Many hours were spent blethering with such as Maidie Dickson, the St. Denis Sisters, Billy Crockett, Billy Cameron, Anne Fields and Sally Logan

I am very grateful to Wally for giving me the privilege of going through the voluminous date-books, papers and photo-graphs that tell the story of his family's thirty years of touring round the provincial theatres. This is only a small part of that story, relating to the Scottish connection, and the major portion dealing with the family as a whole, the theatres in which they played, details of the sketches and pantomimes written by Wal is contained in my book *The 12.40 From Crewe - being the adventures of a touring theatrical family's 30 years in the provinces 1920 - 1950.*

(Copies of *The 12.40 from Crewe* may be obtained by sending a cheque for £5.00 to Randle Cutts at 41 Hereford Drive, Prestwich, Manchester, M25 0AG)

The Three Dancing Dudes and Rita

Reg Maxfield

According to Reg, he and his older brothers Cyril and Percy Maxfield just drifted into the showbusiness career that took them round the top music halls and cabaret spots of the 1930s. The three boys (born in 1914, 1915 and 1916 respectively) started ballet lessons at Nottingham teacher Noreen Bush's school in 1925 and gradually progressed through their grades until by 1931 Noreen Bush's husband, Victor Leopold (a well-known light comedian and tap dancer) saw their potential, produced several routines for the 'Three Maxfield Brothers' and entered them for the 'Dancing Times Exhibition and Cabaret Competition' in the Locarno Dance Hall, Streatham, London. They won Bronze (the prize being a week's engagement at the Ritz dance hall, Manchester). The next step was an appearance in the Leicester Opera House's Dick Whittington. They played for the price of their railway fares, but as Victor Leopold correctly assessed, the experience would be worth it.

We had been seen by an agent in a pantomime *Dick Whittington* who booked us for the forthcoming Baxter and Barter twice nightly tour of *Wonder Bar*. This was a musical play complete with the original stage set from the 1930 André Charlot's production at the Savoy Theatre London.

The cast at the Savoy Theatre featured Carl Brisson, Dorothy Dickson, Elsie Randolph, Gwen Farrar, Enid Stamp-Taylor, Betty Frankiss and Joseph Greenwald as 'Sam Wonder'. The music score was outstanding with the main numbers: *Elizabeth, Wonder Bar, Turning night into day, Alone in a crowd, I've got a plan about you, Who's to blame, I'll believe in you*, and a tango *Tell me I'm forgiven*. The kind of tunes which the audience hummed as they left the theatre and butcher's boys whistled as they made their deliveries.

Among the principals of the touring show was Mignon Morenza (who had been at the Savoy) Peggy Rose, Ian Braested, Fred Wynne, David Lee, Norman Astridge, Monty Golding and Audrey Beauchamp. Included in the cabaret were the Terry Sisters and Peggy Desmond, Six Viennese Dancers, Primrose Ives, The Masked Singers, Three Maxfield Brothers, Bertie Robbins and a full musical comedy chorus.

The novel feature of the show is that it removed the barrier of the footlights the stage being extended over the orchestra well down to the stalls where some rows of seats had been removed. All the characters entered from the back of the theatre down the aisles and up steps on to the stage. All the men in full evening dress and the ladies in glamorous evening gowns.

On stage the tables were spaced out as in a night-club with an area for dancing, the pit band under our own musical director were on a bandstand. We sat at the tables drinking lemonade or cold tea as though it was champagne and whisky, in between dancing with our partner and slipping out for our cabaret number.

The salary for the three of us was £10 a week. After paying the agent's 10% and sending £3 home to our father to recompense for the outlay on our training, we were left with £2 each before paying our digs which cost £1 a week full board. Over the two year's run we played many sea-side theatres which made the week most enjoyable except for the fact when business was slack the men were asked to walk around the town with sandwich boards giving out leaflets advertising the show

After a few weeks I was offered the job of assistant props for a £1 a week which seemed marvellous as I was under the impression that I had only to see to the props. With great pride I opened a Post Office savings account and managed to bank the £1 each week. On the Saturday I realised that there was more to the job than just the props because I was told to report after the second house in old clothes to help, together with some other members of the cast, to dismantle the scenery - one minute you were in evening dress and then as the curtain came down at the finale it was a quick change into old clothes.

The scenery and the many theatrical baskets were loaded into lorries at the stage door, we went with them to the railway siding and off-loaded into box cars, returning backwards and forwards until it was finished. Before the last load my job was to sweep and tidy up all the dressing rooms. We finally arrived back at the digs about two o'clock in the morning.

Train call on Sunday morning was usually quite early and the theatrical profession seemed to take over the railways with various companies changing from town to town. Nearly all the compartments on the train were marked 'reserved' with the title of the show. For some reason the railways had first and third class compartments only. I can't remember any buffet cars, but at all main line stations the train stopped for ten minutes and was met by mobile tea-trolleys using real cups at a penny a cup, newsboys running up and down the platform with the Sunday newspapers two pence each. I recall the sturdy Nestlé chocolate machines a penny a bar.

In later years we sometimes travelled up north across country. The carriages were composed of single compartments without corridors or toilets. They say necessity is the mother of invention so in the end we solved the problem.

The Sunday trains were met by a variety of people touting for the local landladies, some were good looking girls who were snapped up under the impression that they were the landlady's daughter.

After settling into the digs, I had to report to the station to help with the unloading of the scenery etc to transfer it to the theatre. Monday morning was another early start to erect the show, which took all day with a break at midday to visit the nearest pub. I had a lemonade, the others settled for beer at 4d a pint. There was always free cheese and hunks of fresh bread on the counter.

The show had just one set, a replica of a West End night-club and was very intricate to assemble with the extended stage and the electrical wiring. Sometimes it wasn't completely finished until an hour before the start of the first house.

One Monday morning we nearly had a dreadful accident. It happened whilst erecting the skeleton framework of one side of the set. The ropes slipped causing the heavy framework to collapse missing our stage manager by inches. Everyone always had to stand clear while he was directing this operation. The nearest comparable illustration to this was in a Buster Keaton silent film when the whole side of a house fell over on its side with Buster standing in the opening where a window would have been. His scene could have been rehearsed, but was still very risky. Ours was not rehearsed and our stage manager was extremely lucky.

In December 1932 the show was taken off the road for the last two weeks in December and the first two weeks in January 1933. To keep the lower paid members together, the management arranged bookings for this period. Two weeks at Romano's in the Strand and the other two at Murray's Club Beak Street WC2. There were twelve of us in all, mainly from the show's cabaret. For the four weeks in cabaret we stayed in Brixton where we had good digs. Brixton was a popular district for pros mainly on account of the all night trams, especially in our situation with the last show at one o'clock.

Wonder Bar resumed the tour in late January and it didn't take long for everybody to settle down. It has been recorded that some theatres are haunted. My brother would agree after seeing the 'Grey Lady' at the Theatre Royal York. It happened one day when he arrived early at the theatre, on finding the stage door closed he took an alternative way via the front of the house, which was a long tunnel leading back stage. As he approached a junction near the end of the passage something impelled him to glance to the right and observed a greyish shape which appeared to be that of a lady.

For a moment he thought it was a cleaning lady until he realised that the cleaners finished at midday. When she started to float towards him without any sound he decided to run.

When we arrived he was sitting on the stage as white as a sheet under the single batten light which is left on during the day for safety reasons. The stage manager confirmed that he also had seen the 'Grey Lady'. The chorus girls were glad when that week was over, especially as one night my youngest brother draped himself in a white sheet and wandered the corridors moaning. The chorus girls complained to the stage director who soon put a stop to it. I must admit that on Saturday night during my chore of cleaning up the dressing rooms on my own it was very eerie, which made me move like an express train. (The legend of the 'Grey Lady' as related by the stage manager refers to a nun who was walled up alive during the 1600s in a building on the site of the original Theatre Royal built in 1765).

After seeing the 'Grey Lady' Cyril became very interested in the supernatural. He was delighted to find out the following week in Halifax that the landlady was, so he said, a medium. After the show at night we were persuaded to sit around a table fingers touching trying to make contact with the 'Grey Lady' but of no avail – she must have been on holiday.

During the tour two outstanding happy events occurred in 1933. The first was the marriage of Maisie Bonner, one of the Terry Sisters, to Bob our touring electrician, no time for a honeymoon. The second event was the birth of a baby girl to Peggy Desmond the pianist with the Terry Sisters. She worked until a couple of days before the birth. The baby was christened Wanda from the show. It is always a sad occasion when any show breaks up especially after a long run because the atmosphere has been created of a large family and now is splitting up not knowing what the future holds.

The 1929 Wall Street Crash caused a worldwide recession which affected Britain during the 1930s. The Depression did not seem to affect us, or if it did we didn't notice. We were young and not politically minded and also lucky to have regular work. The theatres and cinemas played to full houses, the admission prices were reasonable and salaries were not excessive. The cinemas were the dream palaces where, especially in the 1930s, people could escape from the dreary realities of everyday life to a world of excitement, glamour and romance.

When wireless arrived in 1922 it was forecast that this would affect the theatres, but in fact the public wanted to see the artistes who had broadcasted. The first theatre to broadcast live variety was the Argyle Theatre Birkenhead in 1931. The same worries were expressed when talking pictures came in 1928. Silent films had already been shown since 1910 in music halls that had the facilities to adapt also to sound and cine- variety. (The first all-talking-all-singing-all-dancing film was the *'Broadway Melody* in 1929.)

After *Wonder Bar* we returned to Nottingham and arranged for Victor Leopold to produce a ten minute dancing act which we presented at the Victoria Dance Hall. The resident band was Billy Merrin and his Commanders. Victor Leopold fixed us with a London agent, Reeves and Lamport, our first booking was at the London Pavilion giving us our first taste of five shows a day followed by various dates including a cabaret spot for a bicycle exhibition at the Albert Hall.

Reeves and Lamport advised us to team up with a girl to give the act a greater appeal and suggested contacting Jacquello's Dance Agency on Charing Cross Road. Perhaps on reflection they were trying to get rid of us.

Fate must have taken a hand on the morning we arrived at the agency because Rita White was there looking for two male dancers to partner her in a comedy acrobatic rag doll dance which she had previously performed with two French men. Harry Dennis the Manager of Jacquello's who was an ex-dancer in a variety act saw the potential in combining the four in an act built around the already established doll routine.

Jack Hylton's Band had recently returned from their American Tour and his resident dancer offered to Harry Denis a routine of a new type of tap suitable for three men in a simultaneous dance. An agreement was finalised and so the act was beginning to take shape as we had already completed rehearsing the 'doll dance'. Finally the act was put together and just needed constant rehearsals. The finished product consisted of six dance routines contained within twelve minutes as a non-stop 'ensemble of dance'. Rita opened with a chorus of song *Keep young and beautiful* followed by a high kicking chorus. Dressed in a long red satin dress with long black lapels, split at the front. She had a lovely figure, personality, and a good voice.

As she made her exit, we entered to eight bars of *Who walks in when I walk out* then into our simultaneous tap dance to *Bye-bye blues*. As we made our exit, Rita entered for her acrobatic solo to a waltz *Friends* wearing a white type bathing suit with a bare midriff, the costume studded with rhinestones with long diaphanous sleeves, and gold slippers. As Rita made her exit, my brother ran on to perform a fast tap solo to *Whispering*.

During his solo Rita did a quick change into a short gingham dress, change of shoes and red patches on her cheeks. Percy and I had already changed into gold satin blouses and wine-coloured trousers supported by satin braces with matching shoes. As Cyril came off we ran on with Rita slung across our arms for the comedy acrobatic doll dance, to the tune *The wedding of Mr and Mrs Mickey Mouse*. At the end of the doll dance Cyril joined us also in gold blouse etc for a fast quick fire number to *Rhythm*.

We didn't realise at the time why the non-stop idea was so good, because it didn't give the audience time to applaud the individual numbers, which at the end resulted in three or four curtain calls. Every performer knows the wonderful feeling that applause can give. It is understandable why some old time music hall stars continued to perform even though they should have retired because after so many years the applause had become like a drug.

During rehearsals at Jacquello's a Mr Eric Popplewell came into the studio sat down and quietly watched us then left without a word. A few minutes later Harry Dennis entered with a big smile and announced that we had been booked for the 1934 *Gaiety Whirl*, Ayr, rehearsals starting 28 May for sixteen weeks with nine weeks to follow on Moss Empires.

At first the act was called 'The Harry Dennis Four With Rita' but this caused some confusion as it indicated that the act consisted of five members so after a few weeks it was changed to the 'Three Dennis Boys And Rita'. The *Gaiety Whirl* was a great start for a new act, Rita was seventeen years old, Percy eighteen, Reg nineteen and Cyril twenty. We were already booked for six dates before we were due in Ayr which was a great help in polishing the act because there is a world of difference between rehearsals and a live audience.

The cast of the *Gaiety Whirl* included Dave Willis, Babette O'Deal, Janet Worth, Nora Savage, Stanley Pope, Three Dennis Boys and Rita, Pauline and Diana Owens, The Gaiety Twelve, Benny Loban and his Music Weavers and Jack and Jerry Desmonde. The show was a big success from the start, well dressed, great scenery and well produced. It was hard work changing the programme each week which meant rehearsing daily for the following week's show but at the same time a great learning experience, even having to be the back half of the Loch Ness Monster.

Dave Willis was one of those comics who wasn't keen about anyone getting a laugh when he was on stage. As an example, when Percy was taking part in a sketch and managed to obtain a good reaction Dave Willis had the line cut out - nobody argues with the main comic.

Our digs were pretty basic but still only £1 a week full board. Each Saturday the cast were invited to attend the dance at the Pavilion which was leased by the Popplewells and managed by Ben Popplewell's other son Leslie Popplewell. In the days before the war and television there was a greater interest in meeting anyone connected with the theatre so it was good publicity for the dances and the Gaiety Theatre. The same sort of invitation happened at various towns during the tour of *Wonder Bar* where I always endeavoured to partner Primrose Ives who had been a championship ballroom dancer which improved my dancing so much I became her regular partner.

The season in Ayr is one of my fondest memories, the sands at that time as white as snow, lovely scenery as you would expect in Burns Country, the town small and unspoilt with everyone so friendly. Business at the Gaiety was consistently good because it was a popular holiday resort for Glasgow. There are certain lines or expressions that linger in your memory long after the event. George Lacy was in a sketch in the *Gaiety Whirl* about the secret service in which he says 'Here's my card' other man says 'But there is nothing on it', reply 'I know I'm Secret Service'. There is a knock on the door, George shouts 'What's the password?' answer 'Banana skins' reply 'Slip in'. I tried this on my son's friend many times but after a while she forgot the password and one day said 'I don't know the password' so I replied 'That is the password now, slip in'.

Following the Ayr season the *Whirl* went on national tour beginning at the Glasgow Empire. After Glasgow the show went to the Moss Empires in Edinburgh, Newcastle, Birmingham, Leeds, Stratford London, Brighton, Finsbury Park London and Hull. The *Gaiety Whirl* finished at the end of November 1934. Another sad occasion at splitting up but cushioned by the fact that we had six months work already booked. We were already booked for five weeks in cine-variety in London cinemas which meant five shows a day.

We had two good addresses for digs in London, one at East Ham and the other at Finsbury Park. To avoid changing digs every weekend it was easier to use one of these digs as a base. It meant travelling daily across London but the tube-trains were fast and cheap. Even the trams offered a one shilling all-day ticket with unlimited travel during the day of issue.

It was the advent of the talkies and the super cinemas of the early 1930s, which created cine-variety and became part of the entertainment scene. Speciality acts were ideal for cine-variety especially dancing acts and musical acts.

The custom-built cinemas equipped to stage variety were like palaces, thick carpets, pictures of the stars up the grand staircase, deep seats, rich curtains and spectacular lighting. Many had sliding roofs and as smoking was allowed each seat was equipped with an ashtray. During the depression in the 1930s it is difficult to estimate how much joy, romance, excitement, sheer pleasure and the escapism from everyday life that the cinema patrons experienced.

The main circuits were Gaumont British, ABC, Odeons, Bernstein's Granadas, the Hyam Brothers Trocadero, Troxy, State

Kilburn, the Paramount Astorias, the last name meant six shows a day between two Astorias.

In London a variety act could work a solid six months a year in cine-variety, although a major part was five shows a day (cine-variety was also popular in the Provinces but was usually only three shows a day). The system was three shows at one cinema, the other two shows at another cinema slotted between the three shows, the last show being at the cinema where you started. A coach was provided to transport the three or four acts and a full pit band to and from the two cinemas. The timing had to be right, it would be impossible today with the volume of traffic.

The cinemas opened around midday and as it was a continuous performance it was possible to stay all day. The prices of admission in London were around 6d to 1/6d for which you were entertained by two films, Movietone News, a Laurel and Hardy or a Charlie Chase short, trailer, three or four variety acts supported by a full pit band. At the interval for the sale of ice-cream etc the Mighty Wurlitzer organ would rise up like a monster from the pit filling the cinema with the sound of popular tunes.

The only time we worked to an organ was at the Lido Cinema West Ealing. I was a little apprehensive at band call, or should I say 'organ Call'. The organist was excellent so everything went perfectly. Most cinemas provided a very good café which we often used, our favourite meal consisted of steak and chips, bread and butter and a pot of tea costing 1/3d.

With the advent of war combined with the cinemas showing two full-length films, that was the death of cine-variety.

When we were playing at the Finsbury Park Empire, on the same bill were two American brothers performing a hand-balancing act who were also staying in our digs. They always seemed to have a rubber ball in each hand continuously squeezing them to keep their wrists flexible. One brother chewed tobacco, the landlady was not too happy about that. At intervals from his armchair he would spit into the coal fire. He never missed the target because every time the fire sizzled you knew he had made contact. One thing you had to remember was to avoid his flight path.

By now my brothers and Rita had left all the arrangements concerning the act to me. I suppose because it seemed that I was the one most dedicated to the smooth running and presentation of the act. I had by now built up an address book of two good digs for most towns in Britain, which in 1935 had increased to 25/- a week with 6d for a bath.

When the bookings were confirmed it was advisable to write to the digs immediately before they were snapped up. The landladies always kept a signature book in the hall, which you signed at the end of the week with suitable comments. The previous entries always made interesting reading.

Most pros stayed in digs, even the top of the bill because you could not at that time get a hot meal after the show in a hotel. In Newcastle we stayed in the same digs as Anton Dolin. He asked us to supper one night but cancelled it at short notice. Perhaps he decided one was all right but three were two too many.

One week at Manchester a certain comedian and his wife walked into the digs, being greeted by the landlady with the remark 'Mrs So and So you've changed your hair colour; I liked you better when you were blonde'. There was a constrained silence from the couple all week. Landladies have long memories, but maybe their daughters' memories are longer.

After writing to the digs, the next item was to check up on the train times and inform the baggage man via the stage door keeper the time of arrival of the train for him to transport your baggage to the theatre, usually by way of a long open dray lorry pulled by a shire horse.

Our baggage consisted of two theatrical wicker skips, a dancing mat, a padded wooden box containing photographs in frames for the front of the house, we also had individual suitcases for the digs. The skips cost £5 each and were lined with waterproof material, the corners of the lid protected by buffalo skin. The dancing mat was contained in a waterproof bag to avoid any water reaching the maple wood causing warping, because sometimes the baggage man didn't bother to use his tarpaulin to cover the baggage.

The normal routine for me on a Monday morning at the theatre was to obtain the band-parts from the skip and place them on a board numbered one to ten which had been placed by the stage manager near the footlights. Band call was normally at ten o'clock and was important especially for a dancing act. I always took the band-call going right through the act and then the beginnings and ends of each number to be certain that the conductor had the correct tempo. After checking with the stage manager regarding the set and arrangements for laying the dancing mat, I gave the electrician our lighting plan. Stage lighting during the 1930s was not as sophisticated as it is today. The footlights and overhead battens were coloured. Also, in the wings were lights on individual stands. Situated at each corner of the Gods were the lime-lights which had a disc attached with alternating colours. The first spotlights were blocks of calcium (lime) heated until incandescent when they produced beams of brilliant light. There was always an amount of spluttering until they warmed up.

Then it was back to the dressing room to continue unpacking. After ironing our blouses and Rita's costumes, it was necessary to check all the small details, tap shoes for loose rivets, the dancing mat, the elastic in our shoes instead of laces to make quick changes easier.

Before the days of self-supporting socks we had suspenders to hold up our socks, trousers had button-up flies, zip fasteners were just being used mainly on theatrical costumes, zips on men's trousers came in 1935. Before making an entrance it was advisable to check your flies because it could be very embarrassing as in the case of a baritone who had just started singing when the conductor mouthed at him, 'Your flies are open', which made him cease any arm movements as he endeavoured to cover up that area.

After hanging all the stage costumes under dust sheets and checking make-up, dress studs etc it was time to parcel up the laundry and deposit it with the stage keeper for collection by the laundry who returned it on Friday.

The stage-door keeper who was normally a middle aged man nicknamed 'Pop' was a mine of information and in his small office carried a variety of necessities like stamps, needles and cotton, aspirins etc. He also had the only phone backstage and had an interesting time listening to the girls phoning their boy friends. Before the tannoy system was introduced all theatres had a 'call boy' whose main job was to call the acts in time for their performance also running any errands as required. Some stars who had achieved fame had started as call boys as did Bud Flanagan and Dickie Valentine.

We were booked at the Troxy Cinema, Stepney on 14 January 1935 for three shows a day. We were informed on the previous Friday that we would be doubling with the London Palladium. We were all very excited by this because the Palladium was the Mecca for every British and International variety act. The reason for the sudden booking was to deputise for The Four Brilliant Blondes. One of these girls was Grechen Franklin who was later to take the role of Ethel in *Eastenders*.

The cast at the Palladium featured the Crazy Gang, Eddie Gray, The Hollywood Four, Connor and Drake, Ken Harvey, Renita Kramer, Raye, Ellis and La Rue, The Sherman Fisher Girls and Mathea Merryfield. We had to travel daily by taxi between Stepney and the Palladium and looking back this was our best week financially, £40 for the Troxy with £60 for the Palladium.

Preceding us on the Palladium bill was Mathea Merryfield, a red-haired six-foot fan-dancer with a beautiful figure. She worked with two large feather fans. Whilst waiting in the wings ready to follow her we watched her dance very carefully to see if she was really naked as it appeared, but she was an expert with the fans. It made a very interesting week and has remained a pleasant memory.

We were booked for the Glasgow Empire on 18 March 1935 with Roy Fox and his Band topping the bill. It was a rest playing twice nightly after five shows a day. On the same bill that week was an act Bartlet and Ross. My brother was watching their act from the wings on Monday night and fancied the blonde until at the end 'she' whipped off her wig and in a baritone voice said *Sing up George*. My brother was shocked.

One night during this week at the Glasgow Empire Roy Fox and all the acts were requested to attend a Gala Dance at the main dance hall in Glasgow as a publicity stunt. During the evening Colin

Ross of Bartlet and Ross asked Rita for a dance which upset Terry Bartlet. When Rita returned to our table she told me that Colin had remarked to her 'it feels so strange to have my arms around a woman'.

Like Roy Fox, many big bands toured the Variety Halls during the 1930s, Lew Stone, Jack Hylton, Jack Payne, Henry Hall, Harry Roy, Billy Cotton, Syd Seymour, Ivy Benson and many more. These bands were like a mini-variety show in themselves and would take up the complete second half of the show, the variety acts being in the first half. These visits of the big bands suited the pit band because after the interval they could slip out usually to the nearest public house, returning in time for the National Anthem which in those days was at the end of the show.

The well designed variety theatres like Moss, GTC and Stoll etc had sufficient and well equipped dressing rooms for more than ten acts, allocated according to salary, billing and position in the running order. The dressing rooms could be made comfortable with personal touches. Our theatrical skips were converted into tables, the costumes covered with dust sheets. We carried a kettle and teapot to make a cup of tea between shows, it was surprising how many acts called in for a cup when the word got round. I had bought a 'Three Piggies' wireless set from Bobby Wright of 'Wright and Marion' for £2, which lasted for years.

Glasgow and Liverpool Empires, the Palladium and the Troxy Cinema, Stepney had lifts and showers backstage. What a difference from the old music halls when they had one dressing room for women and one for men and the rest of the facilities were very basic. Even in the 1930s some old music halls converted to take cine-variety were still basic like 'Blue Halls' Islington, Canterbury Music Hall and many more, not much better were the Argyle Birkenhead, Attercliffe Palace, City of Varieties Leeds and the Queen's Theatre South Shields.

It was in South Shields where I had a painful experience. The dressing room in the theatre was small and hot so I was sitting in the nude making up. It was my misfortune to be sitting on a cane-bottomed chair, which had frayed at the front becoming detached from the frame. Whilst I was making up there was movement below which was out of my control. When I stood up the chair came with me, I was trapped, it was agony. I sat down very, very carefully. With the help of my brothers I eased myself out of the trap. Working the shows was rather painful for a couple of days. When I took the chair to the stage manager he thought the incident was hilarious. 'Don't rub it in Zambuk'.

It is strange that everything has its humorous side, providing it happens to someone else. A chorus girl kindly offered me first aid but like an idiot I was too shy to accept, so I had to adopt the strippers' motto 'Grin and bare it'.

In April 1936 we were booked for the tour of the Palladium Show *Round about Regent Street* to run seven weeks in the Provinces and finishing in London at the Holborn Empire. After a week's rehearsal the show opened at the Birmingham Hippodrome. The cast included Naughton and Gold, Dave and Joe O'Gorman, Leon and Lucette, the Six Lias, Betty Bucknell, Three Dennis Boys and Rita, Sixteen Sherman Fisher Girls etc. The pleasant part of being in a touring show was that all the travel and baggage arrangements were made and paid for by the company, we just had to turn up on time for train-call. The show was the expected success after running for nine months at the London Palladium.

In the 1930s the price of a visit to a variety theatre in London was 1/- to 3/8d and in the Provinces 6d to 3/6d (whisky was 12/6d a bottle, a stamp 2d, cigarettes 1/- for twenty, records 2/-, petrol 10 1/2d a gallon, beer 4d a pint, bread 4d a loaf). Theatre programmes were 6d in the West End, London. Moss Empires charged 2d. They had a seal which stated 'Please see this seal is unbroken'. The reason the seal was introduced was because it had been discovered that some attendants had been re-selling the programmes left behind after the first house. We always bought our make-up, Leichners No5 and No9 costing 6d a stick, from Woolworths. They seemed to have a store in every town, the prices being 3d or 6d with an assistant on every counter. My friend lost his job in Woolworths just because he couldn't remember the prices (jest in fun).

I found out years later that the managers of Moss Empires submitted a weekly report to head office regarding the acts, how they were received by the audience, any lateness, change of material, state of the dressing room, etc. Smoking was strictly prohibited in the dressing rooms or anywhere near the stage, although smoking was permitted in the auditorium.

We were clear on all these points especially the clause regarding smoking because our father had promised to give each of us £200 if we did not smoke or drink before we were twenty-one years old. We never received the money but we realized it was for our own good, and it worked.

Many dancing acts carried a dancing mat because although Moss Empires and the modern cinemas had good stages, some old music halls, and music halls which had been converted for cine-variety could be rough and splintery. A dancing mat is comprised of strips of polished maple wood riveted and glued to a special strong canvas backing which formed a mat. They were made in various sizes, ours was approximately 5ft x 15ft costing around £20. After the performance two stage hands turned it over and rolled it up as you would with a carpet. Apart from enhancing the sound of the tap - dancing it was also some protection for Rita in our comedy acrobatic doll dance in which Rita was thrown like a rag doll all over the stage. Sometimes when the stage was not up to standard Rita picked up some splinters in her bottom. After the show it was my pleasant duty to extract these splinters - not to be rushed of course. Rita had a lovely bottom.

The Lord Chamberlain's office was very active during this period, any artiste giving expression to any vulgarity or words having a double meaning or using any objectionable gesture when on stage was liable to instant dismissal.

Some provincial watch committees were also strict because when we were at the Palace, Manchester in 1935 after the first house on Monday night we received a visit from the manager informing us that Rita had to cover up her navel. In 1939 a nude show titled *This is the show* was passed by the Watch Committee, but the title was banned in York. It was not so much the title they objected to as the method of billing which heavily featured the initial letter of each word.

When nude shows were introduced to increase business, although the titles sounded risqué they were quite tame in substance; '*The Nine o'clock Nudes, Nudes of the World, Fanny get your Fun, Bearskins and Blushes, Privates on Parade, Halt! Who goes Bare, Strip-Strip Hooray, Don't Point it's Nude, My Bare Lady, Puff in Boots, Boobs in the Wood.*

We were appearing at the Bristol Empire on 26 February 1940 and on the bill was Claude Lester a brilliant comedian who was the best known alcoholic in the business. On Monday night under the influence of alcohol he got in an argument with a man on the front row which resulted in some bad language and the stage manager closing the curtains. At one theatre the stage manager locked Claude Lester in his dressing room between houses, but Claude had bribed the call-boy to obtain some whisky and a straw which he proceeded to drink via the straw through the keyhole.

When *Round about Regent Street* finished in June 1936 we carried on with cine-variety in London and variety in the Provinces until we were booked for a show *Giggles and Girls* opening 8 March 1937 at the Tivoli Theatre Aberdeen. Early in 1937 Rita left the act for an indefinite period to take care of her mother who was ill. We were lucky to find Bettina Richman who was working solo as an acrobat-contortionist and fitted into the act perfectly.

The cast of *Giggles and Girls* consisted of Jack Anthony, Marie and Laura Carson, Richard Neller and Clarice Clare, Bond Rowell, Three Dennis Boys and Rita, Hilda Meacham and Twelve Sherman Fisher Girls. The tour was for six weeks at the Tivoli followed by one week at the Pavilion Glasgow, two weeks at the Royal Edinburgh, finishing with a fortnight at the Gaiety Theatre Ayr. Dave Bruce took over from Jack Anthony at Ayr because Jack Anthony was to be the comic in the 1937 *Gaiety Whirl* opening 7 June. During the run various guest artistes were introduced: Jules Cheroy, Yeltoni Trio, Ken Harvey, Jenny McAndrew, Christopher and Columbus, Nellie Arnaut and Bros, Renara, Peg Leg Bates, Harum and Scarum, James Calvert, the Act Supero.

On this visit to Ayr our digs were a big improvement against last time in 1934. Good digs with good food was the right combination for a happy week, so the careful recording of recommended addresses was bearing fruit, although some at times presented surprises.

We were booked for the Granada Cinema Dover on 7 May 1934. Our digs were situated on the seafront, and from your front bedroom had a great view of the sea. On going to bed Sunday night the view lost its attraction because the lighthouse illuminated the room at short intervals until daybreak. On reflection I think I would rather count sheep.

In Wigan, we arrived to find the digs next door to a small bakery, the sound of the machinery clanging away during the night wasn't conducive for a good night's sleep. When dawn arrived and the machinery stopped we had to listen to the sound of clogs on the cobbled street of the people hurrying to work, it sounded like a herd of horses. Surprisingly by the end of the week we got used to it. The landlady in consultation remarked that when on holiday she could not sleep because it was too quiet.

We had a commercial hotel recommended for our visit to the Alhambra Bradford and on arrival were greeted by a lovely girl dressed like the waitress in *Allo! Allo* but had a shorter dress. The young lady turned out to be French, she always wore a slave anklet which when examined was inscribed 'heavens above' which seemed to have the general approval of all staying there which included part of Billy Cotton's Band. A year later we returned to the New Victoria Cinema to find the hotel fully booked. Surprise, Surprise!

I was told of a comedian who was so dissatisfied with his digs, before he departed on the Sunday morning he nailed a kipper under the table. According to the state of the digs it would be a while before the landlady sniffed out the kipper's location. I don't think many people dust the underside of a table.

We were staying in some digs at Brixton, on the Monday morning we were awakened by our feet being tickled with a feather duster and with the expression 'come on girls, time to get up'. This was delivered by a 'Boy George' lookalike wearing high heel shoes and a pinny. Later on we asked him about how and when. He told us that when he was fifteen years old he was picked up by an actor

Doll dance with Rita number two, taken from the side of a cinema, 1937

outside the Nottingham Theatre Royal. He then became the actor's dresser and toured with him for a couple of years. The landlady told me that he was the best maid she had ever employed and
also became her companion.

During the tour of *Giggles and Girls* Jacquello's were approached
by the producer of the Palladium shows for the Three Dennis Boys
to team up with three more male dancers to perform a six handed
speciality tap routine also crowd scenes in the forthcoming Palladium show *London Rhapsody* under title 'The Six Dancing Dudes'

Bettina Richman (Rita No2) was disappointed when I told her,
even though it had been explained at the start that her joining the
act was for a limited period. The other three dancers consisted of
Ernie and Gene who had been working a double act and Jack
Lawson who had been partner to Burke of Burke and Head. Rehearsals started in August for *London Rhapsody* taking a fortnight,
and then moving to the Hippodrome Brighton for a two weeks
tryout before returning to the London Palladium for a nine month
run.

The cast included Nervo and Knox, Flanagan and Allen,
Naughton and Gold, Ganjou Brothers and Juanita, Three Wiere
Brothers, Cardini, Gipsy Boy's Band from Budapest (twenty-four
in all), Harry Champion, The Wrestling Bear, The Six Dancing
Dudes, Yolade Fraine, Enid Lowe, Raymond Newell, Rosarito,
McIntosh Three, Omega Trio, De-Rekar and Kortz, Levanda, Avon
Vale Four, Syd Railton, Henry Carlisle, Twenty-four Palladium Girls.

It is unusual to have three sets of real brothers in one show. The
Three Wiere Brothers, the Three Ganjou Brothers and the Three
Maxfield Brothers (part of the Six Dancing Dudes). A similar like
situation occurred at the Granada Cinema Tooting which had the
Five Sherry Brothers, the Three Dennis Boys (Maxfields) all born
in Nottingham including the manager of the cinema.

The full dress rehearsal was held at Brighton on the Sunday. The
general feeling afterwards was that we had a success as all the scenes
were carefully tailored and glossily presented. There was one hic-
cup during the dress rehearsal because an American adagio act persisted in declining to perform their act during the rehearsal. George

Black was adamant and in the end finally dismissed them on the spot. We all enjoyed our fortnight in the sun especially as the show was a hit, and nine months continuous work to look forward to.

In the Crazy Gang George Black seemed to have discovered the magic formula whereby audiences would return and return to see their favourites. They were very popular with everybody because of their friendliness. It was twice-nightly at the Palladium with matinées on Wednesday and Thursday. Over the Christmas period the matinees were stopped to everyone's delight, this was because *Peter Pan* would be playing every afternoon. It must have been very difficult for the stage manager and stage hands having to store and change scenery three times daily, and of course long hours for the orchestra.

The Crazy Gang were always playing pranks on all and sundry during the run. George Black had to put his foot down when the mischief got out of hand. Chesney Allen had to leave the show due to ill-health and later became an agent, he was replaced by Stanley Holloway. It is strange to think that Chesney Allen with continuing ill-health out-lived the other members of the Crazy Gang. Jimmy Nervo was my favourite out of the six and apart from a week at Finsbury Park Empire in 1935, the next time we were to meet was in entirely different circumstances. The year was 1944 when the 15th Scottish Division moved down south in preparation for D-Day. My unit the 15th Recce Regiment being stationed at Angmering-on-Sea. So our last days in England were days by the sea in the sun and in surroundings which might have been created to provide the greatest contrast with the life in the field which was to follow. At Angmering set between the sparkle of the Channel and the dapple of the Downs, houses built expensively for those who could afford seaside holiday homes became the unit's billets. It was indeed life with every modern convenience, kitchens, bathrooms, bedrooms. From our bedroom window we could see the home of Sheila Van Damm the owner of the Windmill Theatre, nicknamed 'The comedians' Dunkirk'. Each Sunday the showgirls from the Windmill would arrive to rest and sunbathe, suitably clothed of course, much to our disappointment.

One evening when Sergeant Bob Holland and I were having a drink in the local pub where the saloon bar was reserved for officers and civilians with the public bar for other ranks and civilians. I knew that all the Crazy Gang had homes in the area, so I kept a lookout for any of them as you could see from each bar into the other. Sure enough later on I caught a glimpse of Jimmy Nervo in the opposite bar. The barman passed my note across to him and he came round straight away. After a drink he invited both of us to return to his house (I should say mansion) where he introduced us to Clarice Mayne, the wife of Teddy Knox, who provided us with beer and sandwiches, it was a wonderful evening.

The Royal Variety Performance of 1937 was held at the London Palladium on 15 November in front of the King and Queen and the Duke and Duchess of Kent. The artistes always appeared free as it was counted as a distinct honour to be selected. The proceeds of the evening always going to the upkeep of Brinsworth House (for retired performers) which in 1937 amounted to £6,342.00.

After the overture and national anthem first on the programme was the opening scene of *London Rhapsody*. The imaginatively conceived and admirably presented Berkeley Square episode, with a numerous company introducing the characters of London life as the city awakes, and Raymond Newell using his fine baritone voice very effectively in the attractive *Sing a Song of London* number. Following on were Norman Evans, Florence Desmond, Wences, George Formby, Max Millar, Jack le Vier, Ethnel Revnell and Gracie West, Ralph Reader's 'Scout Gang Show', Gracie Fields, Will Fyffe, Cicely Courtneidge in comedy items selected from her repertoire with The Six Dancing Dudes and The Sherman Fisher Girls. The Crazy Gang featured in the 'Shadow of Eros' as six flower women, also from *London Rhapsody* a 'Gypsy Camp' production including the Gipsy Boys Band from Budapest, and Chipperfield's bear Bruni. The finale was led by Will Fyffe and included the cast and a full company of the massed pipe bands.

When *London Rhapsody* closed on 21 May 1938 Rita White rejoined the act and it was decided to perform as The Six Dancing

Dudes and Rita to make the most of the publicity from the Royal Variety Performance. This continued until August then we reverted to The Three Dancing Dudes and Rita because it became too expensive to carry seven when after all it was only a padded out version of the original act and also Harry Dennis was producing a show in September and only required the four of us.

The name of the show was *Time Marches On* and included Stan Stanford, Fred McNaughton, The Juggling Pearsons, Le Vadis and Lorna Martin, The St Louis Boys, The Rapid Four, Katie Marsh, Three Dancing Dudes and Rita, The Glamour Girls, The Keep Fit Girls and that great old music hall star Tom Leamore, seventy two years old. The show was a sort of 'Revusical Cavalcade'. It switched in entertainment from 1900-1938 with fourteen distinct scenes effectively staged.

Rita informed us during the tour that when the show ended she would be getting married and leaving the act as her future husband insisted that she finish with the stage. We were all disappointed but agreed it was the right action to take. We were lucky to find our third and last Rita, an ex-member of The Four Brilliant Blondes, namely Joyce Giles who was an experienced acrobatic tap dancer. Luckily she was the same weight and height as Rita White, the only difference being that Joyce had blonde hair and Rita black.

For some unknown reason I had stopped keeping records of the act and collecting playbills because possibly the rumours of war seemed more important. I regret it now although I still have some contracts from November 1939, which were a help in completing my records to June 1940. There are some theatres that we have played that are not on my list and I cannot explain why. One of these was the Grand Theatre, Derby which is in my memory banks on account of a small incident which brings it to my mind. When you are constantly changing digs week in, week out over the years, sometimes getting up in the middle of the night in a strange room to go to the toilet becomes a problem. We didn't carry carpet slippers, dressing gowns or pyjamas because these items would have been excess baggage, so we slept in the nude. You woke up thinking 'Where am I?', the next thought being 'Where's the door?'.

*Three Dancing Dudes and Rita, poster used outside theatres
(drawn by Robert Kemp)*

Getting out of bed the first thing you notice is the ice-cold lino and then the fun begins, groping around stubbing toes on furniture trying to find the door with the situation becoming more desperate until the utter relief on finding the door.

The week at Derby was an example, the seven bedrooms and toilet were on one landing with stairs leading to an attic bedroom which Rita was occupying. Waking in the early hours of the morning to obey nature's call, finding the door this time was no problem or locating the toilet but on the return journey I couldn't remember which bedroom out of the seven was ours. The first one I tried, a voice shouted out 'Who's there?' I muttered 'Sorry' and moved on to the next two which were locked. The next I opened revealed the sound of Percy's peculiar type of snoring which for once I was happy to hear. I had intended for a long time to buy a torch for these situations but this episode made me take action the following morning.

Cyril received his call-up for the Forces in November 1939. We had to appear before a tribunal that decided that we could continue working until Percy was due for call-up. This extension possibly saved us from being at Dunkirk in June 1940.

The only time I dropped Rita in our doll-dance was when we were appearing in cine-variety at the Theatre Royal Dublin in February 1940. I slipped and Rita fell hitting her head, which caused her to black out. The stage manager rang down the curtain. When she had recovered the stage manager suggested that we take a curtain call to assure the audience that Rita was alright. When we went out front the applause was thunderous. The stage manager remarked 'Why don't you keep the fall in the act?' Rita was not amused.

We were booked by Pathe Pictures on 14 May 1940 to perform our simultaneous tap routine at their small studio in Wardour Street for a fee of £16. In 1989 I received a phone-call from a friend to say we would be appearing on television in Jimmy Perry's *Turns*. Our only other appearances in films was in Duggie Wakefield's *Calling All Crooks* and Tommy Trinder's *Laugh It Off*.

Our last week was at the Coventry Hippodrome from 17 June

1940 with Tommy Trinder topping the bill, and realising that the second house Saturday could be the final performance of The Three Dancing Dudes and Rita. The three boys joined the Army July 1940 and Rita (number three, Joyce Giles) joined the WAAF later in the year.

Rita White died 1979
Cyril died 4 April 1943 in an Italian POW camp
Percy died 5 September 1983

Ring Up the Curtain on Yesteryear

Jack Richmond

It is a daunting thought that seventy-odd years have passed since I was taken on my first visit to the theatre by my parents. It was to the Metropole in Stockwell Street, Glasgow and I was all of four years old. The outing had some significance; my mother's cousins, Margo and Tina were dancers in the chorus-line of a pantomime. I don't recall the name of the panto but I can clearly remember being puzzled by the fact that a funny person in female clothes looked strangely like a man! From that night I was weaned on music-hall entertainment, through my schoolboy days by regular visits to the 'Met', the Empress, the Pavilion and the Princess, now the Citizens', right up until theatres changed their style of shows, met their fates through fires or were demolished to be replaced by high-rise office blocks.

Glasgow had always been more music-hall inclined than douce Edinburgh and, being larger, boasted more theatres. Up until the early 1950s 'The Dear Green Place' had no fewer than ten theatres to its name. Five of the theatres staged ballet, opera and drama but the others presented variety and music-hall entertainment in the raucous, bawdy style that the Glaswegians loved. One of Glasgow's most popular comedians was Tommy Morgan, the big, amiable product from down-town Bridgeton. He played all the music halls in the west of Scotland and for almost twenty consecutive summers filled the Pavilion to capacity in his long-running shows with his gravel-voice humour and his creation of 'Big Beenie', the typical, overweight Glesca wumman who stood no nonsense. When Tommy died in 1958 he was succeeded by Lex McLean. His ambition was to play to a packed Pavilion as Tommy had done and this he achieved with his near-the-knuckle comedy and his motto, 'Keep it bright.' 'Sexy Lexy', as he was dubbed, reigned supreme at the Pavilion for sixteen summers until he died in 1975.

In the late 1940s and early 1950s audiences flocked to the 'Met' to laugh their heads off at the Logan Family - Pa, Ma, Buddy, Jimmy, Bert, Heather and her husband Nicky. Ma Logan, a ribald comedienne, had them rolling in the aisles with her creation of 'Fanny, the GI bride.' Those annual shows ran from May until October with a change of programme each week written and produced by Pa Logan (Jack Short). From the late 1920s until the late 1940s a singing and piano duo by the name of Grace Clark and Colin Murray toured the halls of Scotland. In 1949 they changed their act to comedy and became endeared to Scottish audiences as 'Mr and Mrs Glasgow'. Alec Frutin who owned the 'Met' broke away from Christmas pantos and tried a new venture, a tartan show each winter with Clark and Murray as the stars. For many years they played in shows with titles such as *The Skirl o' the Pipes, Wha's Like Us?* and *Abune Them A'*. When the 'Met' was destroyed by fire in 1961 Alec Frutin bought the Empress and, after renaming it The New Metropole, continued with his ever popular tartan shows with Clark and Murray again in the lead. However, in 1964, due to ill health, Alec sold the theatre to Jimmy Logan who named it Jimmy Logan's Metropole. But by now variety was on the way out and the audiences failed to come. The theatre closed and after lying empty for years was eventually demolished.

The Glasgow Empire was a cosmopolitan theatre staging in addition to Scottish artistes the big bands, English acts and American stars. Just as today's pop groups have their ardent followers and

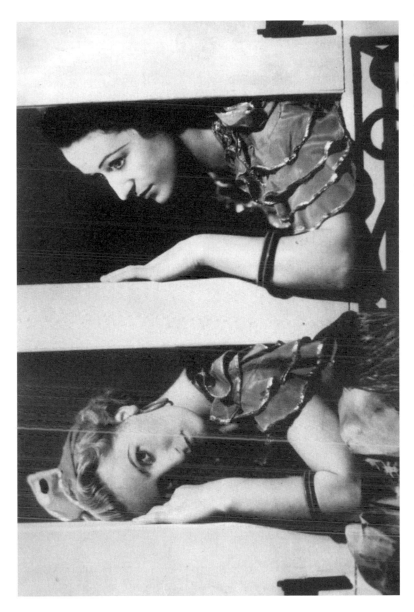

Jack's cousins Margo and Tina as the Ardane Sisters, the act they formed after leaving the chorus-line

rivalry so, too, did the bands led by such maestros as Henry Hall, Ambrose, Geraldo, Harry Roy, and Jack Hylton. Among the many Americans who crossed the Atlantic to play the Empire were Bob Hope, Judy Garland, Danny Kaye, Liberace and Roy Rogers complete with his horse, Trigger. The Empire had the reputation of having a tough clientele whose catch-phrase was 'If you're good we'll let you live.' Known as the graveyard of English comedians, many Sassenachs feared for their very existence.

One of Glasgow's best-loved theatres was the wee Queen's situated in a side-street near Glasgow Cross. It was renowned, or should it be notorious, for its naughty and earthy pantos having a pattern all of their own which other theatres did not or would not follow. Frank and Doris Droy and their merry gang catered for audiences who liked a right good belly laugh and they flocked in droves to those pantomimes. The Queen's show was always the first of the panto season, opening in the last week of November and running sometimes into April of the following year. On the first night the stars of the other pantos which were not ready to open would occupy the front row of the stalls enjoying a night of unlimited laughter. Many ordinary folk made a point of attending that night to see the celebrities as an added bonus to the show itself. Coach parties from all over the west of Scotland followed the Queen's shows and Watson Street was habitually jammed with buses loaded with office-workers, women's guilds and whatever. Frank Droy who wrote and produced the pantos would take note before-hand of parties attending and during the performance would work in gags relating to them, be it from John Brown's shipyard, Lewis's Ladies' Underwear Department, Larkhall Bowling Club, etc. The parties concerned simply lapped up this sort of entertainment. However, there was always the 'unco guid' who refused to go to the Queen's considering to do so was vulgar and in bad taste. I often wonder just how they would have reacted to some of the sketches. For instance I recall one with wee Sammy Murray who always played Dame and could have been likened to Les Dawson. Sammy emerges from his cottage and hails a passing coalman, 'I need two bags but I'm skint this week.' The coalman replies, 'Nae problem, missus' and takes in two dirty bags of coal. Some time later he comes out of the cottage with a happy smile on his face. Sammy, now dressed in bra and long, white knickers, shouts after the coalman, 'See you next week, same time.' He turns to go back inside revealing two black hand-marks on the cheeks of his behind. In another scene Frank Droy and feed Billy Fields play two men lying in the same 'in-the-wa" bed. Frank gets out of bed in his long-johns and goes to the kitchen range to fry some bacon in a pan. Billy in the mean-time has been guddling under the bed and extracts a chamber pot. With his back to the audience he relieves himself then empties the lot down the sink. Frank is now standing with his back to the fire. Billy goes to the range, surveys the frying-pan and remarks, 'Is that your Ershire bacon?' 'Naw,' says Frank. 'I'm only heating the backs o' my legs.'

In another sketch Frank and Doris, his wife, were attempting a love scene, he the wet wimp with no sense of romance, she the hot tart lusting for his body. Getting nowhere, she eventually grapples with him on the settee, pulls his shirt out and wraps it over his head, skelping his bare torso and yelling 'Nature in the raw.' A woman in the audience alongside me turned to her pal and between laughs said, 'It's a good joab it's her ain man.' Compared with what we see today on TV, those cameos would appear to be tame but in the unliberated times of sixty years ago they were indeed risqué. The cast of those pantos was practically the same years after year, with many of them married to one another. The Queen's staged eight-een consecutive pantos from 1933 and I saw everyone except three because for three years I was in India with the RAF. In the Christ-mas panto of 1947 a young song and dance man who did a bit of light comedy got his chance after being released from the army. His name was Jack Milroy, the Francie half of the famous Francie and Josie duo.

Another stalwart of the Queen's pantos was George Clarkson the dancer. His son, also called George, came into the dancing act and together they went under the name of Clarkson and Son. Young George, however, was apt to be breathless during his routines while dad could dance away and at the same time give out endless patter.

Young George broke away from his dad when he married Gail, also a dancer, and together they went into cabaret.

During one of the Queen's last pantos Sammy Murray passed away. In February 1949 he was found dead behind the door of his little flat in the East End of Glasgow, a middle-aged bachelor. His part was taken over at short notice by a total unknown whose name I can't recall who just could not fill Sammy's shoes. He was cast again as Dame in the 1949/50 show and also in the following year's panto. However, the life seemed to have gone out of the Queen's pantos with the absence of Sammy and the 1950/51 show was such a disaster that it was the last of a very long run. Doris had been greatly attached to Sammy and the two worked together to a degree of sheer brilliance. Being a very sensitive person she was deeply affected by his death and she and Frank left Glasgow to work the clubs in the north of England. We never ever saw them back in Scotland again.

Christmas 1951 saw the Queen's with a new brand of panto called *Sammy's Magic Sporran*. None of the old regular cast were in it. A famous Glasgow Principal Boy, Jose Donelli, was called out from retirement and a young Scottish comedian, Billy Rusk, got his chance. However, audiences did not take to the new formula and instead of the usual four months run the closing notice was put up in January 1952. A friend of mine, who saw the show, told me that on the night he went there were no more than forty customers in the stalls. I booked seats for my wife and myself for the final Saturday performance but the theatre was gutted completely on the Friday night bringing to an end something that had become a Glasgow institution.

Another long-running panto was that staged at the Princess. Here George West played the comic for something like fifteen consecutive years until the theatre went over from music hall to legit. Sylvia Watt played Dame for many years until her death when Nellie Wallace took over. The storyline of the panto was not along the way of the usual fairy tales but invented, always of course with the poor widow in search of treasure and thwarted by the villain plus a string of catastrophes. There was always a ship scene with a storm wrecking the ship and the entire cast being thrown on to a tropical island or some far-flung foreign shore. A strange quirk was that the title of the panto always had to have thirteen letters, no more no less, and was the name of the character played by the comedian. So we had *Jinglin' Geordie, Tammy Toory Tap, Sandy Soor Dook, Tam Toddle Bony* and so on.

Before the coming of TV, theatres in Glasgow, like everywhere else were packed, and advance booking was always to be recommended. The Empress had a family atmosphere. Paw, Maw and the weans would go regularly on a fixed night of the week regardless of who was on the bill. It was a case of, 'Oh, we always go to the Empress on a Wednesday night', or a Thursday or a Friday, etc. Before the era of resident shows there was a constant changing of casts each week. A company of about sixteen would put on a show and appear for a week say at the Princess to serve the customers of the south side of the city. The following week the show would move to the Metropole for the folk in the centre of Glasgow then on to the Empress for the west and north. From there it would tour the small towns doing a week at Paisley, Greenock, Motherwell, Hamilton and Falkirk, generally finishing at the Palladium in Fountainbridge, Edinburgh.

Heckling I understood was confined to the Empire where I have been told that the rough shipyard workers turned up with their pockets filled with nuts and bolts which were hurled on to the stage if the artistes did not come up to expectation. I never ever witnessed such scenes and I'm inclined to take tales of such behaviour with more than a pinch of salt. However, I do remember as a schoolboy sitting in the stalls of the 'Met' while Tommy Morgan was doing his solo spot when suddenly a voice from the gallery snarled out, 'Away and work.' All eyes went upwards to where a man in a cloth bunnet was hanging over the edge. Tommy ignored the heckler and carried on with his patter but the fellow persisted and finally shouted, 'Hey, Morgan, I'm talkin' tae you. Away an' work'. Tommy looked up and shouted back, 'No' while there's mugs like you that pay to see me.' The audience rolled about their seats applauding Tommy wildly while the offender was duly ejected by an attendant.

On another occasion Alec Finlay was doing his act at the Theatre Royal, Edinburgh when a coin was thrown on to the stage. This is the insult of all insults reducing the artiste to the level of a backcourt entertainer or a street busker. Alec stopped in his act and in a calm, controlled voice said, 'If there's anybody in the audience with money to throw about there are plenty of well-deserving charities would be glad to have it.' Another great burst of applause. Another heckling was at the Beach Pavilion, Stonehaven. The comedian along with two feeds was doing a song and patter trio dressed as ministers. The line of humour was of an innocent, ecclesiastical nature but a rather irate, sedate lady in the audience suddenly jumped to her feet and called out, 'I object! I object!' There was nothing really out of order with the patter but obviously the lady was a staunch pillar of the kirk and found offence. The two feeds instantly froze but the comedian went on boldly and called out to the audience, 'Just carry on laughin' folks.' which they did. The lady sat down deflated, much to the embarrassment of her husband and teenage daughter who did their best to shrink into their clothes.

In the main, music-hall audiences were from the working class although I suppose some of the better class did have sneaky visits to the number two and three theatres but would not admit it. I remember when I had just started work on the staff of Harland and Wolff and told some of my senior colleagues that I regularly visited the Empress and the Metropole they regarded me as having committed an indecency. However, a few years later when one of them suggested making up a party to go to the Queen's pantomime there was little objection. On the following morning they were all laughing their heads off as they went over the risqué jokes.

The Scottish comedians had to be Scottish - no posh wireless accents, just down to earth. But patter along local lines was essential. Audiences loved to hear digs at local councillors, tram and bus services, shops and stores, Rangers, Celtic or Hibs. The references changed from town to town depending where the comics were playing. Through constant travelling all over the country they acquired a healthy knowledge of the various towns and what they held to provide material.

Mention must be made of the summer shows at the seaside resorts, which were inundated by Scottish families long before package holidays to the Mediterranean had been thought of. Little resorts like Dunbar, Leven, North Berwick, Millport, etc, all had their concert parties which served as training grounds for up and coming talent. The big summer shows were at Aberdeen Beach Pavilion where Harry Gordon, dubbed 'The Laird o' Inversnecky', played for years, the Cosy Corner at Dunoon, Barrfield's at Largs, Cragburn at Gourock, the *Gaiety Whirl* at the Ayr Gaiety and, of course, the Winter Gardens at Rothesay. Here, Charlie Kemble of the famous Rothesay Entertainers played summer after summer with such stars as Jack Anthony, Bond Rowell, Peggy Desmond, Jeanette Adie, Helen Glen Campbell, Mae Wynne, Dave Bruce, Billy Oswald and a host of others. The list seems endless.

I started off mentioning my Mother's cousins and I will finish going into more detail. Margo and Tina began their stage careers when still at school. In those far off days there did not exist such stringent rules about education interference. As young girls they were in a troupe of dancers called the Rosebuds and in the evening would be accompanied by their mother to take part in a little show in a little hall in Glasgow. After their schooldays they went into chorus work and when I was about seven I remember being taken to see them in *Robinson Crusoe* at the 'Met'. Mae Wynne played Mrs. Crusoe and I can still clearly recall in the island scene Mae singing *The House That Jack Built* as thirteen dancers in straw skirts gradually built a small house on the stage. Shortly afterwards Margo and Tina came out of the chorus and formed their own song, dance and guitar act as the Ardane Sisters. At that time and even into the 1940s a show was not complete unless it included a sister act. There were so many around then, the Houston Sisters, the Thompson Sisters, the Jacksons, the Masons, the Bells, they were innumerable. In 1935 the Ardanes got their big chance in a long running summer show and at one time were in the famous *Fol-de-Rols*. They were rarely ever seen in Scotland again. By this time their young sister, Carol, had made her professional debut as soubrette in the summer show at Aberdour. A year later Bonnie joined her and they, too, formed a sister act under the name of Carol and Bonnie Downs. Come 1939 and World War Two and the two sister acts joined ENSA as entertainers to the forces. They saw service in North Africa touring military units with concert parties in their vehicle carrying costumes and props. Around 1942/4 Margo married a Scot who was a civil engineer with the British Sudanese Government and came out of show business. After the war in 1948 Tina and Carol had a double wedding at Caxton Hall, London. Tina married a naval officer and Carol married a farmer from the Borders. Bonnie was the only member of the family who married into show business and she and her husband formed their own act.

It's a far cry from those days of so much entertainment in such a galaxy of variety but now and again at the Pavilion or King's in Glasgow audiences are taken back to relive, if only for a week, old memories with such stars as Johnny Beattie, Jack Milroy and his wife Mary, Anne Fields and the late Walter Carr by their impersonations of the veterans of golden variety who trod the boards of the old theatres. It may be a brand of entertainment of a bygone era but will it ever completely die?

Peggy Desmond

My Story

Dita Maher

Saturday was my favourite day of the week. I had my dancing classes, ballet in the morning, acrobatic in the afternoon and skating in the late afternoon.

I started dancing at the early age of three. I loved every minute of it. My mother played the piano and I made up my own steps. I imagined I was a tree, a flower or a cat jumping off a chair. Being an only child, I had to use my imagination a lot. I had wonderful parents. Father was a doctor in Budapest and I did not see a lot of him, he was always busy. He came to see me before I went to sleep and told me wonderful stories about giants and dwarfs and so on. I was very lucky in my childhood. I was surrounded by lots of love. Because Hungarian is a very difficult language few people outside Hungary learn it. For that reason people who could afford it had a Nanny from another country for their children so that they could be bilingual. I had a most wonderful Nanny from Austria. She was from Vienna. She was kind, patient and funny. I loved her dearly and we stayed friends till she died.

I went to an all-girls school and made lots of friends. We had different religions and when it came to religious education we all went our different ways. I had Jewish friends, Catholic friends, religion was never a problem. On Saturdays our Nannies dressed us in our best suits and we went to our dancing classes. While we were dancing the Nannies went to a small coffee room. One could smell the beautiful aroma of good coffee freshly made. They were gossiping about their charges. One would say, 'My little girl can do two pirouettes, she is so clever.' Another would say, 'That's nothing! mine can do such and such a thing.' How they enjoyed themselves. Every month they were allowed to watch their charges in the class. We would show off the new steps we had learned. I had a Russian teacher who was very strict. He had a whip and if we did not hold our feet in the right position he was not shy to use it.

Mother used to say that I must not neglect my schoolwork. If I wanted to go to dancing classes I must be good at school so I tried extra hard as I really enjoyed dancing. Acrobatic was more difficult. I remember I learned standing on my hands against my bedroom door. It was a little awkward when someone came in. I fell down. Next thing was to learn the crossover where one has to step over one's head. Nanny and a friend held a sweeping brush horizontally between them. I stood on my hands and went over the handle. I mastered this trick until I could do it fifteen to twenty times. Eventually it became my solo bit in the Cancan. I always got a big hand for that trick.

The happy, carefree days of childhood in the 1930s went by. There were whispers in the air, something was wrong. You could not lay a finger on it but something was there. You did not feel safe anymore. Some of the girls left my class and nobody knew where they went. I asked my mother what was wrong and she said that it looked like there could be a war but I did not really understand. I had a favourite teacher who taught us physics. She was a Jewish lady, very popular with the girls because she made learning so much fun. One day she did not turn up at the class and we did not see her anymore at school. I told my mother and a few days later this lady appeared in our home. She stayed in the the maid's room and I was sworn to secrecy. I must not tell anyone or she would have to go to a concentration camp. We were Protestants so we were not hunted.

My Nanny was Catholic and she agreed to hide our friend for a while until she could get out of the country to go to friends in America.

My parents thought I should take a year out before going to college and a golden opportunity presented itself. There were vacancies for young, new dancers in the International Darmora Ballet. Mother knew Madame Darmora from earlier days. She used to play the piano at rehearsals when the usual pianist was ill and I was accepted. I was overjoyed at the thought of travelling round the world and dancing every night. There was so much to see, so much to do. We went into training in July, nine in the morning until two in the afternoon, learning different routines. On 6 December 1938 we went by train to Amsterdam. The Tushinsky Theatre was our first call. We arrived early in the morning, went straight to the theatre and got allocated our dressing rooms. Madame Darmora gave us white sheets to put round the walls. We had to cover over our tutus and all our clothes at all times to keep them clean. She was very strict; no smoking, no drinking, no boy-friends and drugs were unheard of. She used to say that there was plenty of time for boy-friends when you had made it and your name is up in lights. We did two shows per day and matinées on Wednesday and Saturday. After Amsterdam we went to Brussels and played the Vaudeville Theatre. I spoke French, not very well, just school French but I could make myself understood.

From Brussels we came to London and I decided that I would learn English. We all had to do some chores to help keep things running smoothly. I asked if I could do the food shopping for us all. I could learn the language better that way. She agreed to that and I learned a lot. First, I pointed to a fruit, for example a lemon which is 'citron' in Hungarian, 'citronen' in German and 'citron' in French. In English of course it is completely different. The shopkeeper would say 'a lemon' and I would repeat it trying to imitate his accent. Learning that way was fun. I got myself a book on English grammar and between shows I would study. I learned about eight words every day. I kept repeating them until they got into my head. Eventually I started to to make sentences. People laughed at me at times but I didn't mind. Later, when we were in the same show, after the war had started, Bebe Daniels was very kind to me. She showed me pictures of her own daughter and son. She said she missed them terribly but they were safe in Hollywood. She helped me a lot with my pronunciation.

Our first show in London was at the Colisseum and we stayed at the St. Martins Hotel. This was in Upper St. Martins Lane so it was a straight walk to the theatre. I loved London and in my spare time I visited all the sights. I went to the museums. They were at a walking distance. When the others went to the cinema I went to the museums. In our show a Frenchman, Sacha Guitry was the top of the bill. Donald Peers went very well singing *In a Shady Nook by a Babbling Brook*. He had a lovely voice.

We also appeared in a film called *Gaslight* which starred Anton Walbrook In this we did our Cancan on stage in a theatre scene and I came out to the front when it came near the end to do my cartwheels and finish with the splits. I think we took two days to finish the scene. A bus came for us at 6.30am to take us to the studios and after shooting all day we got back about 6pm to get ready to go on stage for our twice nightly show. It was very hard work because we had to do bits over and over again until the director was satisfied. I was paid five shillings for the two days and we never met any of the stars!

After this we were booked to go to Hollywood to do something similar in *Gone with the Wind*. We had our tickets to sail on the *SS Normandie* on 8th September 1939 but, of course, war was declared and the *Normandie* did not sail. So we went into the Holborn Empire, into a show called *Ho Ho*. Max Miller was the top of the bill comic and this was when I met Bebe Daniels and Ben Lyon. On 14th June 1940 it was Bebe and Ben's Tin Wedding Anniversary, that is ten years married, and Max made a speech after the show. They received new gasmasks as presents! *Ho-Ho* finished on 20th July 1940 and the next week we were working at the Kingston Empire with George Lacey and the New Cross and Finsbury Park Empires. A private bus took us from one theatre to another and we changed on the bus. There was little time between theatres

Dita Maher and girls of the Ballet Darmora, London, 1939

because we were doing five shows a day. Next week it was the Elephant and Castle, then Kilburn Empire.

Air raids were now a daily happening. The nights were the worse. We were allowed to take one small bag with our most precious possessions in it to the shelter. Mine was a teddy bear called Zebi which my Nanny gave to me when I was seven, my parents' letters and a change of clothing. We also took a flask of tea which we shared with whoever was next to us in the shelter. Complete strangers became your friends. We were all in the same boat. First thing in the morning we would rush to see if the theatre was still there. It was such a relief to to know that we could still work.

Madame Darmora decided that we should evacuate to Malvern to get away from the raids, to get a little break and so on 22 October we took the train to Malvern and stayed there for four months. It was great to sleep in a bed instead of on a wooden bunk in a shelter. There were lots of evacuees in Malvern including Madame Darmora's niece who was married to Dr Simpson, of Simpsons of Picadilly. Dr Simpson's little nephew, Johnny Mengers, who was about five years old was there and I had the job of looking after him in the afternoon. Every day after morning rehearsals I went down to this rather posh hotel to read to or play with Johnny. Like most boys of his age he was lively but we had lots of fun. I often wondered what became of him; perhaps he inherited the store.

In March 1941 we were told we were going back to London to work at the Palladium in a show called *Apple Sauce* with our old friend Max Miller topping the bill. The show had a great cast and ran for eight months. There was a young Vera Lyn who brought the house down every night with her final number *We'll meet again*. Florence Desmond was the soubrette and when Vera had to have her appendix taken out she stayed with Florence on her farm to recuperate. In between performances I learned to make false eyelashes and made them for all the girls in the show. Strong hair was needed for the base so I made friends with a nice horse that pulled the milk cart. My friend and room-mate, Kathleen, fed the horse with a carrot while I cut a few strands from his tail. The horse was very friendly but used to give me surprised looks when I pat-

ted his head. He certainly did not need false eyelashes, he had beautiful long ones of his own.

When *Apple Sauce* closed at the end of November 1941 we
went into *Babes in the Wood* at the Pavilion, Brighton until the end
of January. Polly Ward was Principal Boy and Jill Manners Principal
Girl. Then it was straight into a variety tour of the Moss Empires
working mostly with Jack Hylton and his Band but Charlie Kunz
and Ambrose also topped the bill some weeks. The summer of 1942
was spent at the Opera House in Blackpool in George Black's *Vani-
ties*. This was a very happy show and we all enjoyed being in it.
Webster Booth and Ann Ziegler headed the cast, Duggie Wakefield
was the comic and Betty Driver, now best known as Betty the
barmaid at The Rover's Return in *Coronation Street*, charmed the
audiences singing *Life is just a bowl of cherries*.

Just before Christmas that year we opened in the *Merry Widow*
at the Opera House, Manchester. I loved that show and the music
of Franz Lehar which was so familiar to me from childhood when
my mother used to play it on the piano. After a month we transferred to London, to His Majesty's Theatre where we ran for nine
months. I understudied the part of Frou-Frou and during rehearsals met up with a chorus boy, another understudy, who was learning the part of Baron Popoff. His name was Dick Emery. After
rehearsals we used to go to a small café near the stage door for
coffee and a sandwich. Being wartime it was usually just spam or
lettuce on the menu. Here we met up with another chorus boy
called Billy Sargeant who told me he was very lucky. He had just
been discharged from the army because he had been shot in the
stomach. I was trying to work out in my mind, how was it so lucky
to be shot in the stomach? I suppose it meant he didn't have to
fight anymore.

By now I had realised that I had to do something if I wanted to
get my mother out of Hungary and bring her to Britain. It became
my biggest ambition. Although I worked in the top theatres, financially I had nothing to show for it. So, I made up my mind to leave
the ballet. I spoke to the boys and asked their opinion. They both
said I should do it and Billy said we could form a double act and I

PROGRAMME

1 The Applesauce Circus
TERRY CONLIN, The DARMORA BALLET, GRAY, AUSTIN & WORTH, BETTINA RICHMAN, LIND JOYCE, THE DOLINOFFS & RAYA SISTERS, JACK STANFORD, JEAN CARR & THE 24 SAUCELETS

2 MAX MILLER tries out a Television Set
Assisted by Beatrice Boarer, Jack Stanford, Lind Joyce and Jean Carr.

3 GRAY, AUSTIN & WORTH

4 Snow Time
"Ting-a-Ling" sung by JEAN CARR
The Dolls ... THE DOLINOFFS & RAYA SISTERS

5 On Guard
2 Home Guards	MAX MILLER and Jack Williams
The Officer	Jack Stanford
A Motor Cyclist	Billy Gray
His Girl	Lind Joyce
The Spy	Jean Carr
The Sergeant	Terry Conlin

If an air raid warning be received during the performance the audience will be informed. The warning will not necessarily mean that a raid will take place and in any case it is not likely to occur for at least five minutes. Those desiring to leave the theatre may do so, but the performance will continue and members are advised in their own interests to remain in the building.

6 VERA LYNN Radio's Sweet Singer of Sweet Songs

7 JACK STANFORD The Dancing Fool

8 The Folies Bergere comes to Oxford Circus
A French Star ... FLORENCE DESMOND
("Mlle. l'Amour" by Eric Maschwitz and Jack Strachey)

Can Can by The Darmora Ballet

INTERMISSION
THE LONDON PALLADIUM ORCHESTRA
Under the direction of FREDDIE BRETHERTON

9 "When You Dream About Hawaii"
Sung by LIND JOYCE
Speciality by BETTINA RICHMAN

10 The Embankment
The Man	MAX MILLER
The Girl	Jean Carr
An Old Actor	Jack Williams
Policeman	Terry Conlin

"A Stranger Came to Town"
sung by MAX MILLER and Jean Carr
(Written by Michael Carr and Jack Popplewell)

11 THE DOLINOFFS & RAYA SISTERS Dancing Dollusions

12 FLORENCE DESMOND
(Miss Desmond's Gowns by Norman Hartnell)

13 MAX MILLER

14 Cheerio ... ... Full Company

AFTERNOON TEAS SERVED IN THE AUDITORIUM, PALM COURT & CIRCLE SALOON

Patrons expecting Telephone Calls or Messages are requested to leave the number of their seats at the Box Office.

Applications for Lost Property found by the Staff may be made between 11 a.m. and 1 p.m. and during the performance.

For Advertising Rates, apply to
P. A. CRAMER & CO. LTD., Advertising Contractors, National House, 60-66, Wardour Street, London, W.1. 'Phone: Gerrard 1404.

Printed by PRATT & CO., 4 & 6, Heddon Street, Regent Street, W.1. 'Phone: Regent 3600.

'Apple Sauce', London, 1941

would double my salary right away. I was scared, a bit unsure of myself, but I knew I had to do it so we made plans. Every afternoon for a month Billy and I got together in the theatre and worked out an act with a beginning, middle and an end. Dicky used to watch us rehearse and was very helpful. We always listened to his suggestions. He used to say, 'One day you will be proud to have known me. I shall be famous.' He was as good as his word. A very talented performer and a natural comic.

My first problem was how to tell Madame Darmora that I wanted to leave the ballet. This proved easier than I thought because I was in a little trouble with her. My first 'sin' was I got caught talking to the boys from the chorus. I was reprimanded for that as we were not supposed to talk to the opposite sex. My second 'sin' was I was seen in Woolworths alone buying a half pound of broken biscuits. We were supposed to go out in twos or threes, never on our own. They wanted to know how often I went to Woolworths on my own and where I got the money to buy the broken biscuits. I told the truth that I walked from Victoria Station so I saved my bus fare and with that money I could buy a half pound of broken biscuits for tuppence. I explained to Madame why I had to leave the ballet. It all boiled down to money. If I couldn't save some money I would not be able to bring my mother out. She was annoyed at first but the boys told me that since my contract had run out years ago I could just walk away. Anyway, to cut a long story short, I stayed in the ballet long enough for a replacement girl to be found and trained to fill my part.

My new life began in autumn 1943. I stayed with Billy Sargeant's folks in London and was made one of the family. We toured round the agents trying to find work. I knew Bernard Delfont and his brother Lew Grade who told me that although they knew my work from the ballet they would have to see our act on stage. So we arranged a 'showcase' appearance in London and invited the agents. The act went down well and we got a booking – at the Opera House, Dunfermline in Scotland! – in a variety show with Pete Martin as comic. I shared a dressing room with Betty Renee the head girl of the Moxon Girls, Maidie Dickson and Kathleen Stanley the soub-rette. Kathleen had her mother with her and I couldn't help thinking that I would soon have mine with me. We liked the show, the audience gave us a nice reception and everything was going fine. It was just too good to last. We were asked what our act was to be the following week. This was resident variety with a change of programme every week. We had no music and no other costumes and Billy got downhearted. His stomach wound was playing up and he said he couldn't cope with weekly changes to the act. I said I would give it a go. I still had a strong Hungarian solo and if I added some Russian steps and music to it, wore boots, it would do for another week. I also had a waltz solo from *The Merry Widow*. It would be a challenge but I could do it.

After Dunfermline, Billy Sargeant came back for a few weeks to try again and we were booked into the Victory theatre in Paisley. I remember Lex McLean was in the show but this was before he had made it to top of the bill. There were two young male dancers in the show, Billy Cameron and Billy Leslie. The work again became too much for Billy Sergeant and he went back to London. Hamish Turner who was producing the show suggested that I join the other two Billys and form a three-handed act and this was the start of many happy seasons for us.

One Saturday morning in the Palladium, Edinburgh I was rehearsing my act for the following week when Hamish Turner, Lex Mclean and theatre manager Dan Campbell came in and asked if I would join them in the bar for a drink. When we went into the bar I noticed they each put a pound note into a glass. I began to search in my handbag but Mr Turner said I was their guest and what would I like to drink? Since I had never been in a bar before and never drank alcohol I just said, 'The same as you.' 'Double?', he asked. 'Yes', I replied. They handed me a glass of this golden coloured liquid, I took a sip and promptly choked. As I coughed they laughed and Mr Turner asked if I was sure this was my usual drink. I had to own up and admit that I had never tasted whisky before so I was handed a glass of lemonade. After a little while I slipped back to the stage to finish sewing a costume for the next week, kept company by the theatre cat, Mouser. This cat literally had the run of the place.

I shared a dressing room with the soprano, Ivy Troy who loved a cup of tea between shows. Mouser knew this and was a regular visitor looking for any milk left over. During performances he often sat on the orchestra pit piano while Helen Fowler, the Musical Director was playing. From the stage we often saw him walking up and down the aisles and from time to time he would jump on to the lap of one of the lady patrons. They were regular customers who sat in the same seats every week and Mouser was a wise old cat and knew who liked him and who didn't.

Later on in that season I did an acrobatic act which finished with me balancing a glass full of water on my forehead. I did the splits and got up again without spilling any of the water. I used a real glass brought from the theatre bar not a trick one. I was petrified the first time I did it in front of an audience and spilled a little water. I tried it again and this time succeeded. You could feel a sigh of relief from the audience as I got up and they gave me a big hand. Mr. Turner came backstage after the first house and said I had done well. Then he gave me a glass of milk and said I should put that in the glass because it would show up better. In the second house I filled the glass with milk and did the splits. Not a drop was spilled but the audience began to laugh and I felt something warm and furry jump on me and lick my face. It was Mouser! He knocked the glass over, lapped up the milk and the audience loved it. I took him in my arms and dumped him in the wings and again we got a big hand. For the rest of the week it was back to using water but with a pink dye. Harold Dayne who often produced shows at the Palladium used to say, 'That cat will ruin my scene one day.'

At last in 1945 the war ended and we all breathed a sigh of relief. Now I could really start to get my mother out of Hungary. Hamish Turner was very helpful and introduced me to Chief Constable William Merrilees. I was in awe of him but needn't have been because he was extremely kind and helpful. He suggested that it would be an advantage if I became a British citizen first, got me to fill up some forms and gave me a booklet on what would be expected of me as a British subject. I went to night school when I was not working and private lessons in the afternoons when I was in a

show. I passed my 'English for Foreigners' with credit and was ecstatic.

One day Hamish asked me, 'Can you cook?' I was forced to
admit, 'Not really.' He then told me to get in the car. I got worried
and asked, 'Are you going to throw me in the Forth because I can't
cook.' 'No,' said he , 'I'm taking you to the 'Dough School' in
Atholl Crescent and they'll teach you.' He explained to the teacher
that he wanted me to learn how to cook mince four or five different ways and make stew and other simple dishes. Years later when
we were married he used to say that that course was the best thing
he ever spent money on. I also went to the French Institute several
times a week and took classes in history, literature and grammar.

After scores of letters, meetings and lots of help from the Red
Cross, who were wonderful, I got word in 1947 that my mother
could come to Britain. There was just one thing. I had to find £100
to make it possible. I scrimped and saved from my wages and in a
few months got the money together. Finally, the message came that
she was on her way. I can't tell you how happy I was. I was playing
at the Empress in Glasgow (this was before it became the Metropole)
and again in a dressing room with Ivy Troy. She made it really
lovely, decorating it with flowers. I got a bunch of lovely red roses
and went to the station to meet my mother. I saw her get off the
train and walk towards me. Then she came through the ticket barrier and walked right past me. She hadn't recognised me! I ran after
her screaming 'Mother' in Hungarian and she turned round in
amazement. She had been looking for a schoolgirl but almost ten
years had passed and I had grown up.

I will never forget the night I stopped the show at the Edinburgh Palladium. Hamish had given me a song to perform. It was
called *Don't forget the Old Folks* and it ended with the words, 'You
lose the best friends you had in this world when the old folks gang
awa.' The words just got to me. I felt the tears welling up in my eyes
and then running down my cheeks. My legs took root on that stage
and I couldn't move. I remembered my father and the last time I
saw him. It was at the station in Budapest when I kissed him good-
bye before jumping on the train for Amsterdam. As the train left the

station I saw him wave his large white handkerchief until I couldn't see him anymore. Now he was dead and I should never see him again. My mascara was smudged and nipping my eyes. I knew I should be doing something but couldn't remember what. I saw the first row of the stalls stand up and clap, then like waves of the sea row after row got to their feet and clapped. I just stood there like the personification of all the sadness of the world. At last, an old stagehand came on stage and said, 'Come on hen.' and led me to the wings Somebody, I think it was Jimmy Donaghue, of Donaghue and Ramsay, went on and said a few words along the lines of, 'Dita lost her father recently and the words of the song just tore at her heart. She was overcome and couldn't stop crying but she's composed herself now and will finish her act.' Helen Fowler played my intro and I went into my dance routine, the waltz from *The Merry Widow.* Again I had a thunderous reception, much more than I deserved for the routine. Hamish who had missed the first part of my act was amazed at the reception I got. He asked Dan Campbell what was going on. 'Dita stopped the show' he was told. 'What did she do? Her voice isn't that great', said Hamish. Dan said that I had been crying. 'Now I've heard everything' Hamish retorted. Dan tried to explain, 'It was the words of that song you gave her to sing. She felt every one of them. It was spontaneous. She was breaking her heart and the audience knew it and responded.'

I said before how wonderful and nice the people who came to the Palladium were and I'll finish with a letter one of them sent to me. Not because it pays me compliments but because the person who wrote it just wanted everyone connected with the show to know how much he enjoyed and appreciated their efforts.

To Dita Maher:
Please be so good as to excuse me in writing you, but, as I have now been seeing you you dancing for about one year, I felt that I must write to you, just to let you know how I appreciate your really skilful acrobatic dancing. As a dancer, you are outstanding, and your tumbling is a real pleasure to watch.

Why the manager does not allow you more scope beats me!

Your high-kicking and the polished use of your hands and head is absolutely perfect.

To my way of thinking, you are the most outstanding person on the stage. I would also like you to mention me to your two very able partners - Billy Cameron and Billy Leslie. I really do think that as a dancing team you three can equal anything in this country.

Also, please convey my kindest regards to Jimmy Donaghue who has a lovely voice but he doesn't use it enough. He is so clear in his diction that he can be heard anywhere in the theatre with ease, which is a lot more than I can say for some of the others.

And, Dita, don't forget to tell a really beautiful singer, namely - Eric Wylie, that his performance is also one of the best. No microphone bogey with Eric, No Sir!

Ronnie McCulloch, Sam Kemp and Hector Nicol are also very good indeed. I would also like to thank Fraser Neal and the Manager for a 'Good Show.'...

They were such wonderful, kind people who came to see the resident variety shows during the war years and just after. They wanted to forget any hardships for a couple of hours and be entertained. When I look at my old programmes for the Edinburgh Palladium and Leith Gaiety I can remember so many of them who came and sat in the same seat on the same night every week. Perhaps it is us who should thank them.

The new comedy materialist

Frank Bruce

As far as maths teacher Bill McDonnell was concerned, his real job started when he got home from work. His daughter Vicki recalls that he was only to be seen briefly at tea-time before he disappeared into his office to work late into the night on a stream of songs, sketches, monologues, scenas, gags and full-blown panto-mimes.

The music-hall bug was in the family; Bill's father Michael appeared as the 'Postie Comedian' in a semi-professional capacity in concerts and smoking parties around Greenock for over forty years, with song and patter routines like *The Hielan' Bargee*, the type of working-man song and patter long popular with Scots Comedians:

> I'm in charge of a Barge, tho' its no very large
> It's as trim as you'll find on the river,
> And I like her so fine, that the name 'Lass o mine'
> Is the one I decided to give her,
> She's a home and a wife, and a good pal to me.

And when I've been a shore, and been out on the spree
I know when I'm broke, with a cargo aboard
A warm welcome waits, where the ould Tub is moor'd &c

Bill started writing scripts as a teenager, continuing as an English student at university in Glasgow, right up until his early death in 1954. He supplied performers all over Britain in what were the ebb-years of live variety theatre. The extra hundred and fifty pounds yielded by an average year's sales was a welcome addition to the family finances.

It was not easy money. According to his records, between 1941 and 1953 Bill made a total of 725 sales. This was made up of 289 items sold part-rights (in other words material sold at a lower price to several performers), 157 sole rights, and 185 'specials' (specially written for established customers). The balance was made up of 'gag set, compere gags, rhymes, rhyme sheets, parodies, medleys, rewrites'. Regular customers like Scottish comedians Jack Anthony, Clark and Murray or Alec Finlay might pay five or ten pounds for a tailor-made song and patter routine, but individual gags sold for five shillings. The norm was one or two pounds for material sold part-rights, like the more than one hundred songs and sketches listed in one of his occasional catalogues, 'Latest laughter lists... Slick, saucy subtle...Refined, robust, rabelesian...'. It includes 'For the light, breezy comedian' over a dozen songs available 'resident part right: 15/- Touring part rights £2.2.0 per song' such as the highly topical post-war song *Nationalised* which he sold several times over:

Then won't the poor kids be surprised
When Registrars say 'Who's the - who sent for you?
Go back for emergency form N.B.2
When everything's Nationalised.

There are character studies, which like most of Bill's material follow well-established music-hall traditions or in other words provided what audiences and performers knew and loved, with a new angle or with topical references worked in. These range from '*The*

Martyrdom of man. A fellow needn't go to the alter twice to be married once too often' ' *'The man for the masses.* He knows all about Labour - aye HARD LABOUR TOO', *'The Quack doctor, The Postman, The town crier, The railway guard*...Terms resident P.R. [performance rights] one guinea. Touring part rights; £2.12.6'. The rest of the catalogue includes collections of 'Merry male monologues', 'Variations in Ventriloquism', 'Diversity in Dames', 'Comediennes', 'Punch packing straight monologues', 'Debonair doubles: Lady & Gent', 'Double drolleries: Two men', 'Minstrel Merriment - complete minstrel show routine', 'Sketches, sketches, sketches', 'Thumbnail skits with quick black-out and strong tags always ready. From 5/- to a Guinea according to number required', 'Quiz questions (Cod)'. The catalogue ends with the following appeal:

Shakespeare wrote his comedy 'As you like it' but his work's done. McDonnell writes his comedy 'As you like it' and his work's never done. By all means visit Stratford on Avon - but don't forget Greenock on the Clyde. Never mind the pilgrimage when I'm gone. Get in touch while I'm here…

As his carefully kept 'script transaction' books and surviving correspondence show, like any other scriptwriter Bill worked hard to market his material. Dozens of approaches were made, as in the following to Box and Cox music publishers:

22nd Dec. 1947
Dear Sirs,
I have just emerged from a panto-rush where material, and vetting of scripts, was most urgent - otherwise I should have written immediately after Harry Pringle's last broadcast wherein MY OWN DARBY AND JOAN was featured. You will know that I did the recitative - a copy of which I now enclose - and that I have done several such for varying types of song broadcast by Harry.
He tells me that you MIGHT be interested in sending out this monologue accompanying copies of the song - whether to artists featuring it or to the public I don't know so I shall await your own

Bill McDonnell

reply, postulating that if you feel like trying the experiment, I shall appreciate it IS an experiment and would therefore be content with a modest fee until public reaction were ascertained....If you are not overstocked, I should like to submit, bye and bye, a complete number - lyric, recitative and music - but lest there be a spate of these, may I add that I could at any time handle the translation of any continental numbers acquired by you where good lyrics in English were wanted, with the spirit of the original preserved. French, Spanish, German or Italian could be undertaken. Also, re. film-songs, I could turn out numbers of a given type or on a theme. Possibly at some time, you'll be able to test me out...

All contacts were pursued, as in the following to Duncan Macrae (a legit actor finding success in variety):

2nd Jan. 1951

...No doubt you'll remember me as the schoolmaster with the hearing aid. We had a chat in Alec's [Finlay] dressing room last year. If you're still interested in finding suitable scripts, I feel you might respond to the two herewith. The angular Sherlock seems just the type and your physique should lend itself to a burlesque life-guard. If I'm right, I'll proceed with patter for DYNAMITE DUNCAN... In the same line, I thought of a Ballerina but will wait to see whether you want to build-up a repertoire of characters or prefer to hold-off until future plans are known....

Scriptwriters relied on a detailed knowledge of performers so that they might attract their attention with material that suited. This ran the risk of offering material in a vein that an established pro had already exhausted. Will Fyffe's manager returned one 1941 submission with the message:

Herewith please find the number you so kindly sent Mr. Fyffe last month; he considers it exceptionally good, but the snag is, he is working two old men's songs and he thinks that it is time that he gave that type of 'character' a rest...

And G.S. Melvin writes from the Hackney Empire in July 1942:

...Re. Land Girl – I already have a Land Girl number. If you have any other character BROAD comedy numbers (but not too blue) I would like to have a look at them...

More annoyingly, a performer might sit on a submission:

11th July 1945
Dear Jack [Anthony],
I got yours with two items returned a fortnight ago and would be glad if you would now send me the three others unless your mind is already made up about them. They have been with you now for fully three months and I suspect that they are dormant somewhere – rather than under your constant consideration.

At any rate, I feel I deserve better treatment and I was rather disappointed at the rejection of 'NATIVE CUSTOMS' which I thought had big possibilities and was written specially in your style. I naturally don't expect you to reconsider it if your mind is already made up – but there is so much alternative work that I might have done.

THAT is really the crux of the matter – that with so many approaches I am forced to concentrate in the most profitable directions. If at any time you think it worth your while to put business on a better footing, I'll be glad to know.

And lastly, in view of the very friendly atmosphere in which I have always been received, may I very sincerely, wish you everything you wish yourself...

When an artist was interested, detailed correspondence often ensued. Fortunately for the theatre historian this was an era when people still conducted much business in writing, in the case of Bill's surviving letters preserving a small snapshot of the innumerable ephemeral and often tangled negotiations which kept the business running. Much ink was spilled over commissioning and schedules – an intricate affair given that pros were often reluctant to commit themselves in advance, and writers did not want to waste time without firm commitments (but had to take work where they could get it):

24th July 1949

Dear Mr. Hingston,

Following my posting of three personal acts on March 20th, I had your note of June 2nd, intimating resumption of correspondence with financial gesture.

Now I am mindful of the facts that originally you took too much trouble not to mean business…I should like however to indicate the position here at present.

I have cleared off my summer show orders beyond 'bits and pieces' requested from week to week by my Clydeside contacts. Normally I should turn to panto work and have indeed completed one important panto order. Specifically, though, I mean that apart from expected and anticipated panto work, I normally go after additional orders. I might not be able to do this if I am to write FOREVER LAUGHTER and I might not be able to write FOREVER LAUGHTER if I take on too many panto commitments!

If you cannot yet be definite re the show, I'll let you know the position here when you do eventually find yourself ready to get busy on it. As already explained, the preliminary preparation will be the harder part for, once it follows a set pattern, I'll know where I am. Firstly, I must get acquainted with the personnel and to that end, you were to send photographs and contemplated cast, barring super-numeraries. The show must be written round the folks in it. I have of course, on file, your earlier letters.

You will recall that we agreed that the wiser plan was to have about four weeks' programmes on hand and, as soon as the first went on, I could get busy on the fifth. The main point would seem therefore to be - have you by now recouped yourself financially to set the wheels in motion and will you make time to help me out re.fixing the basic plans for the programme?…

Then there was the vexed issue of 'rights' as in the following

letter to former oratorio contralto turned successful variety comedienne Suzette Tarri:

28th Sept 1943

Dear Miss Tarri,

Many thanks for latest letter and photograph. Now, let me repeat that I am ready to take you entirely on trust and work from
number to number as circumstances require – but to answer as
requested, I suggest

SOLE RADIO AND VARIETY RIGHTS FOR U.K. – one
year with renewal option – complete number – song and patter or
song and monologue £10.10.0

SOLE RADIO RIGHTS of one complete number – renewal
option £4.4/- or Two guineas for first broadcast and a guinea for
each additional.

SETS OF DOMESTIC GAGS for ad. lib. Use – as many as I
can think up on the required theme and approximately twenty per
set... £2.2/-

EXCLUSIVE USE OF ANY ACT IN PART for radio or variety for one year with the whole number reverting to the writer
thereafter unless option exercised on the complete number after a
year. Approximately half price – £5.5/- but less if less than half
required.

Again I suggest that these terms are elastic, especially the last
one as there may be gags suitable in an act which you know you
won't otherwise use. In such a case, if my script was returned – or
copy of same – with the used gags deleted, I could substitute others
to bring it up to full length for elsewhere. However, I assume that
what you really want is a rough idea of terms expected and a 'gentleman's agreement' re. rights and options....

...As you know, one or two amateur rights make the CAN-
TEEN number and the LANDLADY number available EXCLU-
SIVELY only for radio but re. gags, we both know how these get
around and I suggest the best test re. variety adaptation is your own
experience – i.e. if they are new to you, then they haven't found
their way into the 'halls' yet... Will you let me know when writing

if you are doing panto as I THINK I have a brainwave if I make a good job of it. My intentions were to splash it per STAGE and rent it resident rights but I can hold off if you are your usual prompt self. The title is explanatory 'I'M A PART-TIME FAIRY QUEEN' i.e. munitions by day, fairy by night, and I haven't yet breathed it to a soul…

And again:

9th Jan. 1951

Dear Dave and Joe [O'Duffy],

…Well, I have put new gags into LOVE'S YOUNG DREAM and retyped it completely, also enclosing extra copy for your convenience but mind ye, just this once. … Re. LOVE'S YOUNG DREAM, we'll leave it at £2 as a first job but with an extra guinea any time you happen to broadcast it. That is - if you want nobody else to have use of the act.

Now, maybe I should explain that I have a lot of clients in England - fellows that you never hear about but they get plenty of week-end work in their own towns and must keep changing almost every few weeks. They are always open for good doubles and when they pay a guinea a time to work only in their own town you will see that over a period, I often get quite a bit for each act. That makes it awkward when real variety artists want exclusive use and are not yet in big time re. salaries. Nevertheless, I'm anxious to please everybody so let me know whether you are agreeable to sharing with amateurs or if you prefer sole rights…

With established clients there was a great deal of discussion over possible improvements and ways of making the material suit usually making reference to the artiste's preferred way of working and previous successes. Character comedian Charlie Ellis' manager Charles Spenser contacted Bill in June 1949 seeking material for an autumn production and giving details of three sketch ideas: a girl guide sketch with Ellis playing the guidemistress and drawing on his pantomime dame work, a race-course scene along the lines

Charlie had worked some years earlier, and the Box gag - a stand-ard routine with the comic in the box interrupting the proceedings on the stage. He writes, 'Charlie has played this very successfully, and two shows ago had an excellent script, but of course something NEW is required'. Just six days later, we have the reply to Bill's submitted Box sketch:

I like it very much - it's good, but as you ask me to be frank about my reaction, the only adverse criticism I have is the subject. I think it would appeal greatly in many cases, but personally I am not quite easy in my mind respecting the action on the stage, I much prefer say as an example, a domestic episode or as another the 'old log cabin' principal of the villain, hero, NW. Mountie etc. I trust you will be able to follow my line of thought, but you will appreciate my knowing Charles's work so thoroughly and his every re-action I can feel exactly what is required. I would like to see more movement, and entrances and exits, which can always be a laugh. I know you will appreciate me putting it this way [...] do you think you can now submit something along the lines I am reasoning [...] your further comments will be very much appreciated.

And from husband and wife act Terry & Doric Kendall ('Crazy but clever'):

26.3.52

...All the gags good but will have to delete a few of them oth-erwise the act gets too quiet with the light type of gag - and as one can't get a big laugh with a blue gag off Worthing - it's a question of two or three light gags then a business gag to break up the segment -...we did not intend doing a sailor act this year, but your sailor act is GR. It would save a lot of headache in finding finished and of course I'm getting a bit old in the tooth for dancing finishes but we have to have them as I'm not a real comic...let me know what your sailor act will cost and what you will charge to put a single for Doric straight - she's working as a Scotch school girl with a scooter - she has put two or three gags that she heard Harry Gordon do -

but feels there's no harm as she will only be working it three weeks altogether throughout the season. The hypnotist act we can worry about later. Do you know a little sketch called Proof? Jack [Anthony] & Bertha [Ricardo] worked it for a long while – I thought it might make a little sketch for Doric & I…

26.3.52 Pier Pavilion Worthing
…I'm afraid the scripts you sent me are not quite me! The Scotch school girl has worked in well and they like it. I've vaguely worked out another on the same lines but this time she's staying at a boarding house about which I would like a few gags & they have a musical evening! There's a toothy females who ogles a rather Claude Hulbert type of man & she sings 'The man I love!' to him and he sings 'at last to her'…I also wanted to bring in a rather raucous Irish woman who is a guest …

Inevitably, this way of working could lead to disputes about where ownership of ideas lay. A 1941 run of letters with Scots variety and broadcasting comedian Peter Sinclair 'The Cock of the North' begins promisingly enough in July with Sinclair praising Bill, and promising great things, until Sinclair returns one of Bill's songs saying that it is not strong enough. The song in question was *The glamorous ghillie of Glamis* about a ghillie who takes to the silver screen:

I'm Willie, McSwilley, the Glamorous Ghillie
I've made quite a hit on the screen.
When there's a talkie up north starring me.
Girls write to see if the tickets are free
For a new star is born - he's the Hielan Hill Billy
The man with the magnetic palms…

….As Bonny Prince Charlie I think I'm best
When Flora MacDonald is played by Mae West …

Sinclair says he is going to rewrite the song with new music and offers to return his reworking to let Bill know where he went wrong. By October Bill writes:

…Now re. GLAMOROUS GHILLIE, we must immediately come to a business arrangement. Briefly you will recall suggesting a song I'M WILLIE MCSWILLEY, THE GLAMOROUS GHILLIE, MCSWILLEY THE GHILLIE OF GLAMIS, where you added 'Make him a kind of Admirable Crichton, does everything for the Highland Chief and does him for everything'. THAT is entirely your part.

For my part I started to work on my OWN IDEA of the Hollywood Highland, slightly phoney, and as I reported earlier, I abandoned my tentative title of SANDY THE HOLLYWOOD DANDY to work on G.G. OF GLAMIS. Well, now, my intentions recently were precisely yours as expressed today to rewrite the number, for someone else. If therefore you want to rewrite it to suit yourself, I suggest you buy it and then modify it to your liking. I won't argue over it for I have always maintained that the artiste must feel his material is right but rather than argue I'll place my own faith in the Hollywood Highlander idea by asking you to renounce it or buy it, Please understand that I am NOT misunderstanding your letter, nor am I at all indignant but you will admit that this number has been dragging on since July and inevitably we must get to terms or drop the number. I have no doubt that you can do something with G.G. of G. as originally outlined, but I myself could have sold SANDY THE HOLLYWOOD DANDY and you must admit that the idea is original. I stand or fall on the opinions of an old pro friend in Liverpool on ALL my acts and he tells me the song as it stands is a winner. If you mean that it isn't right for yourself, I'll agree but I'm not convinced that it isn't commercial. The music of course was merely a rough draft to go with the original attempt and would naturally require proper attention NOW.

Re. writing successfully, I thought you knew that I advertise regularly in the STAGE and I'm sorry you haven't managed up this way yet till I could show you the amount of work I have turned out and have on hand. I don't know if you will know all these

names but FREDDY FITTS, NORA FORD, NORRIE NOR-
MAN and JOCK GLEN are a few who have bought sole right
numbers at from three to four guineas. In the past year I have had
over a hundred clients. However, to get to the point - will you let
me have your best offer for that song as it stands and after purchase
'remold it nearer to the heart's desire'...

Sinclair counters that the Hollywood Scot idea is not a new
one, and offers to pay for any part of Bill's material. Bill's response is
angry:

2.11.41
There is still a step from first turn in Happidrome to stardome,
and I doubt if you can bridge it on current shilling successes and
twenty-year-old sixpenny ones. It was here that I hoped to help
until it looked as if you were extravagant only in your promises.
    I am 35 and have been writing for twenty years. You will there-
fore understand that I have long ceased to wag my tail when patted
condescendingly on the head.

By February 1942, he takes a more business-like tone. He writes
of having sent Sinclair two revisions, and argues that the 'crux of
the matter' is that the idea for the song was his: 'Please note I am
claiming only PART AUTHORSHIP and that my lyrics were never
returned to me'. It was another seven years, however, before they
patched it up:

Nov 1949
Dear Pete,
A man may sometimes misbehave
Yet be a Joker not a knave
So take a trick as King of Queens
Then turn up trumps in greater scenes
With sincere good wishes.

Since the start of the music-hall era scriptwriters' relationships

with performers were often strained. The comedians who domi-
nated the bills depended on an army of usually un-acknowledged
writers and Bill was in something of a Clydeside scriptwriting tradition. The industrial west of Scotland was a song-writing centre
for British music hall; two late nineteenth century Glasgow based
magazines carried thousands of songs from the pens of hopeful
littérateurs. According to one song-writer, in 1903 'next to London, Glasgow has the largest and most varied staff of song-writers,
and, I may add, the most prolific authors of the day'. From the start,
however, performers were often slow to pay and slow to acknowl-
edge the debt. The prolific Sandy Melville, author of many late
Victorian Scotch Comics' hits was moved to write in *Barr's Professional Gazette and Advertiser* in August 1903, complaining of his treatment by Harry Lauder:

> Swell houses for the singers and poorhouses for the writers!
> James Curran, my old pal, made fortunes for a lot of self-styled
> comedians, and what did they do? Nothing! Tom M'Ausland was
> the source of inspiration to enliven many a dull hour. He died.
> What did his clients do? Nothing! And both these men wrote for
> Lauder, and rewarded them with – Nothing…

Writers in turn were not averse to borrowing from performers,
as comedian and song-writer Neil McFadyen recalled:

> Stealing melodies and gags is, of course, as old as entertain-
> ment. The moment any comedian produces a new idea it is copied
> by dozens of others and reproduced in one form or another… It
> was quite common for such artists as W. F. Frame to buy a bunch of
> songs at a time, and there used to be the constant trouble of some
> song-writers selling the same song over and over again, till a host of
> comedians found they had all bought the same song…

Troubles over ownership of material are a recurring theme of
Bill's correspondence and he wrote as follows to the *Performer* (official organ of the Variety Artistes Federation) in response to artistes

who had been complaining about having their gags 'lifted':

…Where artistes find exclusive songs, monologues or properly protected business being plagiarised, they have adequate legal redress. Where they find jokes or gags being 'lifted', they have none, nor can I see that they have any grouse. There is no story-teller on the halls with a routine entirely of his own invention. The best of them can, and do, create occasional gags but the demand for stories is so great that the best artistes employ diligent research, either in person or through script-writers, who, in turn, can invent some of their stories and topicalise others, but cannot cope with the demand for entirely new work. I refer only to gags here.…Many of the music-hall complainers are really objecting to the direct lifting of what they have taken trouble to find, a fair enough objection, but the failing is laziness rather than dishonesty. Hence, they have no redress and, as a script-writer, I have never offered gags sole right… I have never used gags heard on radio or that halls and, while in my bright moments, I can create, I still warn acts that the stories will soon get around.

Re. One recurring complaint, surely the time to listen to a theatre-manager is on Monday morning? Then if gags have recently been worked locally, the artiste must substitute others…Lastly, let the moaners get themselves some exclusive SONGS or material other than gags. Then they have the double advantage of real originality and complete protection of material.

In other words, artistes should not complain if they were too cheap to commission original material. Of course, even when they did, they could be slow to pay, and Bill was not alone in complaining of this. He proposed one possible solution to the endless wrangling between writers and performers in another letter to the *Performer*:

…As a script-writer who sought V.A.F. membership for the standing and integrity it conferred, although, as a non-performer, I was unacceptable, may I endorse the appeal of 'Spero Meliora' (who suggested that if a Federation for script-writers were not practicable, the V.A.F. should start a script-writers section), and others.

Surely the V.A.F. is the only properly constituted, freely elected body for finding the right authors for the right artistes – and a body free of all suspicion re. exploitation? Why not a script-writer section? ...

... May we hear more of this proposal soon!

'Merrymac'

For Bill, as for most of those involved in the business, disputes and disagreements were an occupational hazard, but they seem to have been more than offset by the enthusiasm and affection for the business. As well as spending most of his spare time writing material, Bill was a regular at all the local venues, and was always bringing pros back home for tea and hospitality. His wide correspondence with pros frequently spilled over into friendly news, gossip and informal reviews of what was what and who was where, particularly in the case of a remarkable six year twice weekly exchange of letters with Bill Bennett-Hamley, entertainment manager at the Cliftonville Lido in Margate. Bill supplied Bennett Hamley with material, and Bennett-Hamley put business Bill's way, gave detailed accounts of the business in Margate and dispensed advice and encouragement as in the following two letters:

January 3rd 1949

... I note that financially the last year was not as good as one could have wished, but I agree with thee that you have now emerged from the embryo stage and have that seasoned outlook of the lyric writer and also you have not really strained yourself. One reason being, no doubt that you have not had the orders, on the other hand you have tilled some, what I hope is, arable ground with The B.B.C. and also consolidated yourself with Alec and it may be that with some luck you may enlarge your clientele re. Gordon or others of like ilk. That is a consummation to be devoutly wished for. Again, as you say, you have the security of a regular post which enables you to write with a mind untrammelled by mundane thoughts of bread and butter. It may be that the wee mannie will pony up to at least what the stuff was worth at the appropriate time, though I must confess that I like to see the money paid over when the job is done. Anyway Here's to 1949....

Or the following:

14.2.1949
Thanks for the letter to hand yesterday, also for enclosure re. The Butcher Boy. This is a good workmanlike character song and fairly good patter which in the hands of Alec with some care and reasearch into characterisation would develop into a fine little cameo after the type of Lauder's Saftest of the Family and Will Fyffe's Shepherd and Alec's wistful appearance would go very well with it...

The best evidence of Bill's love of the business, however, is the material he wrote. Even reading it off the page after half a century it evokes the atmosphere of live variety theatre in the 1940s and post-war years, as we see in the short selection given below. In the following patter from song and patter routine *The Railway guard* the flow of gags addresses post-war topicalities, mixed with the perennial 'battle of the sexes':

...I wasn't always a guard, you know. I came up the hard way. When I started as a porter, I was up at five every morning with my rag and Brasso, polishing the lines half a mile each way! AYE. And I never once forgot the RED OIL in the danger lamps! Another thing – I never once lost my temper with the passengers. Courtesy pays and when a man is standing on the platform looking at his train just disappearing round the bend, it must be very comforting when a kindly porter goes up and says in a cheery voice 'ER – DID YOU MISS YOUR TRAIN?'... There was a woman hanging over the carriage window one day when we came into a station. I said 'That's a bit risky, missus' so she said 'I'M SICK. I always get sick when I ride with my back to the engine'. I said 'Well, why didn't you ask somebody to change seats with you?' She said 'I couldn't. I was in an EMPTY CARRIAGE'... Another time, a German Prisoner of War came up, all excited and said 'I put my bag on the platform – go for a cup of tea – come back – and my bag is away'. I said 'Now, that's funny. My son was a P.O.W. in Germany. He put his bag on the platform and went for a cup of tea. By the time he got back. The R.A.F. had been over and the WHOLE BLOOMING STATION WAS AWAY'... You know, since we've become BRITISH RAILWAYS, a lot of the old shareholders have been bought out so the Government thought it would be nice to give them all a free farewell trip. Every shareholder and his wife got two free tickets and I was put on the trip to Blackpool. I never saw such bonny ladies all on the one trip. There were ninety-five shareholders and wives all told and after the trip, the Railway wrote to all the wives asking them how they had enjoyed the trip. NINETY TWO WIVES wrote back and asked 'WHAT TRIP'?...

The following 1944 routine for ventriloquist and doll *It's George - by George* is set in an office where the Doll is being interviewed for a job :

Vent: Can you keep your mind on your work?

Doll: Well... it depends upon the kind of work

Vent: What jobs have you done WELL

Doll: I used to be Manager of a troupe of dancing girls.

Vent: You'd keep your mind on your work then, I'll bet?

Doll: AYE. At night I often took some HOME WITH ME.

Vent: And how did THAT job END?

Doll: I resigned when I found three of the girls unfaithful to me.

Vent: AND WHAT THEN?

Doll: THEN? I became BOOK KEEPER at a night club.

Vent: And resigned again?

Doll: No, I got the sack for HONESTY

Vent: Could you balance your books?

Doll: SURE. I balanced em. But the Boss there wanted to

juggle WITH 'EM....

From pantomime script *Alice in Sneckyland* written to star Harry Gordon, and featuring amongst others bird-mimic George McTear:

Harry: Good King Wenceslas looked out – Up at Inver-snecky –
When the snow lay round about – Falling thick and flecky
'For a country walk we'll go' said his wife 'I'm ready'
He said 'You can go – AH'M NO' – AH'M GAUN BACK TO BEDDY
Of course, he was king. If I tried to be King, my wife would CROWN ME. (He yells here) OW! (Long agonised howl).
Sound of girlish laughter coincides with his howl.
Harry: Ye wee rascal. Did you ye throw that snowball deliberately?
Alice: No, Kilty. By mistake. I thought you were a lady.
Harry: Oh, I'm no LADY. With the snow melting down my neck, it's taking me all my time to be a GENTLEMAN
Alice: Oh? Then you ARE a GENTLEMAN?
Harry: WELL...give a gay dog a good name and he'll stick to it. I'm what they call a respected personage up here.
Alice: Oh I know! Like Frankie Sinatra!
Harry: That's it. Or Donald Duck! Only I happen to be the LAIRD OF INVERSNECKY. The title goes back to ROBERT BRUCE.
Alice: Why? Can't you keep up the INSTALMENTS?
[...later...]
Harry: Alice – this old fellow knows more about the birds than anyone ever I met. Hello, George. How are you, man?
George McTear: Can't grumble, Sir. Can't grumble. But it's cold, cold weather for my wee pals in the trees.
Harry: This is a young visitor to Inversnecky, George. Would you like to let her hear what our glens are like in the summertime?
George: Anything to oblige you, sir, especially just after Christmas although it wasn't much of a Christmas for me. Ahhhh! Thank you, Sir.

Harry: And see that you get yourself something to eat instead of the birds
George McTear's bird mimicry here.
Harry: He's a great old lad, Alice. If it's BIRDS, there's nothing he can't do.
Alice: Can he swing on a telephone wire?
Harry: No! You wee wretch. But he can find his own way home.

Finally, from one of Bill's popular routines for his most regular customer, Alec Finlay, *Let Glasgow flourish* (one of Bill's songs which was published by Glasgow firm Mozart Allan) an anthem to the sense of close urban community that was at the heart of music hall and variety theatre:

Ev'ry man glories to think of his race
And speaks of his hometown with pride.
I still get a thrill when I think of a place
Built on the Banks of the Clyde.
Singers find themes in a Land of their Dreams
And tell of strange places in song,
I feel it's time now to try a bit rhyme
To sing about where I belong.

LET GLASGOW FLOURISH for all the years to be
The place where I was born in will aye be dear to me
St. Mungo I adore you tho' I travel far and wide
My home is where my heart lies,
In Glasgow on the Clyde.

There may be places of greater renown
Cities of Glamour that call
Still there is nowhere like Old Glasgow town,
Warm in its welcome to all.
Many a native has wander'd afar
Exiles and others who roam,
All of them saying wherever they are

'There's no place like Glasgow and home.'

Patter: […..] I could yarn all night about the City for "If you come from Glasgow, you know just what I mean" – There's no' a place like Glasgow

Voice interrupts: UNLESS IT'S ABERDEEN!!!

Alec stands nonplussed – from opposite box Willie Dick [Alec Finlay's regular feed] shouts to Jack Holden [variety theatre veteran and feed to Aberdonian comic Harry Gordon]

W.D: How dare you, sir! How dare you interrupt the performance.

Alec: Thanks, pal. What part of Glasgow do YOU come from?

W.D: I, sir, am an Edinburgh man.

(Aside) He seems quite decent, too. ER – are YOU enjoying the show, sir?

W.D: YES – I AM (Alec smiles gratefully). It's such a change from the high-class stuff we get in Edinburgh! (THAT wipes off the smile.)

Alec: And YOU, Mister – are you not enjoying the show?

J.H: I WAS – till YOU came on! I'm here to see my friend, Harry Gordon. Every year, he sends me a complimentary ticket.

Alec: That'll be why you're HERE! ER – who paid your fare?

J.H: Are you insinuating……

Alec: Oh no. NO! But the last time I travelled from Aberdeen, the ticket-collector dragged a man from under the seat. He said 'Forgive me, laddie. I'm an old man. My daughter's getting married in Glasgow tomorrow and though I've no money for the fare, I want to see the wedding'.

W.D: And did the Collector take pity on him?

Alec: Well, just then, the collector bent down and dragged a fellow from under the other seat. He said 'I suppose you'll be going to the wedding too?' He said 'WHO – ME? I've GOT to go. I'm the BRIDEGROOM'

J.H: (Shaking fist) See – for two pins………

Alec: That's Aberdeen for you. Do nothing for nothing.

J.H: Take this fellow off and bring on Harry Gordon.

W.D: By the way, in Edinburgh I had a funny experience. I met

154

a man who looked like Harry Gordon and he bought me a drink.

Alec: THAT'S not like Harry Gordon.

J.H: OFF – I say – OFF!

Alec: Oh, I know that you don't like Aberdeen jokes. Neither does Harry. I told him one at my house and he got up and went home – as soon as he'd finished his tea.

W.D: I rather enjoy Aberdeen jokes. (J.H. is incoherent with rage now)

Alec: An Aberdonian saw an advertisement – SAY IT WITH FLOWERS. Seeing it was her birthday, he went in and bought his lass a packet of seeds.

J.H: It's a lie!

Alec: Did you read the advertisement in the ABERDEEN newspaper – Lost in Union St. A pound note. Sentimental Value.

J.H: See, sir – any more and I'll come down and horse-whip you.

Alec: Ah – I don't believe you've GOT A HORSE.

J.H: What about Edinburgh? Make some jokes about there.

Alec: Oh no! No jokes about my good friends from Edinburgh. They'd take too long to see through them, anyway.

W.D: Just ONE, please. (Willie leans over box, all anticipation)

Alec: Well, an Edinburgh man was sent to a special job – er – in Aberdeen. At twelve o'clock the first day, the men all sat down to their pieces and the Edinburgh man said 'Oh dear. I thought there'd be a canteen and I've forgotten to bring anything'. A big Aberdonian said 'Have you a knife?' and he cut the string off his own piece. 'HERE' he said 'tie this round your finger and that'll remind you not to forget – tomorrow.'

J.H: WHAT? Surely that's not the whole story?

Alec: OH NO! The next day, the Edinburgh man said 'Well. I remembered – all right' and the Aberdonian said 'AYE. But WHERE'S MY STRING?'

J.H: I'm finished – I've had enough!

Alec: That's him away to take his name off the free list.

LET GLASGOW FLOURISH for all the years to be
The place where I was born in will aye be dear to me
St. Mungo I adore you tho' I travel far and wide
My home is where my heart lies,
In Glasgow on the Clyde.

My Dad owned
the Empire

George Woolley

The Empire was a small Scottish variety theatre in the town of
Greenock and, to be more precise, my dad owned half of it –
his brother, David, owned the other half. The two brothers, George
and David Woolley, operated it as a business for quite a few years.
Like all small businesses, the whole family was expected to pitch in,
and so from about 1946, when I would have been about 14, to
when the theatre closed its doors in 1957, I spent quite a bit of my
spare time helping out. I watched the shows, sometimes operated
the lights, helped with renovations and painting, served in the bar
and in fact did anything Dad set me to work at. I would see shows
twice nightly for weeks, but I never tired of the magic of the performances, and the many talented people who gave them – comedians, singers, dancers, musicians, and specialty acts. Most artists were
quite ordinary people off stage, with all the human frailties the rest
of us have, perhaps even more.

The Greenock Empire was designed and built as a theatre, and opened in 1903. Grandfather Woolley bought it in 1933, and family legend has it that the purchase was made by a handshake in a pub. He must have known what he was getting into, however, because he had owned and operated the Argyle theatre in Greenock for six years by that time. The Argyle had not been a money making venture for two reasons as my father recalled later. Firstly, the building was a converted church and never had the right 'atmosphere' for a music hall, and secondly, the seating capacity at about 800, was 200 less than the Empire, and that made the difference between profit and loss when there was a good show with capacity crowds.

The Empire was very successful all through the war. Greenock was a busy port with lots of sailors on shore leave ready to join the locals at the theatre for some light entertainment during those dark days. The business continued to do well until the early 1950's, when like so many other variety theatres in the country, the decline set in.

As things turned out, the church building which was the Argyle theatre, still stands on the corner of Argyle and West Stewart Street in Greenock - no longer a theatre, of course, or a church, but now a discount mattress store- while the Empire was demolished long ago to make way for a shopping mall.

I have many recollections of happy days in the theatre. My first paid job assignment was as the right hand spotlight operator. Uncle David, who handled the payroll, would solemnly hand me a pay packet at the end of the week with some princely sum in it. The little boxes containing the spotlights were perched on the side walls of the balcony, and I had to step up from the seats and scramble into the box pulling the sliding door closed behind me. The lamps were originally powerful carbon arc lamps and there was a certain technique in keeping the upper carbon rod just the right distance from the bottom one by means of the feed handle, so that the light was brightest. You could take a quick look at the carbons from time to time through a piece of smoked glass, something like you would with an electric welder, but after a while you got to tell from the

Greenock unemployed entertained at the Empire theatre in 1933

light beam itself. It was a hot, smelly, spluttering source, but it produced a lovely white light, much whiter than the incandescent lamps which would later replace them.

Instructions for 'black out white focus', where the only illumination of the performer was by means of the spotlights, meant the operators had to be on their toes. Errors were painfully obvious. One night I dozed off on the job up there in the box. It was warm and smoky and well into the second house of the evening, and I was tired. I came back to life with the sounds of someone banging on the sliding door, and I brought the beam back under control. My lapse of attention had occurred during an Al Jolson number when the performer was down on one knee at the front of the stage singing 'Mammee, mammee' with black-out white focus. I was told afterwards that the right hand spot, which was mine, slowly drifted up and up, until it was illuminating the coat of arms at the top of the grand arch above the stage. I don't remember getting into trouble over this, and I kept my job. After all, I did have connections.

For some reason I was later promoted and given responsibility for the operation of the stage lights. The operating platform for these was just over peoples' heads in the wings on one side of the stage. I could see the stage, but not the front curtain. Behind me, I could see the performers standing in the wings and, directly below me if I looked down, I could see someone just ready to go on stage when the curtain went up. There was what seemed at first to be a massive array of control switches and dimmers on the control platform, but it was not difficult once you learned the ropes. I think the worst part was when a comic sketch ended with something called a 'dead black out' right after the punch line. Three large switches had to be tripped simultaneously - two hands and one foot - and all the lights went out. The comics then exited the stage under cover of darkness accompanied by roars of laughter. This was what it must be like to play the cymbals in an orchestra - timing is everything and the palms would sweat a bit as you waited, even although you knew the score quite well by the end of the week.

One night I was up there on the platform and saw my Dad go

mad. I was used to seeing him everywhere around the back stage during the show keeping things working smoothly. This night the first house of the show was just starting. The orchestra had played the overture and had struck up the opening number, *There's no business like show business*. The whole ensemble was on stage and had started to sing and dance and my stage lights were up. I looked down and was horrified to see my dad running across the stage between the lines of the performers. I thought he had 'flipped', but from my line of sight in the wings I could not see the front curtain. This heavy velvet curtain was raised quickly by winding a hand cranked drum up in the flys high on the opposite side of the stage from where I was. What had happened was that the 'fly man' had not shown up for work and Dad, spotting the delay in raising the curtain, took the shortest route to the other side and flew up the staircase to the flys to spin that drum and get the show started. Not only quick thinking, I thought later, but a bold move too. What if the fly man was just a bit slow and the curtain rose suddenly to reveal Dad scampering across the stage? It would be like being caught with your pants down.

Speaking of pants, I can remember looking down from my stage light control platform to watch a performer getting ready to go on stage on cue. He was a tap dancer and one half of a popular double act with his wife who came on stage at the same time from the opposite side. Every night I would look down, and there he was, going through his little nervous ritual before going out before the audience. He would cross himself and almost with the same motion he would reach down and check his fly. I wondered if he was saying to himself, 'God help me if my fly is open'.

The theatre orchestra was a vital ingredient to the magic of the show; they brought it alive. From reports in the *Greenock Telegraph* of the theatre opening in 1903, the orchestra started out with nine members but the most I remember when I was there was five. There was a pianist, a double bass fiddle player, a trumpet player, a violinist and a drummer. Later, as costs had to be trimmed, and dad and uncle tried to keep from going under, the bass fiddle went, and then the violinist. Perhaps it was at that point we stopped calling it the orchestra and just called it the band. The pianist was full-time and was kept on during the summer shut downs, but the other members must have had day jobs, except for the drummer, Jacky, who seemed to be available for other work. I remember he was one of the team helping out with painting during one summer shut down period. We didn't get professional painters in, of course; that would have been too costly. As the deadline for re-opening approached, we were behind schedule and the motley crew worked late to complete the job. Dad would go around encouraging extra effort and would remind us of the joke in the circus business, that if you were caught eating or sleeping there, you were fired. Jacky had been assigned to painting the walls of the stairs to the gallery and had been at it long hours when he was found fast asleep on the same stairs, with his paint brush still in his hand. Jacky was a talented drummer, self-taught probably, and with a good knack for timing. He could not read music, although I was told this was a condition for getting a union card. When the performers were handing out the band parts during rehearsals, Jacky would reach up for the drum music and put the sheets on his music stand. During the performance, dressed in his dinner jacket and bow tie, he would turn the pages of music when the other band members did, playing the part, as well as the drums. The violinist, Danny, who perhaps considered he had a 'feel' for what was acceptable in Greenock, had a large notice posted to the inside wall of the band pit facing the stage, unseen by the patrons. When a comic new to Greenock would try some unsuitable gag, the violinist would silently point with his bow to the notice, 'no dae for here'. The pianist, Billy, was the band leader, and conductor. His characteristic gesture was to raise his right hand, and after a little twirl, bring it down level with his left which was hovering over the keyboard, and hit the keys. This was also the signal for the rest of the band to start, which they did, always in perfect step. The band had been together for a long time, and worked effortlessly as a team, and enjoyed it. It was a pleasure to watch them work.

Billy was a seasoned professional, and usually managed to cover over problems on stage. One night, however, we had a singer of

Scottish songs in the show who had lots of natural talent, but little training. He had a fine voice and was a handsome figure in his highland dress, but I watched with embarrassment as he took three attempts to start his song at the right spot after the band played a brief introduction to the ballad. On Billy's third re-start he got it right. Up at stage level later that night, we could all hear, coming from beneath the stage in the singer's dressing room, Billy's instructions to the inexperienced singer on the finer points of starting a song at the right place in the music. Perhaps this was how many of the acts got to improve their skills. Certainly not all had the advantage of having singing or dancing lessons, or attending drama school.

I seem to remember the few incidents when things went wrong but in reality most of the time the show went smoothly. This was due to the talent and professionalism of the performers, the skills of the stage hands, the orchestra, the costumers, directors, producers, and the theatre management - in fact, the whole team. Night after night, twice nightly at popular prices of admission, the show went on, the magic was created, and the audiences were entertained by live artists. These were good times, and the quality of entertainment was high.

Dad or uncle made a point of seeing any new act before it appeared in Greenock, which involved traveling across the country. They also spent quite a bit of time with an agent in Glasgow making sure they put together good shows for the following weeks or months. They acquired a lot of experience, and knew what went down well with the Greenock audience. Donoghue and Ramsay, The Logan Family, Lex McLean, and of course Chic Murray, who came from Greenock, and Maidie, were sure fire box office successes. The brothers also had to be cold hearted businessmen when a show was not doing well. Termination notices would be posted backstage, and Dad would say it really didn't matter whether a lot of people said they liked the show or not; it was quite easy to measure how well business was doing by looking at the box office receipts at the end of the week.

During this time we lived in Skelmorlie, a bedroom community about twelve miles down the Clyde coast from Greenock, in a big old house Dad and Uncle had bought and then flatted for the two families. They would travel in to Greenock together by car in the morning and back together late at night after the second house was over and the theatre was locked up. On the trip home my mother and aunt would be with them in the car, having travelled in later in the day by bus, and if I was helping, I would be in the car home also. Aunt took care of the tickets and box office, and mum looked after the bar in the theatre. I remember the discussions between the brothers during these trips in the car home – always about the business – how some problem could be solved, or something improved, or whether or not some expenditure could be justified. The brothers, George and David, were very close, and reached a consensus on everything after lengthy discussions. These discussions would continue down in the yard after we got home, as Aunt and Mum were preparing the suppers in their respective kitchens.

As the business declined in the mid to late 1950's, these discussions grew more intense and longer. It must have been a difficult time for them, culminating in a big financial and emotional decision to close the Empire in 1957. I remember Dad telling me at one point that the bar, which was added in 1954, was the only thing that made a profit. He also mused that they would do better to sell the building , put the money in the bank for some interest income, and get jobs driving buses. When they closed the theatre, they borrowed money from Tennent Caledonian Breweries to take over and operate two, and ultimately three, public houses in Greenock, all of which did well. A year later they sold the theatre premises to Greenock Corporation for £6000 and no doubt paid off some of the loans. They were able to transplant their management skills, people skills, and their direct experience of operating the bar in the theatre into a new line of work, and this they did until they retired.

I don't know whether they continued to discuss everything together or not, as I had left home by then, but they probably did. I mention the 'people skills' because I think that was something special they had. Those who came in contact with them during the course of business had a high regard for the pair of them. 'Wonderful people to work with' is one quote from the local newspaper when the closing of the Empire was announced.

I became an engineer, and later emigrated to Canada to work for a very large corporation. This was a completely different life from my Dad's, but I feel fortunate he owned the Empire, and that I was able to spend time there as a young man. The theatre gives me far more amusing stories to tell my grandchild than a career in engineering.

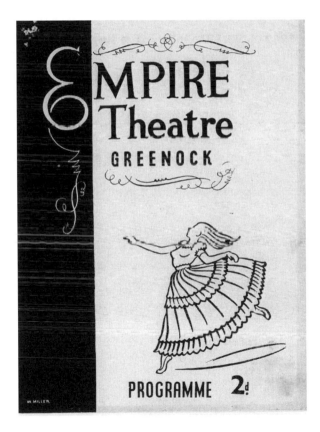

The Voice of Scotland

Carey Wilson

To the uninitiated, a walk into the wings of any theatre built in this country around the turn of the century would be an interesting experience. Three things would be instantly noticeable. The smell, the gloom, and the slope of the stage. The smell, which was not unpleasant, was a combination of dust, glue, size (used to paint the canvas scenery), sweat, and the curious fragrance of stage make-up. The gloom would be pronounced because almost all availabe light would be pointed at the stage, and the slope or rake from the back of the stage down to the footlights. Take a walk on to the stage, and you would be blinded by the lights and hit by a blast of heat, finding yourself for the first time, in the workplace of the variety artiste.

Had you walked through the pass door into the wings of the Empire Theatre in Glasgow on 18 January 1942, having accustomed yourself to the rake and the gloom, you would have seen a spry elderly gentleman in full highland dress sitting by the down-stage entrance. He was perhaps the most famous singer of Scottish songs the world has known, and the chair had been put there at his request so that he could watch and listen to the young man who was standing centre stage, singing, albeit in a very different style, the songs of Scotland. The elderly gentleman was Sir Harry Lauder, and he was the star of a war-time charity concert which had been organised by Will Fyffe and which featured Dave Willis, George West, Jack Radcliffe, Alec Finlay, Harry Gordon, Jack Anthony, Tommy Morgan, Charlie Kemble, Ivor Novello, and the rising star who had captivated Sir Harry, Robert Wilson. It was not the first time that Sir Harry had heard him. They had appeared on the same Bill some nine years earlier, in the company of Tommy Lorne and Elky Clark, when a celebrity concert was arranged by the *Daily Record* in aid of Rothesay fishermen.

A star is someone whose name alone will fill a theatre, and by that definition, Robert Wilson had been a star since his early twenties. It is an old saying that a prophet finds no honour in his own country, and that for anyone to make a real name for themselves, they would have to go far afield, but even from his earliest days as a singer, people flocked to hear him, and if he sang in his home town of Motherwell, the queue at the Town Hall would form early in the day.

Here was a man with an unusual voice. A natural voice that had been trained in the classical style of the day. A voice capable of oratorio, opera, and the light classical repertoire which was still standard fare at concerts throughout the land in those days before mass entertainment became available at the touch of a switch. But there was something there beyond the voice alone. Something impossible to define, and it came from the heart and soul of an extraordinary man who thought little of himself and who believed himself very lucky to have been given a chance to make something of his life. His singing had a hypnotic effect on those who heard him. The way he phrased a song, the way he gave meaning to the words made the listener feel that he was singing to them alone, and his voice had a rare quality which made even second rate music seem somehow profound. To a largely city-bound population, he embodied the romance of Scotland in a way that had never been heard before. In the glare and heat of the lights he would stand, a slim figure of medium height, wearing formal highland evening dress, head slightly raised, his hands sometimes holding his belt buckle, spinning the songs of his native land into long phrases with seemingly effortless ease.

Robert Wilson was born on 2 January 1907 in Cambuslang, but spent his formative years living with his mother and father in the village of Newarthill near Motherwell. His father was a journeyman tailor, and while there was no hardship in the Wilson family, there was no spare cash for what his mother called 'fancies'. There was no musical background either, but regular visits to relations who lived on the Firth of Clyde and who owned a gramophone, instilled a deep love of the Clyde Estuary with its then popular resorts, and of singing, a love which grew into a burning ambition.

That ambition led him to sing with the Carluke Silver Band, and to enter various musical Festivals. He entered the baritone competition of the Lanark Festival as Bert Wilson, and the tenor competition as Robert Wilson and managed to win both, but these early experiences of success made him painfully aware of his shortcomings, and particularly his lack of a musical education. At the age of seventeen he presented himself to Eliot Dobie, an eminent bass-baritone and teacher, who was in charge of the choristers at Glasgow Cathedral, and began studying the elusive art of singing. Dobie was immediately struck both by his appearance and his manner. 'He was pleasant looking, had a shock of wavy hair, a glorious natural voice, and an air of transparent honesty'. Four years later, now his teacher's partner on the concert platform, he was invited to sing at a prestigious concert in Glasgow, when the celebrated English tenor Herbert Thorpe was taken ill, and made such an impression that he was emboldened to throw caution to the wind and become a professional. As it happened he had just been made redundant as junior apprentice draughtsman with an engineering firm, and his erstwhile employer, who had been in the audience at that concert, offered to make an exception and give him his job back. That offer was politely but emphatically refused.

The summer of 1930 provided a change from the comparatively rarified atmosphere of the concert platform, when Messrs Fyfe and Fyfe's famous Rothesay Entertainers gave Robert his first taste of the Variety stage. His efforts were received enthusiastically enough, and he made friendships in that Company which lasted a lifetime, but he soon realised that 'brass neck and a bit of a voice' weren't enough to sustain a professional career, and he successfully auditioned for the D'Oyly Carte Opera Company as a member of the chorus.

At that time, the Operas of Gilbert and Sullivan were very popular, and the company attracted an enthusiastic audience wherever they played. Competition for leading roles was fairly stiff, but eventually he made his debut as the Plaintiff in *Trial by Jury*, and became Principal Tenor. Such was the quality of his singing in that and other roles, that members of the company not on stage would quietly stand in the wings just to listen to him. As one of the leading lights of the Company, the soprano Muriel Dickson recalled, 'There was just something about the way he sang those familiar melodies which enthralled even hardened fellow professionals'.

When the D'Oyly Carte were not performing, life evolved into a series of train journeys, as engagements came his way. The Royal Albert Hall, London one day, the Albert Hall, Stirling the next, courtesy of LMS. There were still lessons with Eliot Dobie, and performances of oratorio, or matinees at Lyon's Corner House, Leicester Square, and tours of the United States and Canada with the D'Oyly Carte, where contacts and friendships were made which were to be influential in later years. Everything seemed to be going well. His voice had developed and matured to a point where he could fill even the largest hall or theatre without need for amplification. His stagecraft had improved, and his diction and breath control were remarkable. A critic of the day noted that, 'While his voice does not have the weight for the true operatic repertoire, in Scots Song he has no peer'. He was principal tenor of an internationally renowned company, had made some recordings for Parlophone, and had managed to scrape together enough money to buy his mother and father a semi-detatched house in Motherwell. Then the first of several disasters struck. While on tour in Canada, he underwent major surgery for a stomach problem, which left him with very poor digestion and the prospect of a lifetime on a very strict diet.

Back in Scotland, he decided that it was time to take the plunge, leave the D'Oyly Carte and go it alone. The Powis Pinder Company in Shanklin on the Isle of Wight provided summer entertainment in the form of a Concert Party. Not quite variety, but each performer had to make an individual impression, and it was here that the kilted persona which had so delighted Sir Harry Lauder came into being. In the first half of a show, he would appear in tails or dinner jacket, singing a light classical selection, and in the second half, resplendent in Highland Dress he would sing Scottish favourites. Writing of his performance in a Burns Night concert at the Royal Albert Hall, a critic reported that 'Robert Wilson was the surprise of the evening. He seemed to bring the wind of the north hills with his song, and with an ease and charm that was a joy to ear and heart'. With a successful season in Shanklin under his belt, and still continuing his travels up and down the country, he was offered a season at the Beach Pavilion in Aberdeen with Harry Gordon, before returning to Shanklin for the summer of 1939. The outbreak of war in that September of 1939, as it did for so many people, changed Robert Wilson's life. He was medically unfit for the Services, and for quite some time there was little or no work to be had. Not being one to sit around waiting for offers, he became a budding entrepreneur and took the risk of booking a hall or theatre and putting on a show, in the hope that people would still want to come out in the blackout. He was now committed to a career on the variety stage, starting very much at the bottom of the bill in a revue called *It's in the Bag* at the Savile Theatre in Shaftesbury Avenue, but as his celebrity grew, the demands for personal appearances at Fetes, Garden Parties, countless charity events, and visits to hospitals left him with little or no spare time, and his concert appearances grew fewer and further between. Some of those who had known his work in earlier years, disapproved of his 'commercialisation' of Scots song on the variety stage, and yet he was able, after a week of 'twice nightly' at the Theatre Royal in Edinburgh, to give a performance of Handel's Messiah in St Giles Cathedral which many felt was 'quite unique and unsurpassable'.

Robert Wilson, about 1938

In complete contrast, and under the auspices of E.N.S.A, he found himself somewhere in France in the company of Will Fyffe and others, entertaining the puzzled local French citizenry. Unfortunately, no one had told the Army they were coming, but they did the show anyway. Robert went over reasonably well, but the wonderful Mr Fyffe found himself playing to mystified silence, and after a few of the hardest minutes of his life, he raised his eyes to heaven, laughed, said, 'Keech, bum, fart !' and strolled off.

Robert became a regular favourite in theatres all over the country. The Theatre Royal in Edinburgh where he shared a dressing room with a very young Dickie Henderson, the Tivoli in Aberdeen, The Ayr Gaiety with Jack Anthony, the Alhambra in Glasgow in the legendary pantomime seasons starring Will Fyffe and Harry Gordon, the North Pier in Blackpool with the great English comedian Norman Evans, the Opera House, Manchester, the Grand Theatre, Leeds, and eventually, the London Palladium on the occasion of the Royal Variety Show of 1947 where he was featured along with Laurel and Hardy, The Crazy Gang, and Gracie Fields.

After long seasons in these big theatres, he would take to the road with a small company of entertainers and play almost anywhere there was a hall, usually giving new talent a chance to spread their wings. When Robert sang, he became trans-formed, singing from the heart in direct communication with the audience. He was incapable of holding back to save the voice, and there were many occasions when enthusiastic audiences both large and small were unwilling to let him go. He never disappointed them.

His recordings of some of the great Scottish Songs became very popular. Songs like *The Road to the Isles, Mary of Argyle, My Love is like a Red Red Rose, Westering Home* and *Bonnie Strathyre* made his name a household word, and yet he was the despair of his recording manager, Oscar Preuss of HMV. Oscar would hear Robert in the theatre, inspired as he always was by the contact with the audience, singing wonderfully the songs to be recorded the next day. But away from that inspiration, he was inhibited by the unaccustomed presence of the microphone, and because of his usual hectic schedule, he would have to record early in the morning when the voice is hardly at its best. Of the many recordings in existence which Robert made over a thirty year period, those which show his voice at its best are the sides cut for Parlophone in the early 1930s, the series of short films made for Pathe Pictorial between 1937 and 1944, and the sides made for HMV between 1943 and 1950.

In the world of variety, where your name appeared on the bill was of great importance and there had to be something else other than just a name. Something for the public to identify with. All the great comics had their catch-phrases, and these would be printed under their names on the bill. Robert started with 'Scotland's Scottish Tenor', then 'Scotland's Romance in Song', and eventually, 'The Voice of Scotland'. It was never meant to mean *the* voice, but rather the one which gave voice to the romance of Scotland, but once it had appeared on a bill it stayed with him. At the age of forty, Robert Wilson at last became a top of the bill attraction. In the Scotland of the war years, comedy was king. The great names of the day, Dave Willis, Will Fyffe, Harry Gordon, Jack Anthony, Jack Radcliffe, Tommy Morgan, were indisputably the star attractions, and it says a great deal for Robert's popularity that he was able to achieve top billing while performers of that calibre were in their prime.

As a top of the bill act, the pressure intensified. Everybody wanted him at once. His tireless work for charity went, as he wished, quite unremarked except by those close to him, who worried that he worked far too hard. A voice is not an infinite resource. It has to be exercised and rested regularly, neither of which were possible if you were doing two shows a night for fifty weeks of the year, getting up at the crack of dawn to be at a recording studio, radio station, hospital, or travelling from one end of the country to the other. Within three years his voice all but disappeared. How he coped with this utter disaster is a mystery. Anyone else would have had a nervous breakdown. Robert Wilson just kept on going, never mentioning the problems he was having, and restructured his repertoire to include songs which were far less vocally demanding. It would have been natural for his popularity to fade, but instead it became even greater. He had a knack of picking catchy tunes and writing words for some of them which made his recordings continue to sell in large numbers. *A Gordon for me, Scotland the Brave, The Highlandman's Umbrella, Way up in Clachan,* and *Down in the Glen* were all associated with him. He also became noted for his highland dress, often changing several times during the course of one show. On one famous occasion he walked on stage to unaccustomed silence. Someone had broken into his car and had stolen the case holding his kilts, and nobody recognised the dapper gentleman in the lounge suit.

As a man, he was quiet and unassuming with a dry self- deprecating sense of humour. He loved comedy and comedians, and the two Jacks, Anthony and Radcliffe were lifelong friends. He played several seasons with Jack Anthony at the Ayr Gaiety when Jack was top of the bill, returning the compliment years later by taking him to tour in the USA and Canada and appeared with Jack Radcliffe in two of his famous *Crackerjack* seasons at the Glasgow Empire. He loved to tell the story of a 'business' meeting with the inimitable Chic Murray, which left him crying with laughter, and not a word of business discussed. The 'business' was the forthcoming production of *Just Daft*, again at the Empire, where Robert achieved his ambition to be a comic by taking part in sketches with Dave Willis, Jack Anthony, Duncan Macrae, and Chic.

As Eliot Dobie had observed all those years before, Robert was transparently honest, and treated everyone he met with the same friendly courtesy. Had you met him in the street at the height of his fame, he would have given no clue as to who he was or what he did for a living. He assumed, mistakenly, that everyone was like him, and this led to many problems when business ventures went wrong. Despite the disappointment he felt when he was let down, it did not change his attitude, and he was generous to a fault, both with those who worked for him, and the many others who found him an easy touch. Should someone ask a favour, a special visit to a sick relative, regardless of the personal inconvenience he would keep his word, sometimes driving many miles to sing to just one person. He rarely talked about himself except to mention a particular song or to tell a funny story, and there is one story he used to tell occasionally which illustrates both his personality and the effect that he

The stars of 'Just Daft' (top to bottom) Duncan Macrae, Dave Willis,
Robert Wilson, Jack Anthony and Chic Murray

had on an audience. As he told it, he was appearing in a wartime show with the American entertainers, Layton and Johnstone, and when the air-raid sirens went off the manager announced to the audience that the show would go on but that as was customary, people could leave if they wished. He then stood in the wings with a bottle of brandy giving each act a snifter as they came off stage. Robert went on and had just started to sing when the first bombs fell. The explosions rocked the theatre and bounced the piano over the stage. The song he was singing was *Oft in the Stilly Night!* What he didn't say was that he didn't stop singing, and that while he was singing, no-one left the theatre, and that when he finished, he was given a standing ovation.

In the late 1940s he took a small company to America, and renewing old acquaintance from his D'Oyly Carte days, was able to book a large Concert Hall and fill it with exiled Scots. There were four of them. Robert, Will Starr, the accordionist, C Archer Mitchell as comedian and compere, and Tammas Fisher, the pianist. This concert was such a huge success that they were able to book another hall in another city, repeating the process all across the USA and Canada. In the Massey Hall in Toronto, the performance started at 7.30 and finished sometime after midnight. Those present said that they had never heard anything quite like it, and from then on those tours of what became known as *The White Heather Group* became an annual event.

Returning from one of those tours, Robert had been invited to attend a function in Glasgow. After what was then a seventeen-hour flight, he should have politely refused and gone straight home. But he had said he would attend, and during the course of the function he was offered a couple of drinks which he foolishly accepted. He wasn't teetotal, but because of his stomach problems, he couldn't absorb alcohol, and it went straight to his head. His car at that time was an ex-army Humber which had self-locking doors, and as he tried to open the door, he was spotted by a policeman, charged and convicted of being drunk in charge of a car. He shouldn't have taken the drink. He shouldn't have been there in the first place, but after the story came out in the Press, it was widely held that he was a drunk. Hardly worth a mention in this day and age, but in the hypocritical atmosphere of Scotland in the early 1950s it was nothing short of a scandal. Robert paid no attention, blaming no-one but himself, and carried on working as before, now with the temporary help of a driver, playing long summer seasons, even longer pantomime seasons, and filling the rest of the year with his now legendary tours to the farthest corners of the British Isles, Australia, New Zealand, the USA and Canada. Name some remote spot and they would say that 'only seagulls and Robert Wilson went there'.

Variety in Scotland was dying just as it was everywhere else, because of the growth of home entertainment and the changing tastes of an ever more sophisticated audience, but those involved worked very hard to keep it fresh and alive. Ten o'clock Monday morning would be Band-call when all the music would be re-hearsed with the pit orchestra in preparation for the two perform-ances in the evening. On Tuesday, rehearsals would start for the next week's programme, when comedy sketches and production numbers would be worked out, involving each member of the cast, and so on through the week until Monday rolled round and the whole business would start again. This meant that each act would have to learn new material and songs in addition to whatever they were featuring in their own spots each week. Of course in Panto-mime seasons things were slightly different. Once the show was up and running, there would be no more rehearsals, but the seasons were long and often involved two and sometimes three shows each day. We think of variety as one act after another, but in theatres like Ayr Gaiety, and the Theatre Royal in Edinburgh, a great deal of effort went into each production. The Gaiety was justifiably fa-mous for its scenery and costumes, while at the Theatre Royal, the producer Jay Morelle wrote special material which was set to music by Gladys Fox, wife of the Royal's Musical Director, Percy Fox. These shows were more like revues, and while there were enough theatres to keep at least some of the many talented performers around employed all year round, there was a never ending search for fresh talent and new ideas.

Using his experience of touring a small company around, both here and abroad, Robert's concept of *The White Heather Group* was that of music, song, comedy and dance presented with all the performers on stage together, rather than featuring himself with supporting acts one after the other, as was customary in variety. The success of this format was dependent on the originality of the performers, and he managed to find a blend of seasoned acts and new blood, which, combined with constantly changing ideas, made these shows a great success. There were many wonderful people involved in them over the years, but three deserve special mention. One was the pianist Tammas Fisher, who played for Robert on and off for about fifteen years. He was a hard drinking ex-army sergeant whose idiomatic playing somehow inspired Robert and helped him cope with the difficulties he was having with his voice. Another was the accordionist Will Starr. If, in this electronic age, you can imagine an audience of three thousand people being raised to almost frenzied applause by one rather frail man playing a button accordion, you will have some idea what Will Starr could do. He played a five-row button accordion, a notoriously difficult instrument. Each button plays two notes. Pull the bellows out you get one note, push it back in, you get another, so the synchronisation of bellows and button is critical. Will could play medleys of Scottish and Irish dance tunes with blinding speed, incorporating unusual changes of rythm, key, and dynamics, all of which combined to make his playing unbelievably exciting. He was a gentle, kindly man, who suffered from the incurable disease of alcoholism which came close to killing him at various times in his life. On those occasions he was saved by being given private treatment, arranged and paid for by his friend and employer, Robert Wilson.

The strain of running what became an almost permanent company became very great, and Robert relied on the honest and loyal support of his 'Road Manager' Jimmy Mackie. Jimmy was a big man in many ways, and did all the foot slogging around the country, arranging publicity, having bills and programmes printed, and booking halls and hotels. He was irreplacable both professionally and personally, and his sudden death came as a great blow. Few people realised that very often, Robert Wilson refused offers of work for himself, so that he could keep the members of the *White Heather Group* in regular employment. But occasionally, when dates didn't clash, he would appear with just a pianist, and do what he loved most. On those rare occasions, the years seemed to fall away, and his voice seemed somehow rejuvenated.

In the late 1950s, the BBC in Scotland started a television show loosely based on the *White Heather Group* format and called it *The White Heather Club* with Robert heading the cast, and it was soon obvious that they had a huge hit on their hands. Theatre commitments made it impossible for him to continue and he was happy to hand over to Andy Stewart, who made the show his own. A couple of years later, Scottish Television came up with *Jigtime,* and once again, Robert fronted the show. His first appearance on television had been on the occasion of the first BBC Outside Broadcast from a Scottish theatre. That was on 15 November 1952 when an edition of *Music Hall* was presented from the Metropole Theatre, Glasgow, starring among others, Jack Radcliffe, Dave Willis, Tessie O'Shea, Harry Gordon, Robert, and Gracie Fields.

He appeared in three Royal Command performances, at the London Palladium in 1947, at the Usher Hall in Edinburgh in 1949, and lastly at the Glasgow Alhambra in 1958. He also had the rare honour of having been invited to sing to the King and Queen on the occasion of the famous Sunset Ceremony at the Palace of Holyroodhouse.

While on tour in Ireland in the spring of 1959, Robert was attacked and robbed as he took a walk on the outskirts of Waterford. He had been clubbed on the back of his neck and, in a severely concussed state, was lucky to survive several days and nights wandering in the countryside. Later that year, he was in Germany with his Company, auditioning for the various Master-Sergeants who ran the entertainment for the American Military Bases there. Most performers hoped to make a big enough impression to be booked for one or two. The *White Heather Group* swept the board.

In the summer of 1960, the *White Heather Group* played another record breaking Summer Season at the Tivoli Theatre in Aberdeen.

The following year they were at the much larger Capitol Cinema , and were such a success that they returned in 1962 for what would be their last and most successful season. In 1963, literally worn out, Robert reluctantly decided to retire as a performer, and gave his farewell performance at the Empire Theatre in Glasgow, typically using the occasion as a showcase for younger performers, and shortly afterwards appeared with his old friend Jack Radcliffe in the show which closed that famous theatre for good. He was involved in a head on collision when returning home from a family funeral in the Spring of 1964, and so seriously injured that he was hospitalised for several months. He never fully recovered and died on 25 September at the age of fifty-seven. Despite his fame and fortune, Robert Wilson was not a wealthy man. His perennial generosity and trusting nature made sure of that. He had entered into several business arrangements on the basis of a 'gentleman's agreement' in which, unfortunately, he was the only gentleman.

All this happened a long time ago, when the world was a very different place, and it his hard to imagine the impact that Robert Wilson must have made when he first appeared on the variety stage. He was regarded as one of the finest lyric tenors of his day.

His unique voice and style spawned many imitators, and even his nervous habit of gripping his belt buckle became standard practice for hopeful Scottish singers. He loved singing, and tried to help and encourage others to make their way as he had. He was a man without peer, who did not know the meaning of jealousy, and whose ego manifested itself only in his stubborn independence, and in his personal rapport with an audience. Why he was like that is a mystery, and there are many who have cause to be grateful for having known him. As his only surviving son, I know that I will never cease to wonder at the happy chance which gave me a glimpse of that world of variety which is now just a memory, and the privilege of having as a father, such a man as Robert Wilson.

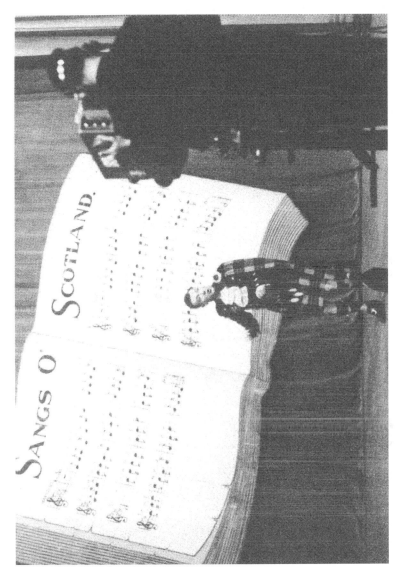

'Scottish Music Hall' being televised at the Metropole theatre in 1952

Canada Calling Scotland

Ray Smith

When Canadians discover that I'm Scottish born and bred, they invariably dig deep into their memory boxes and reel off their favourite Scottish jokes. With the best of intentions, they assault me with an assortment of weird and wonderful accents which would be totally unrecognizable back home. I dare say you are familiar with most of these oldies but goodies such as, being invited to supper by a Vancouver family of Scots emigrants and encountering a beautiful selection of food on the dinner table - all at popular prices! The ravishing young blonde sits beside a Scotsman on a Montreal subway train. and gets totally embarrassed after finding she has been attempting to pet and then feed dog biscuits, to his sporran!

If I received a dollar every time somebody told me variations on those themes, I'd be a latter day Andrew Carnegie. But there's one Scots-Canadian entertainer who knows how to get more mileage out of those chestnuts than anyone else in North America. Back in the 1930's that famed beatitude 'Blessed are the meek for they shall inherit the Earth', caused quite a bit of tittering and finger-pointing amongst the bairns at Canonmills Primary School in Edinburgh. You see, one of their classmates was a wee laddie called Billy Meek. If we knew then, what we know now, that Biblical passage would sound quite different. 'Blessed is Billy Meek, for he shall become a national celebrity on Canadian TV... yea, he shall proclaim a multitude of funny stories... he shall sing the songs that he composeth... he shall make great music upon his tenor banjo... and he shall be greatly blessed, as the 'grand-daddy' of them all... yea, one that belongeth unto the tribes of Scotland, Amen!'

Although Billy Meek looks back fondly on both Cannonmills Primary and Bellevue Secondary schools he was not destined for a brilliant academic career. Says Billy, 'I even failed playtime!' He became a 'pro' at the tender age of fourteen, joining his father Bill and sister Cathy in the family business, which in those days was a music hall act known as The Three Bright Sparks. Billy remembers them doing, 'a wee bit of this, that and the other... a mix of music, songs and dance ending on our big finale, *McDougall, McNab & McKay.*' Bill senior, who was a native of Sunderland, played banjo, spoons and mouth organ. Cathy had the talent to match her good looks and was a whizz-kid on the piano accordion. Billy played banjo and excelled at eccentric dancing, including what he describes as, 'high energy running on the spot'.

Another of young Billy's talents which was a big crowd-pleaser, were his impressions of Dave Willis, then one of Scotland's biggest stars. 'I did Dave as a fireman, a fitba' referee and an air raid warden. Naturally I included the *Wee Gas Mask* song' he recalls. When Dave heard about this young upstart named Meek who had the audacity to impersonate him, he wanted to see Billy in action for himself. Recalls Billy, 'The Three Bright Sparks were summoned to the Theatre Royal in Glasgow.' They went through their paces for Mr. Willis and his manager. 'After our performance, Dave shook my hand and told me to keep doing those impressions. He even hired us for a stint in the *Half Past Eight Show*, so he must have approved.'

The big star made a lasting impression on Billy. 'To this very day, I think of Dave Willis as the nicest gentleman I ever met in Scottish show business.' A close second was that wonderful Glasgow comic, wee Sammy Murray. Billy worked with Sam in the Glasgow theatres. 'Although Sammy was never big-time, the Glesca folk absolutely adored him,' says Billy. And when he died, half the city turned out at his funeral, to pay their respects and say goodbye. Isn't it a shame that we have no permanent visual or oral record of so many of those 'great unknowns' like Sammy...brilliant variety artistes who spent their entire careers toiling in Scotland's smaller theatres.

The Three Bright Sparks were one of Scottish music halls busiest acts. 'We were always lower down on the bill' recalls Billy, 'But we did the kind of upbeat, lively performance that bookers wanted. These days, I suppose we'd be described as a 'feel good' turn. We created a welcoming atmosphere for the entertainers who followed.' They were seldom out of work, appearing frequently at all the major theatres including the Horace Collins circuit. Billy reamed off an exhaustive list; Theatre Royal, Edinburgh, Ayr Gaiety, Glasgow Metropole, Aberdeen Tivoli, Dunfermline Opera House and Dundee Palace. They were always a home-town favourite at the Edinburgh Palladium, where they worked with the legendary Lex McLean. 'That was when all three of us got roped into sketches,' shudders Billy. He also played Dundee with a young Johnny Victory - my personal favourite - whom he describes as, 'an affa nice man to work with.' And the Meek family appeared alongside Gracie Clark & Colin Murray long before they became 'Mr and Mrs Glasgow'. 'In those days, Grace and Colin were well down the bill, doing more of a musical double.' recalls Billy. Other performers of whom Billy has special memories include Tommy Morgan, Tom Cable, Dottie Carr and Charlie Kemble.

But the act wasn't always known as The Three Bright Sparks. 'My sister Cathy and I sometimes went in as a double. Our billing was simply, Cathy & Billy.' At the Theatre Royal in Edinburgh they appeared with *Music While You Work* favourites, Troise and his Mandoliers and with one of Scotland's greatest character comedians, Jack Radcliffe, whose 'Clydebank Riveter' was a masterpiece.

184

They also toured the English theatres, including the Liverpool Shake-speare and worked with Britain's biggest stars, including Gracie Fields, George Formby and Sir Harry Lauder. Little did Billy realize that years later, he would draw upon the influences of both Lauder and Formby on Canadian network TV. When Billy received his call-up papers, Cathy carried on as a solo act. Says Billy, 'Our Scottish troops were getting fed up with Sassenach shows. So they requested something Scottish.' Which explains how Cathy Meek became a favourite with the 'Gallant Forty Twa' when she worked under the ENSA banner, and as part of a touring company called Double Scotch.

But soon Billy swopped banjo for bayonet, completing his basic military training at Fort George before transferring to his beloved Queen's Own Cameron Highlanders. Much to his surprise Billy found that his former career in civvy street, was to come in handy, especially when his sergeant got Billy to 'volunteer' to do a show for the Sergeants' Mess. As a result, Billy was spotted, not by Carroll Levis, but by Bandmaster Pope, who told Billy bluntly, 'Your in the band now, soldier!' He stayed on after the war as a resident musician and comic, and even did a tour of war-ravaged Germany. Meanwhile his mother and father took advantage of Billy's status as OHMS, to emigrate to Canada. 'They didnae reckon that I'd ever find them again!' laughs Billy. But find them he did. In the late 1940s Billy was reunited with his family and decided to see if the streets of Toronto were paved with gold. He was quickly disillusioned. 'I don't know about gold, but they never told me Toronto's nickname was cabbage town. There were plenty of those aboot the place!' The Scottish 'pro' had to find himself a day-job at Eatons Department Store, a Canadian version of John Lewis or Jenners. Bill Senior was in big demand with a professional Punch & Judy, while mother Nellie Meek ran Toronto's best-known dancing studio. In those days Canada's biggest city boasted just one variety hall, The Casino Theatre on Queen Street. But there's no 'pro' like an old 'pro'. Billy quickly got back in the groove and entered an Opportunity Knocks talent contest run by famous North American broadcaster John Adaskin. Billy sang and played *I'm lookin over a*

Billy Meek, Cathy and Dad as the Three Bright Sparks

four-leafed clover and then tap-danced on the wireless. Listeners had to write in and vote for the winning turn. Do I need to mention that this grand old Scottish pro gave his North American competition, the licking of a lifetime? He kept winning all the heats through to the grand final. Surprise, surprise, Billy won. As Michael Miles used to say on Radio Luxembourg's *Take Your Pick*, 'Tonight's star prize is a professional coast to coast radio series of your very own.' Billy embarked upon a regular Canadian Broadcasting Corporation (CBC) network variety half-hour, imaginatively titled *The Billy Meek Show*. With Dick MacDougall as his regular announcer and the Dixie Deans Quintet supplying the music, Billy sang, tap-danced, strummed the banjo and gagged his way into the hearts of Canadians from Newfoundland to British Columbia. Along the way, he taught himself the wee miniature concertina, from which he reproduced the haunting sounds of a great highland bagpipe. Radio fame led to years of public appear-ances across the nation. In the mid 1950s Billy headlined a concert party tour of Japan and Korea, this time entertaining our Canadian troops.

Just when Billy had reached that stage in his career when younger audiences were starting to ask, 'Billy Who?' he got his second wind. In 1968 Canada's very own Scottish stage and radio star became a network television personality. Billy is quite proud of his crowning achievement, 'CFTO-TV in Toronto were launching a British pub music hall series, to go national along the CTV Network. I was hired without audition, [don't tell anyone, but he knew the show's musical director Ken Stanley very well] to play the resident Scotsman.' Billy was quite upset because he had to buy a kilt. 'I'd never wanted to be known as a kilted Scottish turn' insists Billy. 'I wasn't ashamed of my national dress or anything like that, but it just wisnae me!' To this day, Billy avoids highland dress whenever he can. 'It was totally unsuited to the banjo playing, rubber-leg dancing, highly charged, hop skip and jump schtick which I could manage back in those days.'

The Pig & Whistle became the most popular UK-style variety show on Canadian network television, running every week for eleven years. In many ways it was a 'higher class' version of the old

Stars and Garters pub series, which brought English turns like Ray Martine and Kim Cordell to fame in Great Britain. The genial 'innkeeper' who commuted from Blighty to Toronto on a monthly basis to record four shows in as many days was Players Theatre alumnus John Hewer. He had a winning way with such music-hall favourites as *I live in Trafalgar Square* and the fast-paced *Lord Mayor's Coachman*. In addition to Billy Meek, the resident company included singing barmaid Kay Turner, the Rolande Dancers and a popular Irish group, The Carlton Showband.

But millions of British exiles tuned in each week to see and hear many of their favourite UK performers. The guest list read like a casting directory for UK music hall. Such names as David Whitfield, Vera Lynn, Anne Shelton, Reg 'I'm Proper Poorly' Dixon, Tessie O'Shea, Billy Dainty, Tommy Trinder, Denis Lotis, Dickie Valentine, Hattie Jacques, Cardew 'the Cad' Robinson and Barbara Windsor, were no strangers to the Agincourt TV Studios. Here, the show's production 'gaffers' Lorne Freed and John Johnstone, both of whom had produced variety shows in the UK, put them through their paces. Scotland was well represented by such star names as Jimmy Logan, Alec Finlay, Andy Stewart, Allan Bruce and Dennis Clancy. Chic Murray enjoyed a huge personal triumph on the programme. Says Billy, 'Och it was a great pleasure to work with these people. I loved performing with Andy Stewart. He treated me like an old and dear friend.' Billy discovered that Alec Finlay really was 'Scotland's gentleman', off-stage as well as on. [Alec even acknowledged Billy from the stage during one of his Royal Clansmen concerts.] 'And Jimmy Logan made me feel so proud to be Scots.' Jimmy did an unforgettable segment singing *Scotland is waking* while moving through the studio audience carrying a Highland quaich. Many of the Scottish crowd were crying with emotion that night. It makes me choke with emotion of a different kind when I think of the miles of *Pig and Whistle* video tape languishing somewhere in the musty archives of Canadian TV.

Billy, who was born in 1923, has no plans for retirement. In fact he's thinking of going back into the recording studios to tape new material to augment the popular *Billy Meek: Yours For Fun* and

Billy Meek:The Jovial Scot cassettes, which he markets himself. Billy writes most of his own stuff. I'm sure he won't mind me describing his material as a cross between the comedy song styles of Formby and Lauder. Songs like *Jean from Aberdeen, Put me in a rocket* and *The Scotsman's secret* are Billy Meek classics. His favourite North American performers all came out of vaudeville, Jack Benny, George Burns and Red Skelton. And his favourite song is *Leaning on a lampost.* As Billy told me, he was a 'feel good' performer as a teen and he's still a 'feel good' performer six decades later.

And does he have any advice for the aspiring entertainers of today? 'That's cinchy Ray. I always tell them to keep it happy and work clean!' He's a lifelong bachelor, and, since his sister Cathy passed away in Ottawa in 1997, he has no family left in Canada. 'Och but I've got many guid friends, Ray', sighs Billy. When he and Cathy returned to Scotland for a wee holiday a while back, they visited Edinburgh. 'There we were', reflects Billy, 'back hame in Edinburgh not knowing a single soul and feeling like strangers in the city where we were born.'

Another Scottish performer who enjoyed a distinguished career in North America, although he has always made his home in the UK, is that very fine kilted baritone from the Kingdom of Fife, Niven Miller. In *Those Variety Days* Billy Crockett recalls touring New Zealand in a Scottish variety show, headlined by Niven. Although Niven performed in several Royal Command performances, the St Monance-born entertainer was never particularly well known in his homeland. However, in such far flung corners as Australia, New Zealand, South Africa, North America and England – well, that's far flung from where I sit – he enjoyed considerable success. His television series for the Australian Broadcasting Corporation garnered the biggest fan mail in the history of ABC. And his LP, *Presenting Niven Miller* ousted *Oklahoma* from the top of New Zealand's album charts. He was no stranger at the Edinburgh Festival, where he played seven consecutive seasons and his annual concerts at London's Royal Festival Hall led to appearances with Glyndebourne Opera and solo tours of Russia. When he appeared in Halifax, Nova Scotia, his show was sponsored by Her Majesty's

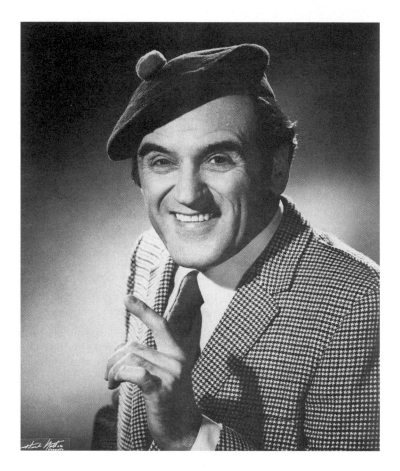

Billy Meek

representative, the Lieutenant Governor.

During the 1970s Niven became a familiar face on network television across North America, when he performed in his own weekly religious series, *Niven Miller Sings*. The half-hour programme of hymns and homilies, sponsored by New Brunswick's Senator Emerson Foundation, led to the release of numerous North American recordings and frequent tours of Canada and the States. Scottish folks across this vast Continent tuned in eagerly every Sunday morning for years, awaiting Niven's familiar signature song, the famous Stephen Adams ballad *The holy city*.

Although many people think of Niven as an opera singer, his concerts left little doubt that this man knew how to entertain an audience royally, in the real 'variety' tradition. I saw him perform at Ottawa's National Arts Centre in a concert tour en-titled *The Four Faces of Niven Miller*. This vehicle demonstrated the baritone's versatility. He sang everything from Rabbie Burns to Schubert, and from grand opera to Broadway ballads and pop. In between his songs, Niven got quite a few laughs with his pithy Fife-accented humour. I will always think of Niven Miller as the star Scottish baritone whose acting ability and sense of the dramatic, made every song he ever sang, whether it was *Largo al factotum* or *The wee cooper o' Fife*, into a crowd-pleasing, one-man 'variety' performance!

Many people believe that 'us yins' who make our homes in North America are even more Scottish than the Scots back home. Our accents are preserved in a 'time-warp', Highland Games, Scottish Festivals, St Andrews Society Dances, Burns Nights and Winter Ceilidhs are huge attractions. They appeal not just to exiled Scots but to people of every race, colour and creed. Scottish butchers, bakers and grocers keep us supplied with comfort foods. International publications like *The Scottish Banner* inform exiles around the globe about the wit and wisdom of the Scots.

And whenever we get a chance to enjoy those Scottish touring shows like *Breath of Scotland*, they are always assured of receiving a hundred thousand welcomes.

On Tour with
Derry and Johnstone

George Johnstone

M ost of our career in show business was played after we left Scotland. Most people have a good reason for leaving home, business and friends; we left Scotland because of an argument over a fiver. We had been working for the same management over a long period and we asked for an increase of £5 on our salary. It was refused. It then became a matter of principle, so we decided to leave Scotland. The problem was where would we go?

This would be 1951. Now, I must go back to the autumn of 1950; we were booked to play an autumn season in the Empress Theatre at St George's Cross, a very beautiful theatre later to become Jimmy Logan's Metropole. We weren't married, so I shared a dressing room with an Irish magician, Jack Kirwan who called himself Mickey Dooley, a weird looking artist, hair to his shoulders, thick horn–rimmed glasses and a Dublin accent you could cut with a knife, but a very charming gentleman. He later told me that when he was younger he was a pro boxer, an ex–bantamweight champion in the Republic of Ireland. It just shows that you can't judge by appearance. We became very friendly and when the season ended he made me promise that we would come to Dublin and he might help us to get work. After some discussion we decided that we would go to Dublin and meet up with Mickey who introduced us to a theatre manager.

The manager's name was Barney Marckey. So Jack said to him 'These are friends of mine over from Scotland, I want you to book them, they are a very good act'. So Barney Marckey said 'Well they can't come in for a fortnight because *The Bells of St Mary's*, the show at the moment is carrying on here for a fortnight but they can come in in a fortnight's time. He said what will they want in money so Jack told him what he thought and it was exactly double what we'd been getting in Scotland. That was a very good start. So we came out of the cinema and Jack said 'Come on let's go along O'Connell Street and you'll meet somebody else'. So along at the end of O'Connell Street at the end of Dame Street was the Irish Theatrical Agency and a gentleman called Percy Holmshaw, an Englishman who looked very like Churchill, even to the cigar. Jack said 'this is a gentleman here whose partners are over to play from Scotland, they're over to play the Capital Cinema now if you can get them some work, Percy, they'll get you commission on the date from the Capital'. Percy Holmshaw said 'Well what do they do?' and Jack said 'They both sing, they both play accordions and George plays the fiddle'. Percy Holmshaw said 'That is the very act I'm looking for for next week. I'm looking for a musical act to go out to the Opera House, Cork for Lorcan Bourke'.

Now Lorcan Bourke was the Deputy Lord Mayor of Dublin and he was also Eamon Andrews' father-in-law. Eamon Andrews had married his daughter, so this was us really in the big time. So we went down on the Saturday to Cork, got digs, turned up on the Sunday – every show starts on the Sunday in Dublin and Cork round about the Republic of Ireland and then we did a band call. On the bill was an act from Newcastle called the Four Graham Brothers also a very, very good Swiss juggling act called Selovis who juggled while he was riding a bicycle and finished up playing

Tipperary on an accordion riding the bicycle. We did a very, very good week indeed; we had an absolute ball. So Mrs Bourke, who was managing the show, said 'we'll be seeing more of you that's for sure'. So we came back to Dublin, went down to see Jack and he said 'we've been hearing about you, you've done very well at Cork and I'm quite sure that a lot of people will be wanting to talk to you'. So we started our job at the Capital and on the Tuesday a gentleman called Vernon Hayden came in to speak to me. Now Jimmy O'Dea was the top comic in the Republic of Ireland. So Vernon said Jimmy was in a Christmas show at the moment and would like you to join us in a tour when he comes out of the Christmas show. I said 'Oh, great, marvellous'. Vernon said the tour would be opening at the Opera House, Cork. I told him we were just back from there, he said it wouldn't matter just change your stuff a bit. So we went on tour with Jimmy O'Dea. We opened for two weeks in Cork, two weeks in Limerick, two weeks in Belfast, two weeks in the Shakespeare, Liverpool and came back to Ireland and played Clonmel, Dundalk and Sligo.

We had a very interesting experience on the opening night of the show at Clonmel. Jimmy O'Dea always did a police show and he got a sergeant's uniform from the local Garda and Vernon Heydon had been busy all afternoon getting the show ready for night and he said 'George when you've had your tea would you call in to the Garda station and get the uniform for Jimmy'. I said sure. So we called in at the Garda station. I got a funny feeling when we went in – there was two elderly constables sitting in front of a roaring fire they were both grey haired men and they looked at me and said 'Aye what do you want?' I said 'I've called in for Mr O'Dea's uniform that you give him'. He asked 'Are you in the show' and I said 'Yes we are' and so he said 'What do you do?' I said 'we sing and we play instruments'. 'Oh' he said 'that's terrific' he said, 'Give us a song'. I said 'Wait a minute, you're joking'. 'No' he said 'we're not. Give us a song and we'll give you the uniform'. So I said to Roma 'Sing' I said 'Sing. Don't cause any bother'. Roma started to sing *Loch Lomond* and we got wonderful applause from the two men at the finish. I said 'Now can we have the uniform please?' 'No' they said 'you haven't sung'. I recognised defeat and I sang *Westering Home* and they were delighted, gave me the uniform and said 'When the show is over tonight come in and we'll have a very, very good night here'. I said 'Aye, that'll be right'. So when I went down to the show I said to Vernon 'Never you ever ask me to do that again'. He asked me what happened so I told him and he laughed and said 'don't forget George you're in Ireland'.

During the tour with Jimmy O'Dea we had been writing to managements and papers in England to see if we could fix up any work and extend our line of work and the name O'Dea seemed to open doors that might have been closed otherwise. We managed to fix up dates at Bolton, Halifax, Huddersfield, Liverpool, Hulme and Blackpool. Now the manager of the Grand Theatre, Bolton, (which was the first variety theatre that Roma and I ever played in England) was an old man called Alfie Booth who was known to the entire profession, had been in the job for years and years, and knew the business backwards. He gave us our first date. From that we got the Palace, Halifax and the Palace, Huddersfield. During these dates we got an invitation from a man called Jimmy Brennan in Manchester who owned three theatres, the Hulme Hippodrome, the Liverpool Pavilion and the Queen's Theatre, Blackpool, so these three theatres came immediately after Halifax and Huddersfield.

The first of the three was the Pavilion, Liverpool and top of the bill was Tessie O'Shea, 'Two ton Tessie'. I arrived on the Monday morning at Liverpool to do the band call and I went along the dressing room passage passed number one dressing room and Tessie O'Shea was standing in the middle of her dressing room looking quite lost. I thought I'd be bold; I said 'Good morning' – she said 'Hello, do you work in the theatre?' I said 'I'm a member of the cast. We're working with you this week. My partner and I are the musical vocal act'. 'Oh' she said 'Good. What's your name?' I said 'George'. 'George, will you do me a favour?' I said 'Sure'. She said 'Will you stand up on that chair and open that window for me?' That was the very first favour I ever did for with Tessie O'Shea – the only one actually. I thought to myself I can tell everybody now that I opened Tessie O'Shea's window. She was a lovely person, she had a wonderful act, so friendly and at the end of the week we felt really good about working with Tessie.

The second week was the Hulme Hippodrome in Manchester. Now Hulme is in a very working class district of Manchester and the top of the bill that week was a young girl making her first top appearance, she'd never topped the bill before, a lovely little girl she'd a very sweet voice her name was Joan Regan. We never did meet her because of minders, she was surrounded by minders all week, never even got speaking to her.

The third week was at the Queen's Theatre Blackpool and we met a wonderful artist that week, a lovely artist probably the finest gentleman I ever met in showbusiness, Frankie Vaughan. After his first week and topping a show I must tell you how it happened. When he made his entrance the whole theatre was packed with young people, young girls and when he made his entrance from the back of the stage he ran down and I think the number he opened with was called *Lucky Seven*, he got the first two bars out and the first row of girls immediately shrieked and fainted and the first song went through with ambulance workers and girls getting carried out. I've never seen anything like it in my life. The noise was tremendous; shrieking and bawling all over the place and then when Frankie did his *Give me the moonlight* and did his high kick, the older ladies in the audience started to shriek. So we had a very wonderful week of shrieking and fainting young ladies, and shaking elderly ladies when he did this routine.

He had a piano player called Bert from Middlesborough and when it came to *Give me the moonlight* Frankie used to sit beside him to start it off and Bert would start the shrieking. The noise was tremendous but what a wonderful artist he was. I went in on Tuesday morning to the theatre looking for mail and Frankie was in the theatre and he was talking to a couple of lads in the building, 'George' he says 'Would you like to buy some trousers?' I said 'Yes, I certainly would'. He said 'I have a tailor friend got a shop along the road from the theatre here and he sent some material to be cut for sports jackets and the firm he sent the material to made a dreadful mistake and they cut it for trouser lengths. So he's got a shop full of trousers that he can't sell. Let's go along and see if we can buy some, I'll get you a good bargain'. So we went along to the shop on the front at Blackpool, Frankie spoke to his friend and said 'Right boys, what do you want?' The trousers were black and white check and brown and white check, obviously cut for jackets. I got two pair of each – ten bob a pair, this was before decimalization. Ten bob a pair, that was four pairs of trousers for £2. I wore them on the golf course for years. That was a marvellous bargain.

At the end of the week we were all really sorry to part with Frankie and took great pleasure in saying that Frankie Vaughan was not only a wonderful artist but he was a lovely honourable gentle man. Some couple of years later Roma and I were playing at Derby Castle on the Isle of Man for a week and Frankie was playing the Palace, Douglas, for a week. I went along the front one morning and Frankie was sitting on a seat on the front and he had on very dark sunglasses – I recognised him so I looked at him and he took his glasses down his nose a bit and he looked at me he said 'I know you don't I'. I said 'Yes you do'. When I told him who I was he said why don't you sit down beside me. Well, I spent an hour with Frankie Vaughan that day on the front at Douglas talking about anybody and everybody and he was absolutely a wonderful gentleman.

Jimmy Bennett's uncle was the bookings manager for the Collins agency in Glasgow, the top agency in Scotland, which gave us promotion into the very top work (the Collins agency in Glasgow was the brother of Collins in London who was the father of Joan Collins). As I described in *Those Variety Days*, this led to a very big tour in *The Coronation Scots*, fourteen weeks in Cragburn then a twenty-six week tour of the English number twos.

At the end of that tour we got a booking at a cabaret in Blackpool called the Ocean Room. This Ocean Room was in the Tower, at the top of the Tower in a special cabaret room. We were booked for a short season. And of course, when you go to Blackpool everyone sees you. People come round and they knew every show. And a gentleman called Peter Webster came in to see the show. Now Peter Webster had a franchise on the central pier in Blackpool and he was also Jimmy Clitheroe's manager, the Clitheroe Kid. So Webster liked us, he said 'I'm putting up a tour with Jimmy Clitheroe, would you like to join the tour?' I said ' Yes, Love to.' He said 'It will be Jimmy Clitheroe, Ronnie Hilton and the Tanner Sisters. That will be the top of the bill'. I said 'Oh, great. That sounds marvellous'. So we went on tour with the Clitheroe Kid, and got to know Jimmy Clitheroe very, very well indeed. He and I would go golfing together. Now he was very small, tiny, and he had special golf clubs made to suit his size. Never hit a long ball, but hit a ball down the middle, and a lot of golfers used to say Jimmy Clitheroe never shouted 'four', he shouted 'two'.

After that the Tanner sisters got us work in the clubs. They put us onto Les Booth, a great concert secretary in the north of England and he fixed us fourteen days and nights work. We started work in the Palladium of the Clubs, Guisborough in Yorkshire. That was the first club that started booking names, a working men's club outside Rotheram. We'd to double Guisborough and the Scala club in Doncaster. And I didn't know the distance between them. So moseying around in the dead of night trying to find the difference between Doncaster and Guisborough was a panic. The Scala club in Doncaster was a big long club with a stage door, and you had to walk right through the club to get to the stage with all your gear. And if you did badly, you had retrace your steps through the club with all your gear, with the whole club looking at you accusingly.

We finished up the fourteen days on a Sunday at Attercliffe Non-Political, and it was up a stair, and the as soon as you went on the stage the dressing room was on the right, and there was no water in the dressing room, only a jug of water. It was a very poor district and we could smell the disinfectant from cleaning up on the Saturday night. We did the Sunday lunch and then we did the Sunday evening. And the Sunday lunch we did four spots and we died, we got no applause. So we asked if he wanted us to come in at night and he said the ladies came in at night. But the ladies were worse than the men. We got nothing. We did five acts that night, and when we came off to the sound of our own feet leaving the stage. Roma was in tears and I was raging. And the secretary came to us and said, 'When can you come back? I'll give you another two pounds.' I 'said are you joking. He said every thumb in the club was up – that was the accolade. I can still smell that place.

Some clubs are very, very difficult to play. If you hadn't been brought up in theatres, then clubs are extremely difficult because, in the first place, they expect more time from an act than theatres want. It's nothing to want half an hour or forty minutes to do an act. You've got to pad, you've got to talk, you've got to do all sorts of things to keep the act going for the length of time that they want. But, having said that, they are a good place for making money and as one artist used to tell me 'When you go up for your money at the end of the show, don't forget that you're earning more money that night than some of these people who are maybe booing you get for a week down a mine or working in a foundry or something, so be nice to them. So if your act doesn't go too well, just a case of 'heid doon, and haun oot' and be as nice as you can to them, take your money and go. But' he said 'the work is very, very difficult' and it took us a long while to become accustomed to clubs after learning our business in theatres and the timing of theatres. Time didn't matter all that much and if things happen every club had what they call a compere and they were up in a sort of pulpit and the things they used to say were beyond all comprehension. If any of you have looked at the television at Colin Crompton and that wonderful show where he was the compere, it is just actually portraying clubs like they were. I was at a club one night and the soprano wasn't very good and the crowd was a bit noisy and I heard this compere shouting to the club 'Be quiet. Quiet everybody. If you don't be quiet I'll put the soprano on' and that really sums up what would happen in a club.

There was one old club around from Sheffield Wednesday Football Club up a hill round from the football ground. It was a very big club with a very large membership and we used to go on a Sunday. They liked our act for some reason or another, and they used to book us on Sunday and we used to go quite regularly, four, five, six times a year to this particular club. And every Sunday we went there a member of the club had died. There was such a big membership that they were dying all over the place and every Sunday morning the compere got up and announced that member so-and-so had died through the week and will the members please stand and have a minute's silence. So the club stood up dutifully and had a minute's silence. There was a five-piece band who were all out of tune with each other. The band played *Abide with me* and then the compere said 'And now gentlemen, straight from Scotland, Derry and Johnstone'. So we had to follow a minute's silence and a band playing *Abide with me*. We didn't have an earthly; it was dreadful but that was club business and eventually we got accustomed. We worked at material. We realised that we had to change, we couldn't expect the clubs to change. There was good money to be earned and everybody who could do it was playing clubs and that included stars.

We actually played at a club in Manchester for a week. We had a week's booking for a pair of clubs in Manchester and we opened in a club in Workden, that is a part of Manchester. I think they called the club the White Bull or the Grey Bull and they had a cast headed by Dennis Lotis, who was the big BBC singer of his day, a wonderful singer, a lovely singer. When he turned up as a star we were all waiting for the band call and we noticed it was just an upright piano. So a wee man came in, took his jacket off and hung it over the seat, pulled up his shirt sleeves (and he had on one of those silver bands that used to keep your shirt sleeves up) took the lid off the piano, sat down and said 'Right, who's first? I don't read, I can't read music but I can busk anything, who's first?' Dennis Lotis was standing there with a big pile of BBC arrangements. That was actually the sort of thing that happened to you.

Now each night a week we had to double, and we got a club to double with, a late night club called the Oasis. Now, I won't go into much detail about it; it was all right, they treated us all right. I noticed on the first night we were there that there was quite a crowd of young women in the club. A man would come in and make a signal, and one of the girls would get up and walk out and she would come back to the club about an hour later. This went on all night. It went on all week. The girls were a marvellous audience

200

and towards the end of the week I realised the kind of club it was. The girls were all working girls and they were doing their work in the evening. They were all getting called out one by one to go out and do a job and come back again. It took us a while to get accustomed to that but we got used to it and the girls were absolutely marvellous, so it was fine.

We played clubs in our time from Newcastle to South Wales, through Birmingham, the Midlands, Stoke, London, all over the country. We played workers clubs and social clubs and any time we were wanting to work we just arranged clubs. And as the old adage went 'get your head doon, get your money and go'. Some nights it was marvellous, most nights it was mediocre and some nights it was dreadful but it was only for a night.

By the time we got our act going, the first act we did you did a smooth type of ballad and stuff and at the finish of the night we had two accordions and the fiddle and got them stamping around. That was really the stuff that got you through and we learned it was a hard business. We learned another business in clubs, it was totally different but we learned the hardness of facing an audience, breaking an audience down and getting them on your side. And when you did that, when we learned to do that we could go to the clubs and Roma and I made a lot of money in clubs right through the whole of the UK, more money than ever we'd made in theatres in the UK. You would earn the same money in a weekend, a Friday a Saturday and a Sunday as for a week's work in a theatre.

The money was good at that time because you were a bit of a name, coming from the theatres. So it was quite a lucrative job at that time and a lot of artists stayed in the clubs, they didn't come out. After the theatres closed hundreds of artists were out of work and would have stayed out of work had the clubs not been around. If you could arrange your act and arrange the time, you could work, you could earn a living and I have got to say that without the clubs then many people like ourselves would not have existed in the business. We could earn a good living if we could come to terms with it.

During this time a man called James Crossini contacted me; he had seen our act in Blackpool. James was an escapologist. He told me, I forget just which one, but he told me he had either been stage manager to Houdini or to Murray, escapologists, and he knew all the mysteries. He himself wanted to tour the Great Trunk Mystery and he was looking for an act that could do a good act and also could spiel the Trunk Mystery. So he said 'Would you do it, would you be interested?' I said 'Yes, sure. How long is it?' He said 'Sixteen weeks touring around the number twos in England'. I said 'Fine. You'll have to tell me what to do'. He said 'I'll show you it but I want you to promise you'll never tell anyone'. So I gave a promise. I do know the Trunk Mystery but I'm not going to tell you, it would be unfair – I gave my word.

What I had to do was – the trunk was brought on stage and Crossini came on stage and I started telling the people what was going to happen. Crossini was going to be tied up and put into the trunk. The trunk was going to be locked and then covered with a cover and you would see what happened. So I had to get two members of the audience, two men usually, came up and examined the trunk. They knocked at it, examined it thoroughly, it was all right. The trunk was absolutely solid. Then I said right would you tie Mr Crossini up, we opened the lid, they tied Crossini up and they put him into the trunk, they pulled down the lid and put a heavy lock on the lid and I kept the key. I started the spiel again and during the spiel he was free, it was as quick as that. He was just lying in the trunk waiting.

So then I brought a young girl on dressed in a bikini and she stood up on top of the trunk. I started to spiel to the audience and this young lady was standing on the trunk and we went to pull a cover round the trunk: 'The young lady will go under the cover. Then we will take the cover away and see what has happened!' Up she got, put the cover on and down she went and by that time he was out and she was in the trunk. I spieled away for a couple of minutes then took the cover away and of course the girl had disappeared. I said to the two boys on the stage 'Right, lift the trunk and see if Crossini is still there'. They said 'Yes, he is still definitely there' and I said 'Right, unlock the trunk'. So we unlocked the trunk and up sprung the girl – she was in the trunk and at that time Crossini had run round the theatre and come in at the front door having a yell at the front door; 'Right I'm here, I said ladies and gentlemen the Great Crossini'. This I did for sixteen weeks.

It was a marvellous business actually, he did it very, very well and after sixteen weeks I think I could have done it myself. But during that run every show at that time had to carry nudes. The audiences demanded that there were nudes in the shows and we were carrying two girls who were nudes and they posed around the show at various parts of the show and we were finishing the first half of the show with a cowboy scene. Now Crossini took his props around, including the trunk, in a big van and he had two horses made, wooden horses, for this cowboy scene and they were at the top of the stage where there was an opening. And we had a comic called Ken Wilson, a good lad, a great comic, and he was to make an entrance dressed as a cowboy, walk down and do some cowboy patter. I was dressing with him and he said 'I'll need to say something as I pass these two girls, they're sitting up absolutely naked each one on a horse and I'll have to say something'. I said, 'Well I'm sure you'll think of something'. So on the first night, the opening night he made his entrance, he stopped for a moment, he looked up, he said 'That's a mighty fine horse you've got ma'am' and he carried on walking down to the stage and got a roar – absolutely great!

During the season, while working with Crossini, we got another offer from Ireland and this time it was from an up and coming comic called Jack Cruise. He was becoming the biggest comic in Ireland at the time and he was running a summer season at Butlins, outside Dublin, Mosney they called the camp and he asked me would Roma and I join the show and then do a tour. When we heard about it we were touring with O'Dea. I said fine, so we settled the money and went across to Dublin, to Mosney and did eighteen weeks at Butlins holiday camp. The whole show took an hour and ten minutes, that was all they wanted, so Cruise and I golfed all day and we did an hour and ten minutes at night in Butlins with a night off. It was a great job and after the season at

Butlins he went on tour with the company and it was the usual tour; two weeks in Cork, two weeks in Limerick and then we went to the Opera House in Belfast for two weeks. Then we went back to a place called Mullingar, to Sligo, to Dundalk and to Tipperary. Now I had very often heard it sung and very often sung it myself but I didn't realise there was a place called Tipperary. I stayed there for a week and I went down one night with Cruise and played to packed capacity business and we'd come back from the golf course and he said he was going in for a paper. There was an old lady in the paper shop and Cruise hadn't given her any passes – he was doing such good business. This old lady behind the counter said 'Mr Cruise how is your business?'. He said 'I am doing capacity we are turning them away in hundreds.' 'Ah well' she said 'Mr Cruise, if your publicity had been good you would have been turning them away in thousands.' I said to him, 'That old lady deserves a pass you know, that was a beautiful crack'.

We left Tipperary and went to the Royal, Dublin and we did an eight-week season with Radio Erin. Eight separate weeks doing a show once nightly called *Holiday Hayride* and this took us right up to Christmas; an absolutely marvellous time in Ireland. This was 1955 and during the winter I did a season in the clubs with very good money, actually playing very good clubs.

In the summer I booked a season in the Isle of Man, that was the summer of 1956. We played the Crescent Theatre in Douglas and it was one of the most beautiful summer seasons from a weather point of view. In 1956, you may not remember it, but there was practically no rain at all, it was a record. Roma and I were staying with an Isle of Man man and his wife and he was a real Manx man. I think he thought there were fairies in the Isle of Man; I'm not going into the matter, but he could be right. He said 'The Queen's coming and she is going to come on a Wednesday and' he said 'it always rains on the Isle of Man when the Queen comes.' I said, 'Well I don't know it is a beautiful summer just now and there's no sign of it.' She arrived on the Wednesday and the *Britannia* sailed into Douglas Harbour at ten o'clock in the morning but at nine o'clock it clouded over and started to rain. It rained all day and the

Britannia left at six o'clock, the clouds parted and the sun started to shine. That is the gospel truth and after that I said to Charlie, that was the landlord's name, I said 'Charlie I believe you, I think there must be fairies in the Isle of Man.' I said 'That was absolutely marvellous and unbelievable.' He said, 'Ah, but you haven't heard the worst of it George. An old, old tale on the Isle of Man goes back a long time that says a Manx man is entitled to shoot a Scotsman on sight'. I said 'Charlie let's forget it please, let's just have a pleasant summer!'

During 1957 we did a long tour with a comic who called himself Little Tommy Green and we worked all summer making a lot of money. He must have kept it under the bed because when we went out on tour with the company he carried on until the money was finished and that was the company finished when his money ran down. We did a long, long tour with him on all the English dates again during 1957; it practically went on the entire year. It was a great tour - no business, but a very good tour. That went on to 1958 when we started working for a Belfast colleague, called James Young. That was a name that I don't think will ever die in Ulster. He's dead now himself, but James Young was one of the finest comics that I've had the pleasure of working with and he used to pack the places. He was the king of the Belfast Empire. So Roma and I spent 1958, 1959 and 1960 working for James Young around Ulster; Belfast, Bangor and all the dates around Ulster, from Derry right round, and everything you could possibly think of.

In 1961 we got a call back to Scotland from Chalmers Woods and he asked us would we appear at the Queen's Hall, Dunoon with Clark and Murray. We did, we had a very good season and at the end of the season he asked me if Roma and I would go to Rothesay for 1962 and would I produce the show. I said yes I would.

Now I touched on this in *Those variety days* – in 1962 and 63 we appeared at Rothesay with Chalmers Wood Rothesay Entertainers. In 1964 Roma and I did something that we'd always wanted to do and in fact I think every artist wants to do it sometime during his career; we put on our own show, at Bangor in the County Down.

Now James Young had been doing the show for years and he decided that he wanted to do something else and he asked me did I want to take the place over? So we did and every year from 1964 to 1970 Roma and I produced our own show called *Showtime* at the Little Theatre in Bangor, Northern Ireland. It was very successful, very successful indeed, the people in the district loved it and during that show we actually employed Scottish comics. For the first two years I had a comic called Joe Long who had been at Rothesay with me. In 1966, 67, and 68 we employed a Scottish comic called Neil Owen. Neil unfortunately died rather young; he dropped dead in a public house in Craigneuk. In 1969 and 70 we employed Jimmy Fletcher who was a very well known little comic around Scotland who also played the moothie. So these were the comics during the time we played in *Showtime* in Bangor. We also employed a very well known ESP artist called Zarida who went down a storm with the Bangor audiences.

At that time in 1970 things were becoming very, very difficult because of the troubles and we decided that there wasn't much point in going on as things didn't appear to be getting any better. So we decided we would give in. We told the proprietor of the theatre that we would finish in 1970.

During the 1970 season I had a letter from Lorcan Bourke whom we had appeared in Dublin for. Our first date in Cork we played for Lorcan – he was Eamon Andrew's father-in-law as I told you previously. Now Eamon Andrews owned a country club at a place called Portmarnock outside Dublin and Eamon wanted to know if we would become the resident cabaret act for a month at the country club for him, so we said yes we would be delighted. We went down to Portmarnock at the end of the Bangor season which took us up to Christmas and this actually was to be our very last appearance in Ireland, a beautiful country with friendly, hospitable people, but we just never returned to Ireland.

In 1971 we got the offer of a long tour with Mecca all round the United Kingdom. Actually they were all bingo halls most of them by that time, but they were doing bingo plus a cabaret. So we got the offer to do this and we had a long, long tour in 1971 and we finished up in a very beautiful theatre in the Strand in London, the Lyceum, which used to be very famous for its shows.

We'd finished that and because of that we got the offer of a variety tour round the London clubs. Now I've got to explain that the London club tour was a tour that was sponsored by councils in London and each council put on a night in the Civic Hall. What they did was they employed a well-known London 'top' and to support that 'top' they put on an act from another part of the country and we toured with Tommy Trinder and we finished the first half as a Scottish act which was an absolute change from anything that Trinder did. The show proved very successful, it ran for six weeks and it was finishing up in the Walthamstow Civic Hall.

An American came in one night into the dressing room, he knocked and said 'I like your act I, I like it very much. Would you like to play for me?' I said 'Well, what do you do, what do you book'. He said 'I am the booker for the American forces in Europe'. He said 'Have you got any work arranged?' I said 'Yes, I have work for the next three weeks'. 'Well' he said 'who's the agent?'. So I told him. He said 'Forget it. Any agent will do as I ask him to do because I give a lot of work round the American forces'. So I gave him the agent's name and three weeks later Roma and I were standing in Victoria Station, London en-route for Europe.

We landed first of all in a place called Frankfurt and what happened was the show went on in Frankfurt and the American agent gathered in all the entertainment officers from around the country and from other places. They all came in to see the show and if they liked it they bought it. So what happened was they bought a show and they supplied the money for the show to go to their club wherever they were situated. So this is how they got the money for the show; it was an excellent idea actually. So we were fully booked at the end of that week.

We spent eight weeks in Germany and each week we shifted hotels in Frankfurt, Mannheim all round whether the American forces were. We stayed in very good hotels and we were coached in first class coaches around all the sights. It was a lot of travelling, we were constantly tired because we'd hundreds of miles to the date and hundreds of miles back but then it was autobahn and there was no changing of gear it was just a matter of running there and running back. The clubs themselves were peculiar because they were enlisted men's clubs and they were all young men and were pretty noisy. Then there were NCO's clubs and they were family clubs with a family audience and they were extremely good. Then there were the officers' clubs and they differed from place to place, some of them were a bit toffee-nosed, others were absolutely great. It was just a matter of chance whatever site you were on.

Now at the end of the eight weeks the colonel ordered us, to Athens. He said 'I want you two to go to Athens, to join the show at Athens, now how do you want to go? Do you want to fly or do you want to go by train?' So we said 'Well I think we'll go by train because we'll be able to see the country'. So he said 'All right you join a train at Cologne at midnight and you travel overnight to Munich and you'll catch the Acropolis Express from Munich at eight fifteen in the morning'. I said 'Wait a minute now sir, what if the train runs late and we can't get on that eight fifteen?' He said 'George, the trains do not run late in Germany; it's not allowed. You'll be there in time for that eight fifteen'. So we got on the train at Cologne at midnight – we had sleepers – arrived at Munich at five minutes to eight the following morning, dead on time, as he said, we got the eight fifteen Acropolis Express to Athens.

Now this express travelled all through Germany, all through Austria, all through Yugoslavia. We stopped at Belgrade to change trains because the train from Belgrade to Athens was on a smaller type of line. So we went into Belgrade and walked around the place and found it a bit depressing. Actually it was a bit duller than most of the cities, however, everything was very, very cheap. We rejoined the train at Belgrade and we travelled then through the rest of Yugoslavia down into Greece. We stopped at Salonika and from Salonika we travelled right through to Athens. The whole journey took two days on the train and it was one of he most interesting journeys I have ever made in my life – absolutely wonderful.

When we reached Athens we were put up at a first class hotel in a part of Athens called Vaula, a sort of West End of Athens where a lot of moneyed people came for their holidays, beautiful beach and of course beautiful weather. The only trouble was it was in the flight-path for aircraft going into Athens airport and it was a bit noisy especially in the mornings with the noise of the planes coming in. We had no travel, it was like a holiday; we could walk from our hotel to the club where we were working so it was like a rest. Athens itself is a very beautiful city. The only complaint I had about Athens was the standard of driving. I considered the drivers were mad, completely mad. If you had to cross the road you did it really at the expense of your life. It was probably the worst driving I had ever seen up until then. We ate in the club, beautiful food. It was really a wonderful eight weeks and after all the travelling in Germany it was absolutely superb. However, at the end of the eight weeks we were told that we were going to Crete for a fortnight.

We sailed from Piraeus, which is the port of Athens. We sailed overnight to Herakleion in Crete. When we arrived at Herakleion we remembered the name of the hotel; it was the Astoria Hotel and when we started in the business in Scotland, the man we started with owned the Astoria Ballroom and Hotel in Glasgow, so it was like old times. During our stay in Crete we met marvellous audiences, they were really wonderful and one night we had our first experience of an American standing ovation which happens all over America when the people like you. Roma was singing *Danny Boy* and when she came to the end men stood up shouting and applauding and then they started moving toward the stage and I think Roma felt she was about to be attacked. She shouted to the men 'What do you want me to do?' The men shouted 'sing it again honey, sing it again'. So Roma sang *Danny boy* again. At the end of the two weeks we flew back to Athens, but it was only to get ready to travel on to the next part of the job.

This proved to be probably some of the most interesting work I have ever done in my life. Since then and up till now I have never done anything like this. We flew to Turkey, and flew into Izmir, one of the main ports of Turkey with a very big airport. Now, Roma was travelling on her passport, it showed one accordion; when you are travelling like that your instruments are shown on your passport. So Roma, as I say, had this passport with one accordion and we came up to the official where they were doing the business with the passports and luggage, and the Turkish man looked at Roma and looked at her passport and he pointed to the accordion. He said, 'No, no, you no. Him two', pointing to me with two accordions. And I should have been showing the two accordions on my passport. Roma started to argue with him, she said 'No, I play the accordion'. The official wouldn't have it. He said 'No, no him, him two' Roma said, 'No, I play it'. The man got a bit exasperated and said 'All right, you play, now'. He told Roma to play the accordion so that was right up Roma's street – Roma was a bit of an extrovert that way. Off came Roma's anorak, took the accordion out of the case put it on and started to play *Scotland the Brave*. There was a crowd of American service men who were en-route, either coming in or going out of Izmir and they started to shout and cheer and dance and for about two minutes the whole of Izmir Airport stopped, with Roma playing, marching up and down by this time, playing *Scotland the Brave* and the Americans dancing and shouting. When she stopped the Americans gave her a big hand. She put the accordion back in her case and said, 'Well can I play it?' and the Turk looked at her and he just stamped her passport, closed it and said 'Thank you'. She put her accordion back we passed through the customs and we were walking out towards a mini-bus that was waiting for us and the Turk shouted 'Madam' – so Roma turned – he shouted 'Have a good time in our country'. I often wondered if he was having a joke at out expense. However, if he was I reckoned the score at that time was Roma 1 Turkey 0.

When we arrived in Turkey it was Ramadan which was a very holy festival around Turkey at that time. It was November and all the men at the mosques were praying all day long they were in, and of course the noise from the minarets at night – you could hardly sleep and there were doors opening and closing in the hotel, men bringing out their praying mats to face Mecca to pray. This was going on all night so we really didn't get a lot of sleep in Izmir. Izmir I found was very hot and very dusty but the club was good, the American club was good – we were fine, we did the job well and were told to go on to Karamousel. Now Karamousel is situated on the Sea of Mar-mara opposite Istanbul and there's a ferry running every hour from Istanbul to Karamousel and back. So we jumped on the ferry one day and got across to Istanbul. I wanted to see the Blue Mosque but when we got there, being Ramadan no-one was allowed into the mosque, so we just didn't get a chance to see the mosque inside but from the outside the Blue Mosque looked absolutely fabulous. From Karamousel we motored down to Samsun and Krabzone, they are both situated on the Black Sea.

Now at that time America had listening posts on every hill in Turkey where they were listening to planes coming out and in in Russia and we had a lot of travel up and down hills to all the various posts to do our work. From Samsun and Krabzone we moved on to Ankara. We found Ankara a curious mixture of old and new. Middle-aged and elderly women were wearing yashmaks where you only saw their eyes and a breathing space for them to breathe, young girls were knocking around wearing, not mini-skirts but mini-mini-skirts, leaving very left little to the imagination actually. Once again the driving was deplorable, it was even worse than Athens.

It was December by this time and we were appearing at the NCO's club in Ankara. When we walked on I was wearing the kilt and there was an utter roar of applause went up; I couldn't understand it. It went on for about a minute of applause so I stopped and I thought what's up, what's causing this. There was a table down in the corner, they were all British and they were actually from the British Embassy and they were down drinking in the club, so we had a marvellous time. They came in a couple of nights later and said they had been telling the Ambassador that there was a Scottish act on the show at the NCO's club and he said 'ask them would they be prepared to bring in the New Year up at the Embassy Club at Hogmanay'. We said we would be delighted. So on Hogmanay night after the show in the NCO's club a land-rover appeared for us with the Union Jack flying in front and we were escorted up to the club in the British Embassy. Now in Ankara the time is one hour exactly before London, so at twelve o'clock in Ankara it was eleven o'clock in London. They kept us in another room and the people met in the club didn't know that we were there. At twelve o'clock when the bells were ringing twelve in Ankara the doors opened and Roma and I walked in playing the accordions dressed in the Scottish outfits and the whole place erupted. They hadn't seen anything like it in all their New Years there so we had a most marvellous hour. It was so good they decided they would like to do it again. So we decided we would go back into the room and at twelve o'clock British time when big Ben sounded on the radio we would do the whole thing again. Big Ben sounded twelve o'clock, we marched in again playing *Scotland the Brave* and we brought in the New Year twice that night. It was actually a superb evening.

We were in Ankara for a fortnight and after the show on Hogmanay night at the Embassy, Roma and I were out every afternoon visiting British homes and having a most wonderful time. We had very, very wonderful memories of Ankara. From Ankara we moved on to Adana. Now Adana is situated on the Mediterranean Sea of Turkey and I was sitting one afternoon in the hotel we were in, I was looking at the programme of the places around Adana and I saw a place called Tarsus. I enquired in the hotel was this the home of St Paul, they said yes, St Paul was born in Tarsus fifteen kilometres away from where we were. I said to myself I wasn't going to come all this road and not go down to see where St Paul was born. Some of us in the company got together and got a taxi to take us down to Tarsus. St Paul's home has gone but the well is still there where he drew his water. From there we went down to a place called the Falls of Tarsus. I don't know if this is true or not but it is rumoured that Christ met St Paul at the Falls of Tarsus. If that is true, then Roma and I stood on the bridge at the Falls of Tarsus in Tarsus where St Paul was born.

At the end of our period in Adana that was the end of our tour in Turkey so we motored back from Adana to Izmir, and we flew back from Izmir into Athens for the last part of the tour. At Athens we got on to a mini-bus and we drove to a place called Patris which is the other side of Greece and from Patris we sailed overnight to

Brindisi in the south of Italy. We landed at Brindisi, we did a club overnight and then we motored from Brindisi up to Naples.

Naples is the home of the American 6th Fleet and it's the biggest club in Europe for the Americans. It was an absolutely massive club, three clubs in the one ground – the enlisted men, the NCO's and the Officers' club – and the Officers' Club had to be seen to be believed. It was actually made in white marble with a beautiful staircase up to the entertainment room. It was absolutely perfect and I had a wonderful experience in the NCO's club one Friday night. The 6th fleet had come in from sea on Friday morning and the club was packed with sailors and their girlfriends. We were in the middle of our show, Roma and my particular show, and I heard a voice shouting, sing *Old Man River*. I thought I would just carry on and ignore it but they kept on saying sing *Old Man River* so I stopped. I said 'Would the gentleman who is saying that please stand up'. 'No'. I said 'Sir would you please stand up'. 'No'. So I appealed then to the audience, I said 'Ladies and Gentlemen isn't it fair that this gentleman should stand up when he is shouting at me?' 'Yes, sure, stand up'. So this guy started to stand up and I honestly thought he would never stop getting up, he must have been about six feet ten and built in proportion. I took one look at him, I thought well do something quick, I said 'Sir did you say *Old Man River*?' 'Yeah I did'. 'I said all right thank you very much, Roma give me a G7 quick' and I sang *Old Man River*. I could just imagine this guy standing at the stage door waiting for me coming out and what would have happened after it, so I was delighted to meet his request.

We were a month in Naples and we moved then from Naples to a site called Camp Douglas, which is just outside Pisa and, of course, we went to the Leaning Tower of Pisa and we walked up right to the very top. It's a wonderful place but I was a bit affronted by the dirt. It was very unkempt inside and didn't appear to be very well looked after but the view when you got to the top was absolutely out of this world and we couldn't go to Pisa without going up the Tower. So up we went and that was actually was the end of our work for the tour.

213

We got very friendly with a couple who were with us. They did a rolling skater act on a mat – Monica and Walter – and they had a car. So we decided that we would go with them from Pisa through Turin up over the Alps into France to Grenoble and up through France to Calais to get home. So that we did and it was absolutely a very, very wonderful end to a very wonderful tour.

When we got to London I had to go up to the office to collect some money. So when I got to the office the man who had given me the job in the first place was there and he said 'That was great, you did a marvellous job, it was a good tour, every one was absolutely delighted. Now would you like another job, would you like more work?' I said 'Well, yes but we've just done the whole tour.' 'Oh', he said, 'it's not the tour there's another company very interested to book you. I've been telling them about you' and he told me about an office to go to in London. I went to the office in London and we were booked then by a company, the biggest travel corporation in the world at that time. The company was called AARPMRTA; AARP means the American Association of Retired People and this company was fronting fifty-five million American retired people and arranging holidays for that amount of people. They offered me the job of European social and entertainments director with an office in Spain.

One month later Roma and I were in Torremolinos carrying out our first part of the duty for AARP. AARP had arranged with Spanish hoteliers spread right along the Costa del Sol for cheap rate holidays from October till May. This was the slow time in Spain and it kept the waiters and other staff working in the hotels. Now this going on from October till May, at a cheap rate, meant that Americans could live cheaper for eight months of the year in Spain, taking into account the cost of heating and living in America in bad weather conditions. So a great many Americans took advantage of the long stay from October till May. They were coming over in planeloads from John F Kennedy, New York to Malaga and each planeload was approximately three hundred Americans. It started with six hundred people and at the height of the season round about Christmas it was up to seven thousand American retired people

214

spread between Malaga and Marbella, right along the coast of the Costa del Sol.

As the season went on and crowds were growing, our artists were booked; cabaret artists who could do the job and who were resided in one hotel and they went out every night to different hotels to do their cabaret act, which meant there was entertainment every night in every hotel along the coast. Our job was to arrange the social and entertainment along the coast. This meant arranging classes in Spanish dancing, Spanish language, we had debating classes and bridge classes, bingo plus cabaret and dancing every night. We also arranged for people to go on other tours from their hotel on the Costa del Sol. We went to Morocco, to Tangiers, to London, to Bonn, to Paris and then returned at the end of the tour to their hotel on the Costa del Sol and this was all done on cheap tickets. We were in Torremolinos from October till May till the season ended. The following season we were asked to go to Sorrento in Italy and we did exactly the same job in Sorrento the only difference being that the tours were to the Amalfi Coast and to Pompeii and the excavations around Vesuvius and also out to Capri to Gracie Fields' grave.

We got a contract from the Aznar shipping line based at Bilbao in Spain for one of their very beautiful ships called the *Monte Grenada*. This was the first cruise ship we had been on; it sailed between Bilbao, Liverpool, Vigo, Funchal, Lanzarote, Tenerife and La Corruña and back to Liverpool. It carried cargo and passengers. The cargo was tomatoes and bananas from the Canaries and the passengers were British from Liverpool and Spanish from Vigo. On the road back we dropped the Spanish passengers at La Corruña and carried on the cruise to Liverpool. This was a most beautiful 12,000-ton small ship, beautifully appointed. In the cinema on the ship the screen was right across the bow of the ship, two decks down. If you sat watching the cinema and the ship started to plunge everyone got sick, so the cinema could only be shown when the sea was calm. We had a marvellous time on this ship and were very sorry to leave it.

The next cruise line we were on was a Norwegian/American

sailing out of Miami on one of the most beautiful ships afloat at that particular time – a ship called *The Song of Norway*, famous round the world for its beauty. It sailed between Miami, the Caribbean - San Juan and St Thomas, one week's cruise and back to Miami. We transferred then to *The Nordic Prince* which was a sister ship of *The Song of Norway*. *The Nordic Prince* sailed between the Caribbean down to South America, the Caracas, Guadeloupe, Port au Prince on Haiti and back to Miami. These were beautifully appointed 25,000-ton ships carrying mostly American passengers. We got to know Americans very well of course through our touring in Spain and we knew exactly what entertainment they liked. We had a very good time indeed; some of the ports we visited were very interesting.

At San Juan I went ashore and I went a walk up the hill. At the top of the hill I came to a Church of Scotland church and I walked in as the door was open looking at the place and a Scottish voice behind me said 'Can I help you?' I said 'Well yes you can I'm a Scot, I'm off the ship in the harbour'. So it was a Scottish minister from Dundee and we had a very pleasant time and he said 'Any time you are in San Juan come up see us and we might be able to take you round the place and show you the sights'.

Caracas was a very dangerous port. You had to be careful not to go ashore alone otherwise you could be attacked. Guadeloupe I found to be a smelly place; when you got out the ship and out the gates there was an open drain right in the middle of the main road and they were selling fruit and vegetables from stalls right along the side of the road not far from the drain. Port au Prince in Haiti was probably the most dangerous port of all because in Haiti there was the voodoo, the black magic. You had to be very careful; you had to go round in a crowd otherwise you would have landed on the top of a mountain as a sort of sacrifice!

When we left that we went on then to the Baltic Shipping Company and this is where we did most of our cruising. The Baltic Shipping and the Russian Shipping Company whose home port was Leningrad at that time. We sailed on the *Kalinin* the *Mikhail Lermontov*, the *Oddessa*, the *Leonid Brezhnev*. The *Kalinin* which was a smaller ship did the Canary run but included Morocco the Costa Blanca, Casablanca, Gibraltar, Lisbon and back to Vigo and back to Southampton. We did our first world cruise on the *Mikhail Lermontov*, a 25,000-ton ship sailing from Southampton. This ship later sank on passage between Australia and New Zealand. It struck a rock not shown on the map. We cruised out to Sydney, Bali and the South Sea Islands, back to Sydney and then up via Hong Kong and home. We did our second world cruise on the *Leonid Brezhnev*. We then played a northern ports cruise including the Norway fjords, Finland, Leningrad itself. Leningrad was a very beautiful, clean city. It had been totally demolished during the Second World War by the Nazis and the Russians re-built the city brick for brick after the War back to how it actually was pre-war and prior to the bombing.

When we finished cruising with the Baltic Shipping company we managed to get a job with a French company on a ship called the *Calypso*. This ship was cruising between Los Angeles, San Francisco, Seattle, Victoria, Vancouver and three ports in Alaska, Juno, which is the capital of Alaska, Skagway, and Ketchican which is one of the main shopping ports in Alaska. When we cruised into San Francisco the first place we made for was the cable cars that we saw on the television programme the Streets of San Francisco. They are there, they are just exactly the same cars so we boarded the car and we rode right up the hill to the very top of the hill and, as it showed in the television show, men and women just jumped onto the car for a run up the hill and when a conductor went near them they jumped off. This was really interesting. So we got to the top of the hill, found a marvellous Chinese restaurant took the tramcar back to the ship. The following journey into San Francisco we took a ferry sailing from San Francisco jetty across to Alcatraz, that very famous prison and we toured round Alcatraz all of it – a very forbidding place indeed. We even saw the electric chair where they executed the prisoners who were on Death Row. This was quite a business seeing this prison, closed now of course, but open to tourists as one of the attractions for people going to San Francisco.

When we got up to Alaska one of the main ports was Skagway which is the start of the Yukon Trail where the gold rush and the miners started their journey up the Yukon Trail. We went up – you go one way by coach and the other way by plane. If you go up by coach you come down by train down through Dead Horse Gulch and all the places you read about on the Yukon Trail where the men battled for so long and died getting gold. But the one thing I noticed about Alaska – I expected lots of snow, this didn't happen and I understand that the world is warming and the snow is receding very, very slowly but minutely receding because of the heating. We sailed in on a Tuesday; we went in to Glacier Bay, which is one of the great attractions in the world. The ship sails into the land-locked bay sand you're completely surrounded by glaciers; a magnificent sight.

Now at the end of that cruising season we sailed back to Los Angeles and flew back to London. Now that actually was the end of our cruising, we returned to the north of England, to Liverpool and in 1987 and 1988 we did two summer seasons at the South Pier, Blackpool and in 1988 we found that that was the start of Roma's terminal illness. That finished our working career.

I would like to go back to 1966 when we were doing the summer seasons of our own at the Little Theatre in Bangor. In June 1966 I was over in Bangor doing some work preparatory to the opening of the summer season and I wanted to come back to Greenock on the Sunday and I found that I couldn't get a flight from Belfast to Glasgow. But by chance there was a boat making a special journey from Belfast to Glasgow over-night, Saturday to Sunday morning. I was able to get a passage on the ship but I couldn't get a berth and was up all night. At half past three in the morning I was standing on the deck. It was a most beautiful summer morning, the sky was absolutely blue, there wasn't a ripple on the Clyde and as we came round Ailsa Craig, up past the Mull of Galloway and the Mull of Kintyre, right up to Gourock, I could say that I saw scenery that morning that was on a par with anything I saw on our journeys around the world.

Not so long ago somebody said to me if you had your life to live over again would you do it all again? I said yes I would do every bit of it again and with the same woman because without Roma none of it would have been possible.

218

The Tall Droll and the Small Doll – Chic Murray and Maidie Dickson

Annabelle Meredith

My brother Douglas was born on 27 April 1946 at the Dickson family home, 3 Montague Street in the south side of Edinburgh and I was delivered by my grandmother Murray in her house 21 Bank Street, Greenock on 9 May 1948. Because of this she always referred to me as her 'May blossom'. Strangely, the Murrays had lost a daughter in infancy and the Dicksons an infant son and I was born in Greenock and Douglas was born in their home.

I don't remember Douglas or me ever thinking that we had an unusual upbringing. True, we lived with and were mostly brought up by our Dickson grandparents and our parents were away a lot of the time, but it had always been like that. To us, it was normal. Mum phoned us every night when they were away so the bond was there between us and them and we realised the nature of their work from early on. In the early fifties, before mum and dad could afford a car they used to come back to Edinburgh, to 3 Montague Street, usually on a Sunday after a resident season somewhere. Nana Dickson would make sure Douglas and I were dressed in our Sunday best and, full of excitement, we would go round to Clerk Street to meet them. We stood in the doorway of the camera shop to wait for them coming off the tramcar, carrying their luggage with wee Maidie lovingly holding on to her accordion which was nearly as big as her. When they left for another engagement, again usually a Sunday, we would wave out of the window of Nana and Granddad Dickson's flat until they were out of sight. There was always a feeling of sadness and a lump in our throats as they left. Time seemed to drag until they came home again although we were happy with the Dicksons. Nana Dickson was strict with us but also loving. Granddad Dickson was a 'softie'.

Hugh Dickson had lied about his age so as to serve in the First World War and was called up for the Royal Navy in the Second World War becoming a Chief Petty Officer. In civilian life he was chief heating engineer at the Sick Children's Hospital in Edinburgh. He met and married Anne Sinclair. She was a cleaner working for a Mrs Rae of the well known music shop, Rae, Macintosh & Co in George Street, Edinburgh. Mrs Rae thought so highly of her cleaning lady that she was allowed to buy one of their pianos and Mrs Rae arranged for weekly payments to be paid. On 23 April 1922 the Dicksons had a baby daughter. This was Maidie and through her Anne Dickson fulfilled her dream of a stage career.

Dainty Maidie Dickson showed exceptional talent at a tender age and her parents were not slow to spot this. She had an innate feeling for music, dance and general entertaining and could quickly memorise the melodies and lyrics of all the 'standards' of the age. Her first public appearance as an entertainer was at the tender age of four at Leith Hospital. Two nurses had to drag 'wee Maidie' off the floor where she was performing for the patients. Her first professional appearance was at the Capitol Cinema, Manderston Street,

Leith. When she was there she would notice that there was a man who was allowed to stand in the wings to see the acts. This was the famous boxer Tancy Lee and it was a privilege that only he had.

Maidie was a natural tap-dancer, referred to years ago as 'buck dancing' and was taken to a dancing teacher called Alec Barnes who lived in Sandport Street, Leith. The story goes that Maidie's mother and grandmother took her at four years old to see Mr Barnes about dancing lessons. Mr Barnes hesitated seeing this tiny child and, knowing how young she was, thought perhaps something less intricate than tap-dancing should be taught. However, he decided, as Maidie's grandmother and his mother were fellow Leithers, he would give it a try. Maidie, of course, turned out to be his star pupil. Perhaps because of her size and age her shoes, which were made by a firm called Peebles in the Grassmarket, had ebonite soles in-stead of taps.

When the Dicksons were in Burntisland one summer when Maidie was six, she performed with the Gilroy Entertainers at the little open air theatre on the front. Gilroy was a friend of Will Fyffe and when the great man happened to be visiting his friend at Burntisland Gilroy asked 'Dainty Maidie' to perform for him. Will Fyffe gave Maidie a pound note and signed it to her 'Tae a clever wee lassie, yours aye, Will Fyffe'. She still has a photograph of her and her father holding the note but not the actual note and often wonders if her father spent it.

In the late twenties and thirties Maidie was a very busy little performer. A press cutting in a scrapbook, probably kept by her mum, says underneath her photograph; 'Maidie, the little Scottish dancer of Jimmy Stewart's 'Young Stars' company who although only ten years old has given over 500 per-formances... and has been performing since she was five.' She also appeared with Betty Brandon's 'Jolly Girls' who were well known in Edinburgh for their work in aid of charities. It's fascinating to go through this scrapbook to see the different places she performed and the different ways she was billed. At the Capitol, Leith in March 1930 she was 'The Wonder Child in Song and Dance' - note she wasn't quite yet eight years old. Often she was 'Daintie Maidie - Child Comedi-

Young Maidie

enne' and sometimes simply 'The Scottish Marvel'.

In the summer of 1933 she appeared in the Summer Show at the Prom Palace, Portobello with the comics Pete Martin and his half-brother Charlie Holbein billed as 'Britain's Youngest Variety Star'. The local paper reported;' On Tuesday evening in addition to the splendid programme provided by the Prom Entertainers, a delightful rendering of songs was given by Miss Maidie Dickson who is also an accomplished dancer... The company would like to take her on tour but owing to the fact of her being of school age this is impossible. She is a clever little artiste and every encouragement should be given to her.' Young Maidie also appeared with Andre Letta's Royal Entertainers based in Bath Street, Portobello. During one season an up and coming young Welsh singer called Donald Peers was also on the bill. She lived with Andre Letta and his wife, Peggy Desmond, in their house behind the theatre during the season and this was not always a restful experience. The pair's frequent arguments were of epic proportions.

At the age of thirteen, Maidie was signed up by Scottish impresario Pete Davis to go into the pantomime *Puss in Boots* at the Palace Theatre, Newcastle as a singing and dancing speciality act. She remembers her digs were just behind St James's Park football ground. Because of her age Maidie had to go to school in Newcastle, which she hated, and had to be out of the theatre by 10 p.m. therefore was unable to appear at the finale of the second house. After the panto season was over Maidie was again signed by Pete Davis to go for a summer season to Bangor in Northern Ireland. As a youngster Maidie was also on the same bill as the legendary Harry Lauder. This was a show at the Theatre Royal, Edinburgh for a charity known as 'Jocks Box'. Sometimes Maidie as a teenage performer had to go through to Glasgow to see the agents to get work It was known that the artists would regularly go to Green's Playhouse for coffees and the agents would approach them to do Sunday night concerts at various venues. One agent was known as 'Wee Fergie' and would book you for St Francis Catholic Hall for the handsome sum of 'Three Hauf Croons'. This he would indicate by putting his three fingers inside his jacket and all the while

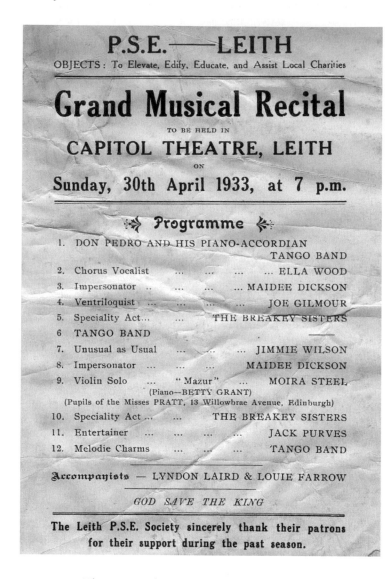

'Pleasant Sunday Evening', Capitol Theatre Leith

staring you straight in the eye meaning, 'Take it or leave it.'

By the time Maidie was booked into the Greenock Empire in 1943 she was a seasoned veteran of the variety circuit. Perhaps it was fate that she was sent to the Murray home at 21 Bank Street where she met the love of her life. Charles Thomas McKinnon Murray, known to one and all as Chic, was the son of William Murray and Isabella whose maiden name was McKinnon. She was a very intelligent lady who came from a large family and dad used to tell my brother Douglas and me that they were known as the wild McKinnons of Greenock. Although Chic was born on 6 November 1919 he used to always claim that it was on 5 November and that was why the fireworks were set off. His dad died when Chic was fourteen and as they were extremely close it had a profound effect on him which I think remained with him always.

Chic as a youngster was encouraged to learn the organ and played it at the local church services and this early introduction to music served him well in future years. He formed a skiffle group while working at Kincaid's Shipyard in Greenock as a riveter although before they were married, which was in St Giles Cathedral on 27 April 1945, he told Maidie he was a marine engineer.

o oooo ooo

This system of dots was his coded message 'I Love you' which he sent to Maidie when she was away on tour - always using the little brown envelopes in which he got his pay! While performing with his skiffle group, aptly named 'Chic and his Chicks', he developed a good singing voice and found he took a natural harmony. He also yodelled effortlessly and in harmony. This harmonising and yodelling became a big part of the double act of Chic and Maidie. This double act had a natural advantage. On stage there was this big man of 6 feet 3 inches towering above the little 5 feet lady in front of him. One of their favourite pieces of business exploited this. Occasionally 'Dainty Maidie' would look round at Chic and gave him a loving smile - very show business like - and the audience would wait for the reaction. When Maidie turned her head away Chic would time the response perfectly and direct a dirty, disdainful look down at her. The timing of the reaction varied but the

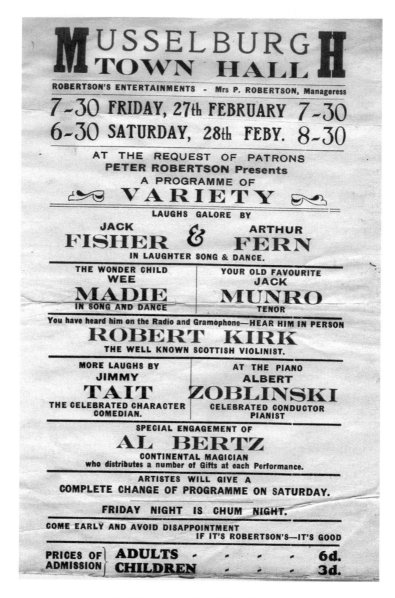

Maidie on the bill at Musselburgh

audience would wait knowing it would come.

Mum and dad also bought a flat at 3 Montague Street, the top flat. I loved that house. It had a wonderful atmosphere and was very 'showbizzy'. Often some of the acts appearing at the Empire, which was down the road, would come to visit. Two I remember were the boxer Freddie Mills and Dickie Henderson who were both very nice persons. The room dad rehearsed in was covered in tartan wall-paper, had a comfortable suite and white Indian carpet and a real coal fire. Now, dad was not really very good about the house but how loved to prepare this fire which he took hours to set. Each paper was twisted carefully, each piece of coal placed with precision after checking the way its grain ran. Chic also had a piano in that room and he would play and sing all day. The audience would be the four walls as he sang such songs as, *I'm going to drink my coffee from an old tin can, I'm alone because I love you, Rock-a-bye baby days* which was one mum knocked out often in their variety days and gave dad great scope to display his yodelling skills. This was the type of number that would usually close their act, often bringing the house down.

Sometimes mum and dad would be able to do a Christmas season nearer home, in the Glasgow or Edinburgh Empire. Those days were sweet memories and often Douglas and I could go to the theatre with them. Tom Arnold was the producer when dad played the fairy-godmother in *Cinderella*. On the opening night at Glasgow Empire dad was to suddenly appear on stage through the trapdoor. Because he was such a big godmother he bumped his head and he and the stage hands were left huddled together still out of sight with the cast and audience waiting in anticipation. He did eventually appear wearing a ballet tutu, white leotard and plimsolls wielding a wonderful bendy wand he made for himself. However, he looked a bit dishevelled with his big blonde, curly, Shirley Temple style wig all to the one side. This wasn't dad's first appearance in *Cinderella*, in 1949 he and mum had played the Ugly Sisters. That must have been something to see!

Disasters, or near disasters, are not unusual in pantomime. Dad could always see the funny side of things that went wrong during performances and loved to tell the story of when he and mum were in *Dick Whittington* in 1950. Archie Lewis, the Jamaican singer with the Geraldo band, was playing the Sultan and in one scene was to come on and simply say, 'Oh my, what a size of a cat!' However, while the scene was being set up he had to sing a couple of numbers in front of the closed curtains dressed in his dance band suit. On the first performance he dashed off at the end of his spot to make the change from his tuxedo to the turban, robe and other trimmings, got into a fankle, missed his cue, rushed on stage and came out with, 'Jesus Christ, what a big cat!' On the same bill was an American animal act called Jean Detroit and his Chimps. Marquis was the name of the star chimp and he was a great mimic. At the finale during the national anthem dad saw Marquis put his forefinger in the fishnet tights of one of the chorus girls and start to rip them. In attempt to save the day Chic decided to distract Marquis and quietly blew a raspberry at him. Marquis, of course, loudly blew raspberries throughout *God Save the King*.

My earliest memories of being taken to variety shows are of the early fifties. I adored going back to see Bank Street when mum and dad played Greenock Empire. Greenock always had a welcome for them. It was as if they knew that Chic and Maidie were destined for the top. Douglas and I would stay up with grandma Murray, sitting beside the kitchen range. Sometimes we would be allowed to attend the matinées on a Wednesday and Saturday and it was then that we got to watch the acts from the wings, being well warned not to be seen by the audience. We thought this was a great thrill.

From almost as long as I can remember I was always fond of Tommy Morgan. He thought very highly of mum and dad and they were often in his shows at the Glasgow Pavilion. It was Tommy Morgan who whispered into my ear, 'Your mum and dad are going to be big stars.' That certainly came true. On my fifth birthday Tommy pulled me up the back stair of the stage at the Pavilion at the Wednesday matinée and commanded the audience to sing Happy Birthday to me. What a memory, with all the cast on-stage at the finale of the programme.

It is well known that a lot of comics are very serious characters

Chic and Maidie with Douglas and Annabelle

when they are not on stage. This was certainly not the case with dad. Life was not dull with him around and the only thing you could expect was the unexpected. For a long time I believed the story he told me that I had been left in a bag with a note to mum and dad attached on a hook at the stage door of the Greenock Empire. When Douglas and I were young and had a long car journey ahead of us to London, Wales or wherever mum and dad were playing summer season, he would keep us amused with daft songs like: 'There was a wee man that had twa bums, sing nickerty, nackerty noo, noo, noo and he shows them off to all his chums. Singing, Hi Willie Wackerty, ho John Dougall etc…etc….' Restaurants often brought out the best - or the worst - from him. If the waiter came up to him and enquired, 'Aperitif sir?' Chic was certain to reply, 'Why? Is the steak tough?' In 1962 or 1963 mum and dad were providing the comedy in a Summer Show at the Windmill theatre in Great Yarmouth with Billy Fury, Karl Denver, Joe Brown and the Bruvvers and the Vernon Girls. Harry Secombe was appearing in one of the pier shows with Ronnie Corbett and they invited the four of us to lunch one day at one of the big hotels in town. Can you imagine a luncheon party of Harry Secombe, Chic and Maidie and little Ronnie Corbett? They were irrepressible and the whole affair was hilarious and unforgettable. It didn't really matter but the food was very good as well.

Mum gave up touring in the middle sixties to run the hotel she and dad had bought in Edinburgh. Like the flat in Montague Street there was a theatre just down the road. This was the Kings, and many of the performers would call in. One star stayed there in secret. This was Robert Wilson, a good friend, whom mum and dad took in after he had been attacked and robbed in Dublin. When he came back to Scotland mum and dad collected him and he and his wife lived in the hotel out of the range of the newspapers until he was better. When he was leaving Robert gave mum a silver cigarette box, which she still has.

When dad died the huge affection in which people held him was shown by the enormous coverage in the media. I remember Johnny Beattie saying to me that he had never known such a press

Happy smiles from Chic and Maidie

for a Scottish star. Top comics called him 'The comedian's come-dian'. Billy Connolly had always heaped praise on Chic before and after his death and he and Johnny gave dad a fitting farewell to this life at his funeral and wherever he is now, the host as always, will be the winner. Happily, Mum, 'Daintie Maidie', is still going strong and we see a lot of each other. She really is a Scottish Marvel and it's a privilege and pleasure to dedicate this to her and to dad's memory.

Further Reading

Bruce, F, Foley, A, and Gillespie, G, eds., *Those Variety Days: Memories of Scottish Variety Theatre*, Scottish Music Hall Society, Edinburgh, 1997

Bullar, G R, and Evans, Len, eds, *Who's who in variety: A biographical record of the Variety Stage*, The Performer, London, 1950

Devlin, Vivien, *Kings, Queens and People's Palaces; An Oral History of The Scottish Variety Theatre, 1920-1970*, Polygon Edinburgh, 1991

House, Jack, *Music Hall Memories; Recollections of Scottish Music Hall and Pantomime*, Richard Drew, Glasgow, 1986

Hudd, Roy with Hindin, Philip, *Roy Hudd's cavalcade of variety acts: A who was who of light entertainment 1915-60*, Robson books, London, 1997

Irving, Gordon, *The Good Auld Days; The Story of Scotland's Entertainers from Music Hall to Television*, Jupiter, London, 1977

Littlejohn, J H, *The Scottish Music Hall, 1880-1990*, G.C. Book Publishers, Wigtown, 1990

Mellor, G J, *The Northern Music Hall*, Frank Graham, Newcastle Upon Tyne, 1970

Napier, Valantyne, *Glossary of terms used in variety, vaudeville, revue and pantomime 1880-1960*, The Badger Press, Westbury, 1996

Yule, Andrew, *The Chic Murray Story*, Corgi, 1990,

Wilmut, Roger, *Kindly Leave the stage! The story of variety 1919-1960*, Methuen, London, 1985